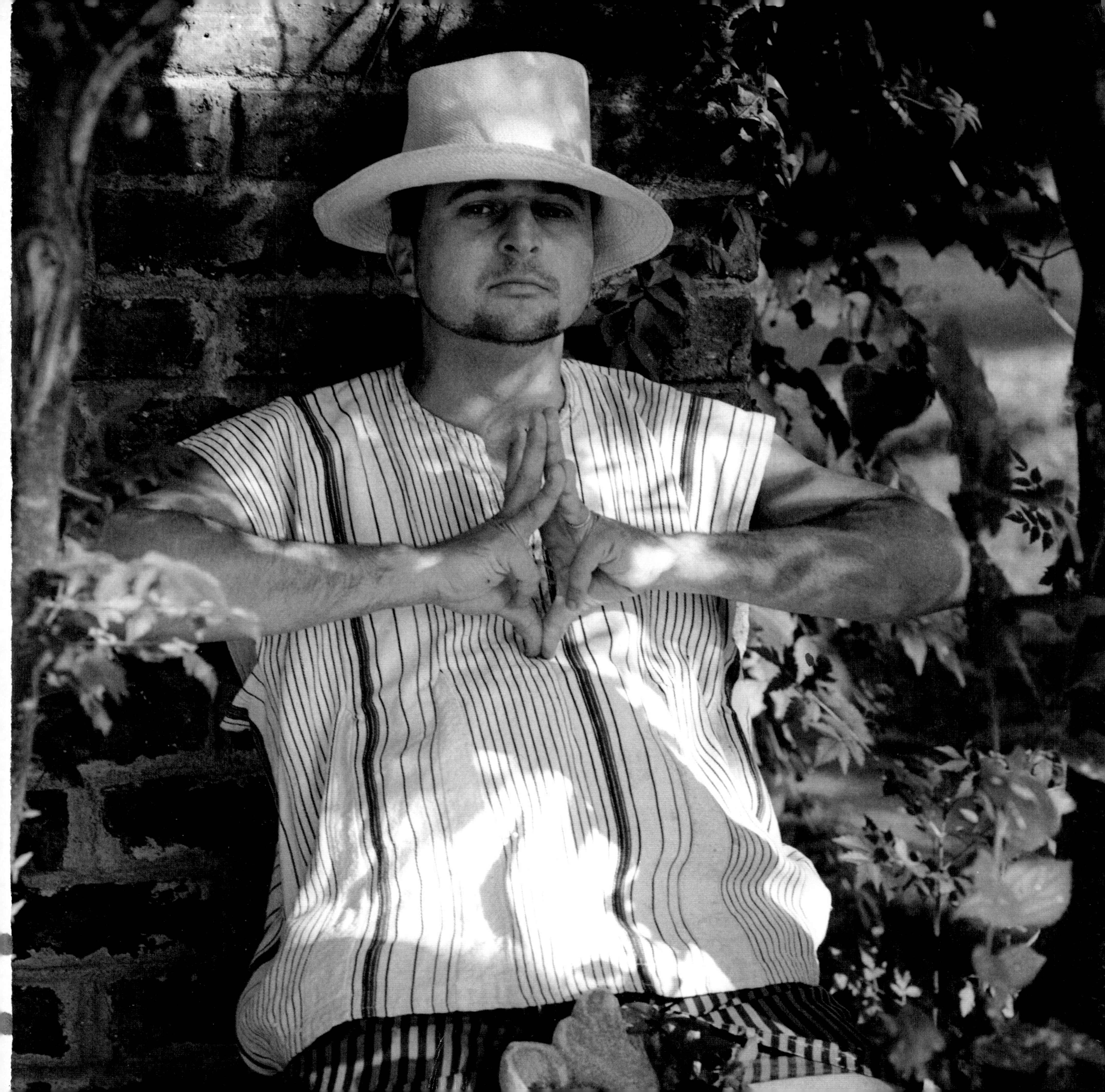

BEEZY BAILEY

Brian Eno

Richard Cork
Roslyn Sulcas

CIRCA

First published in 2019 by Circa Press

Circa Press
50 Great Portland Street
London W1W 7ND
www.circapress.com

ISBN 978-1-911422-12-9

Printed and bound in Italy

Design: Herman Lelie
Layouts: Stefania Bonelli

Contents

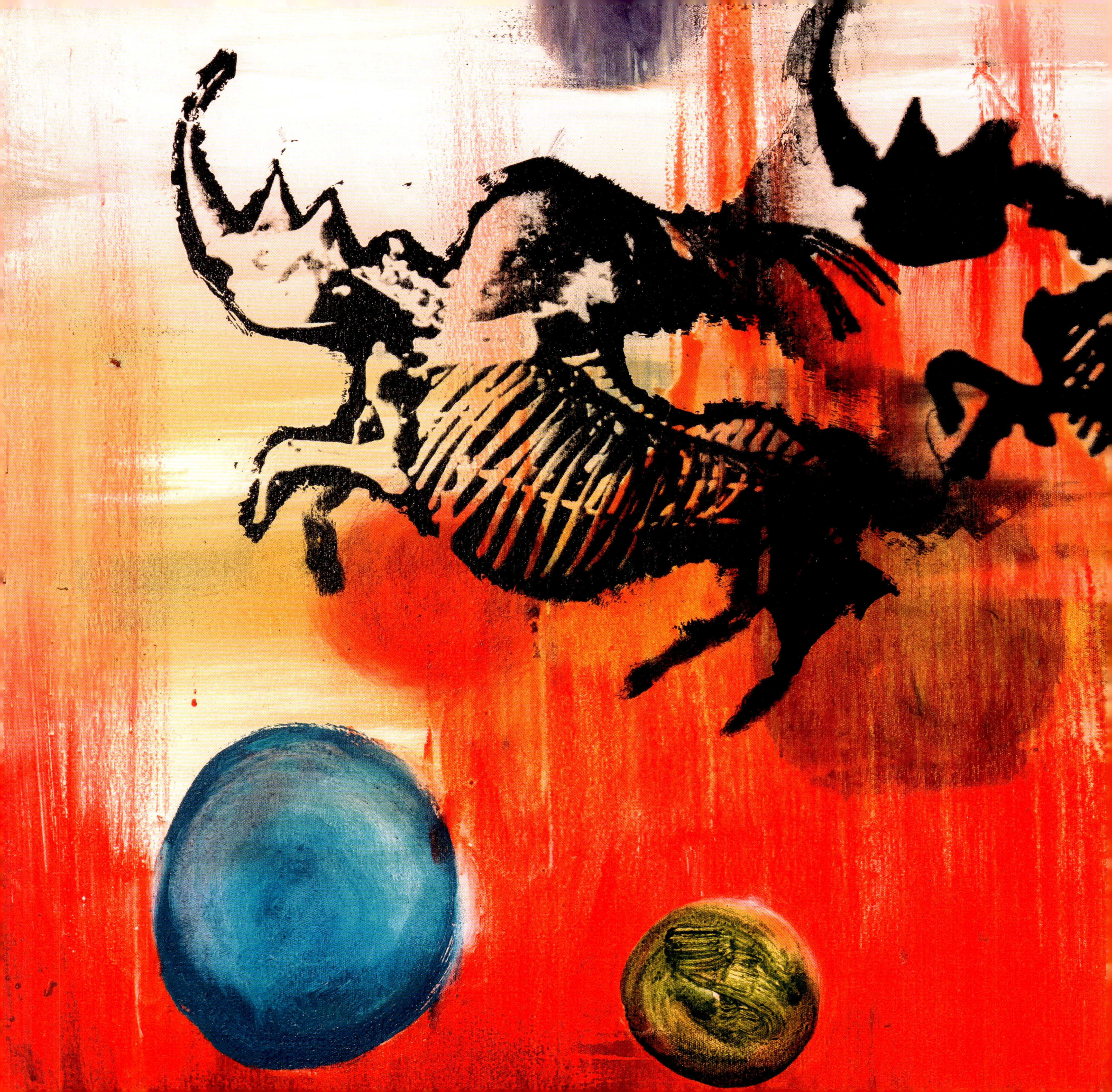

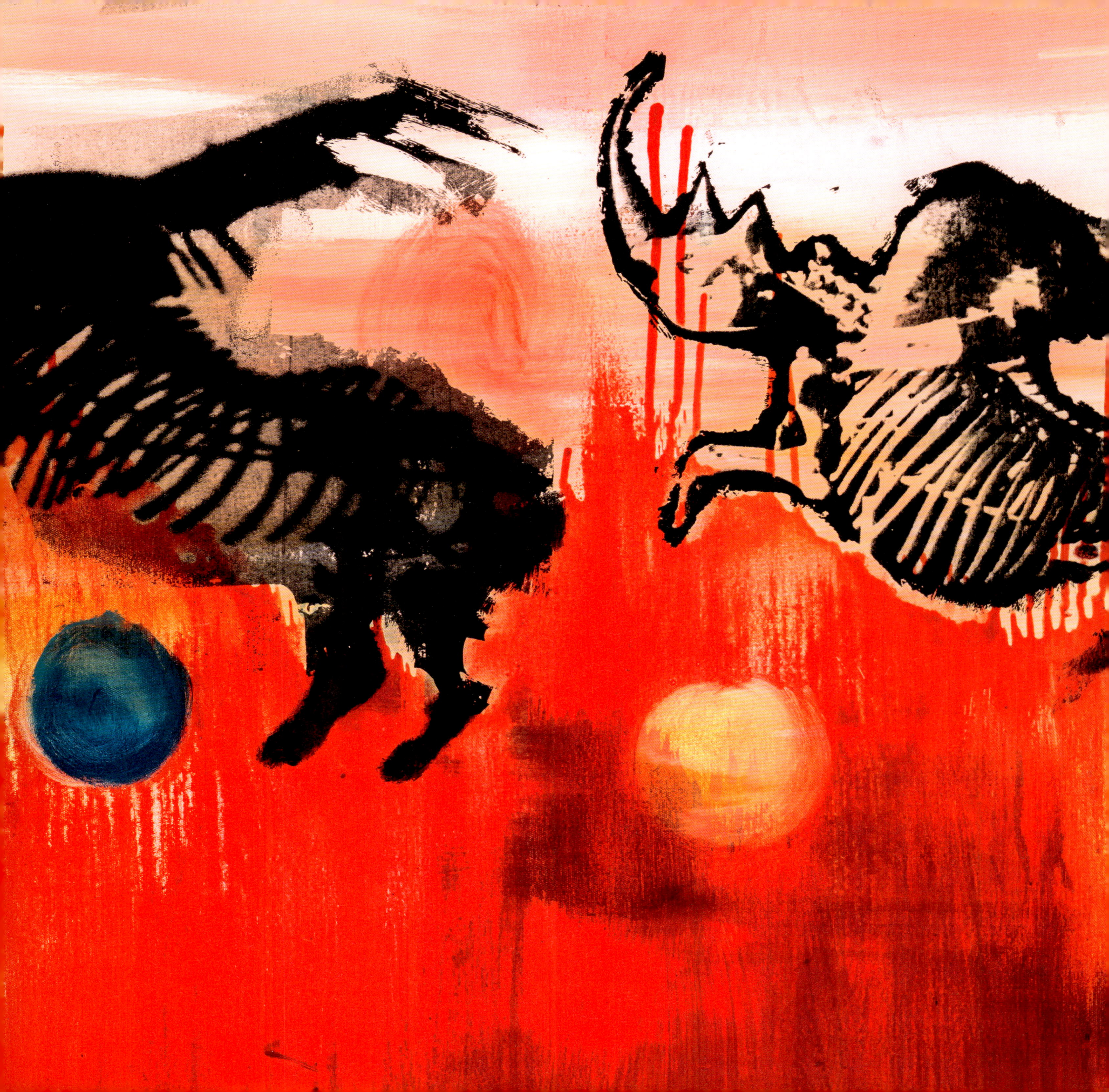

Foreword

Beezy Bailey makes his art from joy and laughter (and sometimes from terror). Like a chef gleefully throwing ingredients in by the handful without ever measuring them, he revels in his gift and has confidence in it. He conjures up new worlds, tiny and huge, peopled by bird women, snake men and lizard children, and bursting with bright new music.

He paints just as he cooks: with exuberance and lots of strong, rich colours. He's an African artist, as colourful as the tropics, and as full of life. He comes to visit in purple suede shoes, a violet trilby and red hot pants.

When he works he does so in short, intense bursts. It's sensational to watch because everything can change completely in seconds. He's not precious, nor hesitant. Better to ruin a picture completely than not to see how far he can go. He's like a jazz player taking a solo. After a long burst he takes a break to read and look at pictures and phone people and eat and drink. But the corner of his vision is always sizing up the painting, waiting to pounce. Turning back to it, picking up the brushes, he develops an evil twinkle in his eye and starts slinging and scraping, and singing and dancing, and looking for all the world like a demonic child who has just discovered he can make spells that work.

He makes African jazz in paint, garish as the midday sun, and dark as the deepest night.

Brian Eno

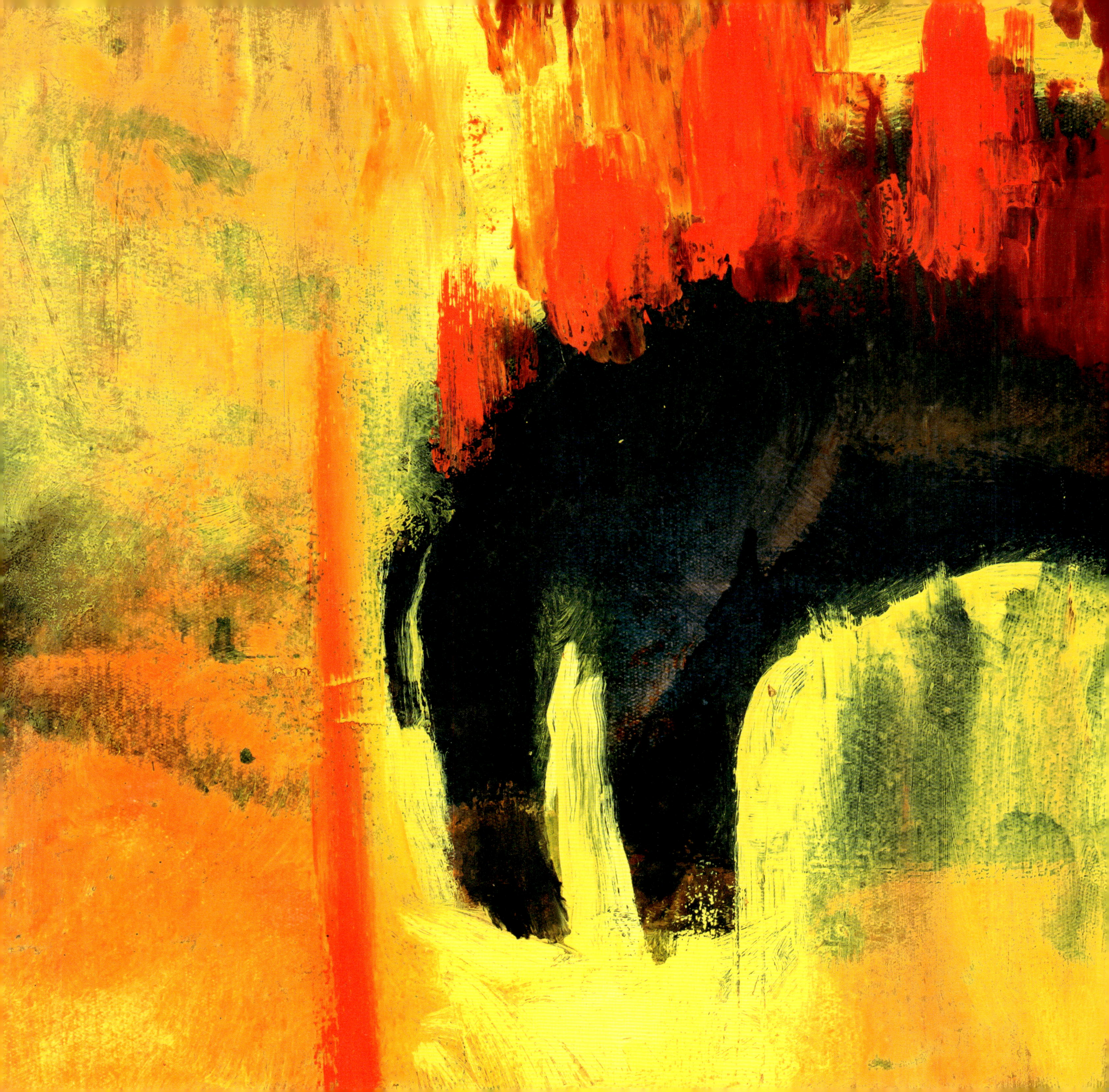

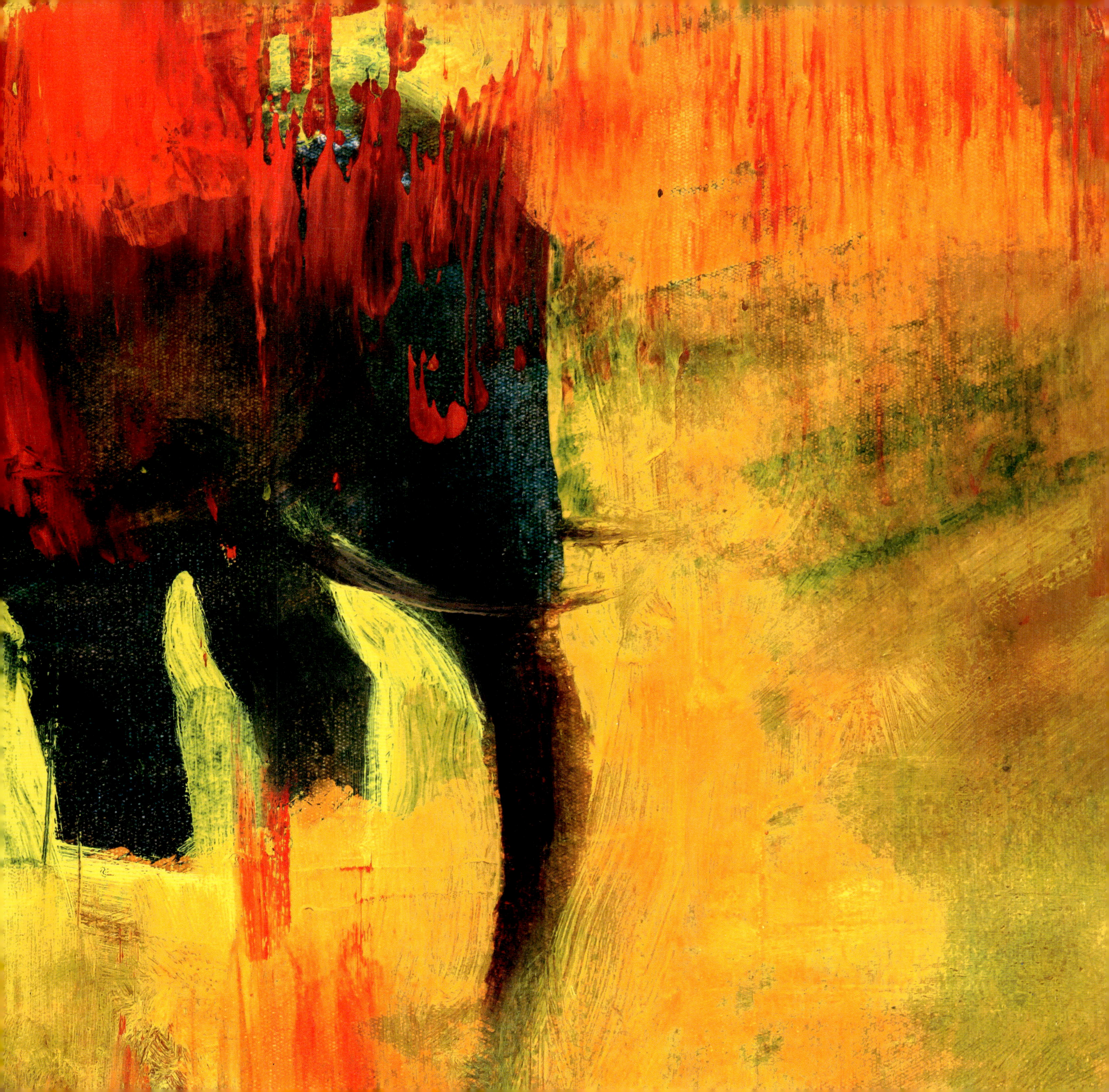

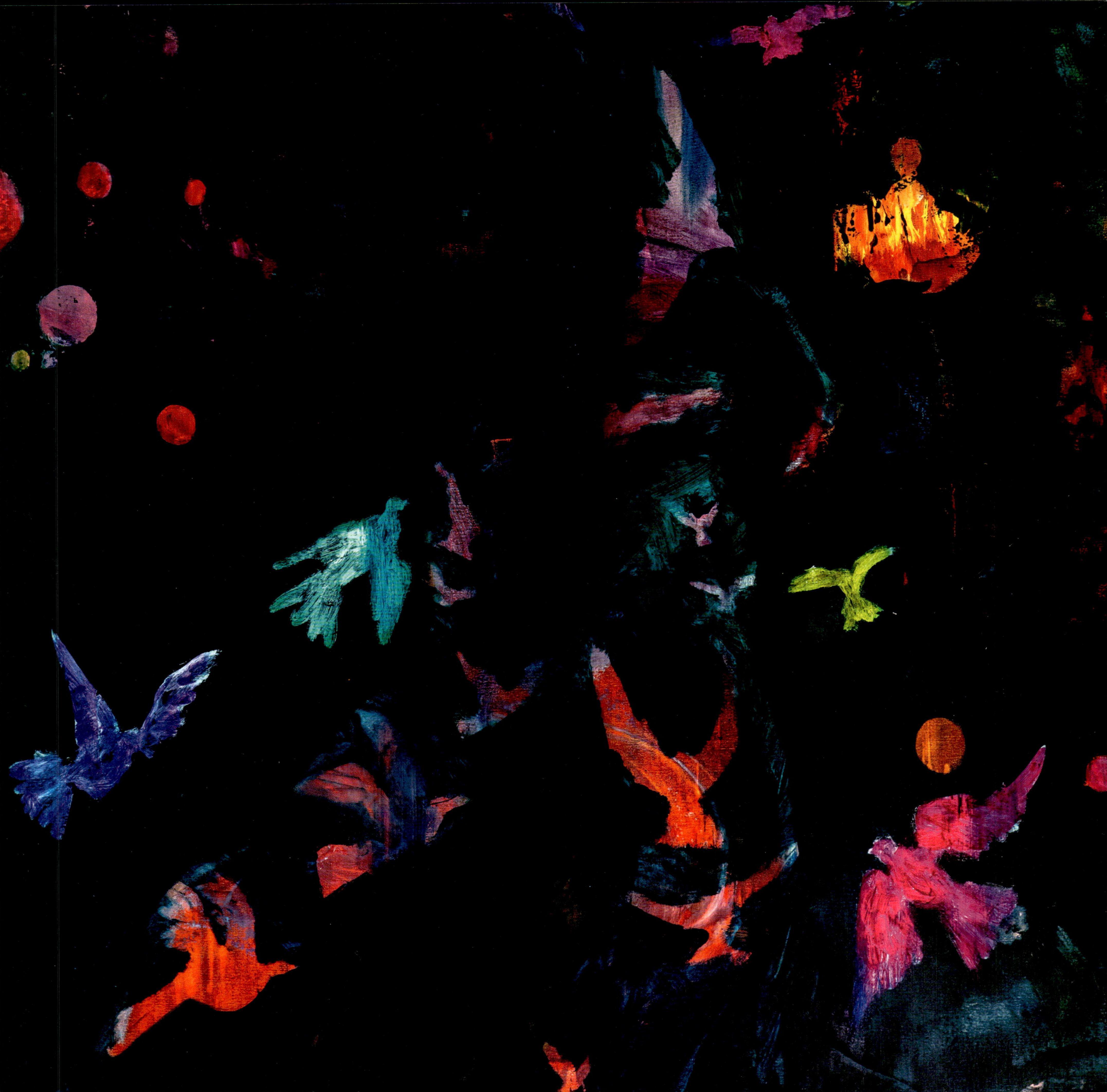

Beezy Bailey: Probing with Impulsive Flair

Richard Cork

Looking back over Beezy Bailey's restlessly inventive career as an artist, we soon become fascinated by a defiant unpredictability. At every turn his work is filled with surprises; there is a fundamental urge to challenge the status quo. Unlike so many painters and sculptors, who formulate an identifiable style and never stray from it throughout their lives, Bailey discovers stimulus in leaping around. He never stays still, and this sense of freedom gives his output a darting, inquisitive quality that sharpens our curiosity.

No wonder his nanny gave Bailey the nickname that has stayed with him as an adult. In her opinion, the little boy was 'always so *beezy*!' And making visual images took up an increasing amount of his energy while he grew up in Johannesburg. His very first kindergarten report complained that he 'prefers to sing when the rest of the class is playing with plasticine, and to draw when they have outdoor activities. William [he was christened William James Sebastian] does not obey orders. He appears not to hear'. His mother Barbara later recalled that 'poor little Beezy was always in trouble, at school and at home'. She described how he 'played long imaginative games by himself and either sang or kept up a running commentary, so that when he was silent it usually meant he was doing something that he shouldn't'. His subsequent involvement with performance art was prophesied in childhood, too, for Barbara affirmed that 'Beezy has been a highly original and fancy dresser since he was about six. He always wore a hat: a tam o' shanter, deerstalker, Nigerian hats that [his father] Jim had brought him, or an opera hat that could concertina flat'.

At that time, South Africa was a profoundly divided country. In 1960, only two years before Bailey's birth, the notorious Sharpeville massacre had alerted the entire world to the brutal horrors of apartheid. White policemen ruthlessly gunned down black protesters during the tragic day at Sharpeville, and Bailey had every reason as a child to become acutely aware of this bloodbath. After all, his radical father Jim Bailey was a passionate supporter of *Drum*, the aspirational magazine that became an immensely popular voice of black opposition to apartheid. He not only financed *Drum* and became its principal champion, he also befriended key fighters such as Nelson Mandela, while defending the magazine against its powerful and malicious opponents. The battle to promote *Drum* depleted the fortune that Jim had inherited from his father, the 'Randlord' tycoon and art collector Sir Abe Bailey. But Jim was doubtless inspired by the bravery of his mother Mary, who had become an outstanding female aviator in 1928 when she flew a pioneering solo flight from London to Cape Town and back.

As a boy, Beezy would likewise have been intrigued to learn that Jim had been an RAF pilot in 1939 and had fought in the Battle of Britain. The first plane flown by Jim must have become a special source of fascination to Beezy. Armed with a rear-facing gun turret, this fighter 'flew forwards and shot backwards'. And in 2007, when Beezy had a solo exhibition at Everard Read in Cape Town, he coined the phrase 'being blown backwards into the future'. They were the first words of a statement written for the exhibition catalogue, where he explained that his work proposes 'a way of dealing with the historical moment we find ourselves in; by looking backwards, examining where we come from and what we have been through, we may be able to move wisely forwards'.

While he was growing up and struggling as a dyslexic with classroom work at school, Bailey must also have found himself drawn into the excitement of flying when he heard about the airborne adventures of his father and grandmother – hence, perhaps, the prevalence of references to rising, falling and floating in his mature art. Flight in all its different meanings clearly entered his wild imagination at an early stage, and never left his dreams. He also became aware of the remarkable collection of British sporting art that his grandfather Abe had amassed. It amounted in the end to more than 400 works and he generously ensured that, after his death, they were all given to the South African National Gallery in Cape Town. His collection still constitutes the largest bequest ever received by this gallery, and young Beezy's familiarity with these sporting images may well help to account for the remarkable proliferation of animals and birds in his own work.

Not that he preferred traditional art and rejected Modernist alternatives. On the contrary: by the time Bailey reached the age of twenty-one, he was delighted to have lunch with Andy Warhol at The Factory in New York. Fascinated by Warhol's reliance on images of the contemporary world in all its diversity, from Marilyn Monroe and Campbell's soup cans to the gruesomeness of electric chairs, Bailey felt immensely encouraged by this meeting. In particular, Warhol made positive remarks when Bailey showed him some photographs of his own work. So their New York lunch strengthened his resolve to become an artist, and three years later he gained a degree at the Byam Shaw School of Art in London.

During the 1980s, both painting and sculpture had benefited from a widespread sense of renewal among young artists in Britain. So Bailey would have been stimulated by this vitality during his London years as a student. Then, in 1985, he told his parents that: 'I went to the De Kooning exhibition last week, and tears blocked my vision. Never have I seen such pure agony. His feeling of dissatisfaction drives him into bounds like no other painter, so honest is he. Very inspiring.' A year later Bailey met another hero, Francis Bacon, and after graduating began to define his mature identity in a large charcoal work called *New York New York* (p. 89). Although draughtsmanship plays a key role throughout this dream-like image, photographs taken by Bailey himself are collaged onto it as well. Warhol is seen floating like an angel above the skyscrapers, and one of the photos pays tribute to Keith Haring, the tragically short-lived artist whose shop in New York would eventually inspire Bailey to open his own Art Factory and Shop in 1998 as an attempt to narrow the divide between fine art and popular culture.

Back in 1987, Bailey's innate rebellious streak prompted him to paint a self-portrait called *Running from Rome* (p. 39). He shows himself as a blanched, etiolated and naked figure clutching a stolen mask while racing away from an authoritarian classical temple in the distance. The swift, impulsive handling of oil and bitumen shows just how removed Bailey must have felt from the whole notion of academic propriety. He wanted to aim at a more expressive spontaneity, and another work, *Transcontinental Love* (p. 41), proves that Bailey was not afraid to explore painfully autobiographical content. Here, with a jet flying low over the sea, he portrays himself as an isolated, melancholy centipede abandoned in the desert. Sand is mixed with the paint, and Bailey mourns the loss of all his girlfriends over the last seven years.

Travelling continually between South Africa and London, where he held his first substantial solo show at the Vanessa Devereux Gallery in 1988, Bailey felt dislocated. A painting called *Clown Elliot in Dover* (p. 35) shows a Zulu dancer friend who performed with his dancers at the exhibition opening. The brightly costumed Elliot sits slumped in a landscape inspired by both Dover's cliffs and African huts.

Dance and music are recurrent themes in Bailey's work. He inherited his love of music from his mother Barbara, a talented keyboard performer who recalled how Beezy as a child 'sang all the time he played'. Bailey's response to music would lead him, in 1995, to collaborate with David Bowie on paintings and drawings that were shown in London and Basel. A passionate art collector, Bowie undoubtedly relished this opportunity to explore his own lifelong love of visual mark making with a painter as responsive as Bailey. Art had always been important to Bowie, who once described it as: 'a stable nourishment. I use it. It can change the way I feel in the mornings. The same work can change me in different ways, depending on what I'm going through'. Bailey would have readily agreed with these words, for he likewise experienced a wide range of contrasting impulses. In one mood, he was ready to become captivated by a mythological fantasy. Yet he also felt equally prepared, in another frame of mind, to involve himself with the cause espoused by *Drum* magazine.

In 1991, Bailey contributed to *New Directions*, a group exhibition of sculpture at the Centre for African Studies and Michaelis School of Fine Art, in Cape Town University. But because the Cape Town show contained anti-apartheid images, the police closed it.

This censorship did not stop Bailey secretly creating an alter ego: a black woman named Joyce Ntobe. According to Bailey, Ntobe had been taught art as a schoolgirl by a missionary woman. Then, after getting a job as a domestic worker for a couple who lived in Camps Bay, Ntobe was encouraged by her employer to develop as an artist. Bailey's wife Nicci, herself an artist and art teacher, pretended to be Ntobe's employer. But her submissions were rejected from a national exhibition called the Triennial. Without knowing that Bailey had created Ntobe, the South African National Gallery spotted three linocuts among her rejected work and immediately acquired them for its permanent collection. They depicted her life as a domestic worker, and when the gallery's curator wanted to find out more about Ntobe, Bailey revealed the truth. After he criticised the hasty rearrangement of the chairs to cover up past bias at the gallery, and denounced it as 'political correctness, or policing creativity', the story quickly grew into an international media scandal.

Bailey went on to have three group exhibitions with Ntobe, the first one held at the AVA in Cape Town. By this time he was focused on raising his two children with Nicci while developing as an artist. Nicci played an instrumental role in his creative growth and became to a certain extent his muse, acting as an insightful and fearless critic. Guiding his progress, she knew his work better than anyone. Bailey has also been stimulated by his children Jasper and Saskia, both of whom are creative in their own spheres – Jasper is a photographer, and Saskia (at the age of nineteen) has been commissioned by a publisher to write her memoir.

As the twentieth century approached its end, the irrepressible Bailey took the surprising decision to base a whole series of paintings and prints on Lee Ping Zing. His bearded face fascinated Bailey after he found it on a Chinese ceremonial funeral banknote. Because he had never visited China, it became a fantasyland and impelled him to embark, over a five-year period, on an extended sequence of images. In 1997, a silkscreen showed the moment when *Lee Ping Zing Goes to School* (p. 59). He looks hesitant, and doubtless reflects the feelings of insecurity experienced by Bailey himself during his difficult period as a schoolboy. But outright fantasy quickly enters this series. Another silkscreen portrays Lee Ping Zing as a mermaid juggling love hearts in Swazi countryside threatened by a storm. Subsequent prints show more peaceful scenes, where Lee Ping Zing kneels in prayer before one of the ceremonial notes, which are burned at Chinese funerals to ensure that dead people benefit from riches in their afterlife. An equally optimistic silkscreen shows Lee Ping Zing with beams of sunlight projecting from his head accompanied by silver doves symbolising peace. Yet a more ominous mood is conveyed in a painting of Lee Ping Zing's birthplace, where a dragon from the same note thrusts out its claws in a woodland scene also inhabited by other clamorous animals. Whether playing a guitar as a rock star, or taking tea beneath a double-headed moon, Lee Ping Zing can undoubtedly be ranked among the most intriguing characters in Bailey's work.

By this time Nelson Mandela had been released from prison and, through a triumphant and fully representative democratic election, become South Africa's first black president. But Bailey, who would later devote a whole body of work to celebrating Mandela's advent, was under no illusions about his country's fragility. In 1999, as part of a public sculpture festival to commemorate Heritage Day, he received a death threat while draping a celebrated equestrian statue of the Boer general Louis Botha in the traditional apparel of a Xhosa initiate, worn by young men when they go into the bush to be circumcised and initiated from boys to men. Bailey wanted the symbolism of his intervention to illustrate the transformation of his country from apartheid 'boy' to democratic 'man'. So he transformed this imposing work, which stands prominently on Stal Plein outside the Parliament building in Cape Town, with a traditional hat, face paint and a striped blanket. Angry white Afrikaner passers-by shouted 'this is disgusting!' But the City of Cape Town had given Bailey permission to drape the general in this provocative new garb during the festival. So although Bailey felt 'slightly shaken' by an enraged passer-by who threatened to shoot him, he put the finishing touches to his work on the Botha statue and explained that it symbolised 'the initiation of our country into democracy and in the spirit of the African Renaissance'.

Mandela's inspired presidency came to an end in the very same year, and Bailey was acutely conscious of South Africa's continuing vulnerability. The tension between hope and anxiety filled his imagination, becoming clear in a turn-of-the-century series devoted to the overall theme of *Learning to Fly Again*. Adopting the idea that humanity was once able to soar through the air, Bailey filled these energetic paintings and prints with images where people took to the sky. He likened it to discovering how 'to walk again after an accident', and explained that flying 'symbolises the angelic in us, the spiritual side of our lives'. Bailey even explored the possibilities of performance art on a memorable day at the Durban Art Gallery Red Eye function in 1999. After singing his own pre-recorded song, he was painted blue and given silk wings, goggles and a propeller hat before leaping on to a stage where a group of actors was waiting. This performance, the result of a fruitful collaboration with theatre director Brett Bailey (no relation), was called *Blue Zulu*.

The largest of the prints based on the flight theme are carved into Masonite board using an angle grinder. They show near-naked figures flapping purple wings, wearing brown coats with umbrellas and aeroplane attachments, surging upwards powered by propellers and even soaring through space with skis on their feet. One print, which uses gold leaf as well as silkscreen, also includes Bailey's photographs inspired by the Italian artist Mimmo Paladino. They focus on African men and women reaching upwards as they prepare for flight, and in *Take Off* (p. 37) he also uses hand-coloured gouache for an image of a small plane carrying three visible passengers: a black man, a white woman and a bird.

During the early years of the present century, Bailey collaborated in stimulating ways with artists as diverse as Brian Eno and Zwelethu Mthethwa. But he also became increasingly preoccupied with the 'fallen angel' theme. While insisting that 'it is not for me to explain the contents of my work', he did declare in 2007 that his involvement with this particular theme 'relates to the demise of the white male in South Africa who thought he was higher than the Almighty'. Now fallen from grace, he is 'forced to search his soul'.

Bailey's disturbing explorations of this theme have taken the form of sculpture, executed in bronze with patina. One is given the optimistic title *Walking Tall* (p. 94), and the figure certainly attempts to stay upright by stretching out both arms with apparently decisive vigour. The legs, however, are attenuated to a disconcerting extent. They might easily collapse, and in another bronze called *Fallen Angel* (p. 95), not even a thrusting pair of wings can prevent this inverted figure from plummeting headfirst to destruction. At the same time, though, the doomed and emaciated victim appears strangely icebound, and Bailey himself once declared that 'each of my works is a frozen dream'.

At this stage of his career, tragedy predominates. Even a large painting of a she-wolf suckling two abandoned human children in the countryside turns out to be Bailey's interpretation of Romulus and Remus. In his version of this ancient story, one of the twins is black and the other is white. Despite everything the kindly she-wolf gives them as an adopted mother, one of the twins will grow up and kill the other before proclaiming himself the founder of a nation. Bailey explained that 'as with the fallen angel, there are African political and historical connotations in this myth that weave their way through stories of the images'.

Although he felt enormously relieved that 'our very young democracy had emerged from the dark age of apartheid', Bailey continued to be appalled by the prevalence of arms deals. He loathed the way in which arms, 'bought for huge sums of money', were then 'used to kill people. The invasions of Iraq and Afghanistan illustrate my point. Wars are created unnecessarily in order to sell arms, mostly poor peasants die in the wake of this monster'. Hence the diabolic character of a tall, sinister sculpture called *The Arms Dealer* (p. 29). The body of this macabre creature, made from driftwood and finished with ink-blue patina, looms before us in an eerie pose. His hands hold out a military boat, cast in bronze from a plastic juice container discovered on Cape Town beach. The vessel, which came from China, may look small, and the arms dealer's oil-painted face adopts an apologetic expression. Yet Bailey ensures that the overall mood of this sculpture is both creepy and malignant.

Fear is once more evoked in *Doll Man* and *Doll Woman*, figures testifying to the potency of two ghostly African bronzes that Bailey first encountered in his father's collection. Although they were supposed to be spirits who made people feel afraid, these figures were equipped with human limbs. Bailey was also stimulated by a merry-go-round he saw in Coney Island, New York, where bee figures had human legs. So he purchased two dolls and attached their limbs to carved wooden figures. Then they were cast in bronze, and the spectral quality of their heads and torsos contrasts eerily with the chubby innocence conveyed by the child-like legs and arms.

These apparitions could hardly be further removed from the style Bailey continued to deploy for the paintings by his alter ego Joyce Ntobe. In 2008, he had a joint exhibition with her at the Everard Read Gallery in Johannesburg, and an artist's statement purportedly written by Ntobe explained that her paintings were based on 'photos I took in Gugulethu and Khayelitsha after the recent floods'. One large painting, *Shack in the Grass*, is a forbidding image of a rudimentary dwelling covered in rough metal sheets to defend its occupants from the water. 'The floods are terrible, our children become sick', declared Ntobe's statement, before emphasising that 'the people there suffer so much'. But she also worked as a conceptual feminist artist, creating an installation of eight Mother Earth figures in resin containing objects relating to her life as a black woman.

In 2011, Bailey explored an optimistic and at times celebratory mood in his solo exhibition called *Icon – Iconoclast*, a tribute to Nelson Mandela. It was held at the Everard Read Gallery in Johannesburg, and the catalogue's introductory texts opened with an enthusiastic piece written by Mandela's comrade Ronnie Kasrils, the former Minister for Intelligence. In its most eloquent passage, Kasrils described how the 'symbolic tapestry of South Africa's haunting landscape, secretive mists, visceral imagery of birds and broken shacks, weave and float around the elusive, multi-dimensional charisma of a man who has always reminded us that love is central to liberation, and the masses, not great men, are the true creators of history'.

One of the exhibits, *Rainbow Men* (p. 109), was based on Joyce Ntobe's oil painting *Shack in the Grass*. But this time Bailey added a silkscreen sequence of images in the blue sky above, based on photographs of a grinning Mandela embracing the equally appreciative Joe Slovo, who had been Housing Minister and a prominent anti-apartheid activist. Various silkscreen photo shots were used in the paintings throughout Bailey's show, which revealed in this respect just how much he still recalled the stimulus provided by Andy Warhol. But Christopher Till, Director of South Africa's Apartheid Museum, rightly pointed out in the catalogue that Bailey had submerged these photographs of Mandela 'within the painterly canvas plane', thereby giving 'the printed image a gestural and personal signature consciously absent from the photograph'.

One of these paintings, *Homecoming* (p. 108), fills most of the canvas with the same photo showing Mandela and Slovo hugging each other. Yet there is no feeling of repetition there. Far from it: each of these six images is handled in a different way by Bailey's oil and enamel. The photos are also placed within a freewheeling landscape, where aeroplanes dive through the sky like fish in the sea. Throughout the show, Mandela's iconic figure is seen not as an isolated presence, but as an integral part of South Africa. In *Prisoner of the People* (p. 113), his laughing face appears eight times on the canvas, emerging defiantly from the strong, vertical bars of the prison where he was confined for so many years. Behind him, simplified images of land and sea glow as if celebrating their liberation from apartheid. Even when a painting shows rain in Africa, with a turbulent sky unleashing a storm on the dark and empty countryside, this affliction is offset by four images of Mandela. Garlanded with plants and flowers, he gazes to the right as if viewing a future filled with potential.

By no means all of these images show him smiling and at peace. One of the most moving works juxtaposes the desolate shacks in a Ntobe painting with photographs of an elderly, frail Mandela leaning on a stick and wearing a T-shirt emblazoned with the words: 'I am an HIV treatment supporter'. He looks anguished, as if imagining the effects of this devastating illness or recalling friends who had died after contracting HIV. But there is no doubting his determination. One image, *Ghost Boxer* (p. 111), shows the young Mandela wearing gloves and bracing himself for a boxing match. His body seems to be melting into the derelict townscape beyond. Yet he could equally well have emerged from the damaged house behind him, filled with a sense of positive resolve about the fight for freedom ahead.

Bailey never forgets how difficult Mandela's task really was. Another immensely poignant painting, called *Stormy Weather* (p. 107), sets Mandela in the context of a gale-force storm, where an isolated figure struggles to carry on walking through a weather-beaten landscape. Above, Mandela's face is juxtaposed with that of a twelve-year-old white boy, who reaches out with both hands to touch the president's cheeks. He smiles, and is doubtless moved by this gesture of affection. For the boy is blind, and is using his hands to explore Mandela's face to discover what he looks like. The full significance of this moment is emphasised by Bailey's decision to spread three images of the blind boy's communion with Mandela across the full width of the canvas.

With hindsight, we now know just how much of Mandela's legacy was betrayed by Jacob Zuma. Hence the feeling of desperation conveyed by the figures in *Goodbye Jacob* (p. 119), a poignant 2018 painting in which Bailey vividly exposes the deep sense of national frailty that Zuma left behind. Everything appears transient, and Bailey knows precisely how to summarise this fleeting quality in his swift, spontaneous brushwork. Dante's vision of hell will not leave him. In a larger recent painting, he refuses to grant us any of the redemptive light that animates most of his work. Instead, the only brightness found in this new version of Dante's Inferno emanates from the flame-like harshness destroying the figures as they plummet through an otherwise unalleviated gloom. Almost all of these helpless victims are inverted. And however hard they try to touch or grasp each other, Bailey ensures that each one of them is alone.

Even so, the majority of his new paintings are horizontal rather than upright, and they combine a roaming cosmic vision with an acute awareness of specific tragedies occurring on our own planet. In one of the largest canvases, *Summer Snow on Pluto* (p. 203), Bailey evokes an alarmingly unpredictable climate as well as the bullets that hurtle through space and threaten some of the most ancient and impressive creatures on Earth. In the distance, a handsome elephant can be glimpsed. But his existence is clearly at risk, and the future of another elephant in *Lonely Walk* (p. 204) is just as uncertain. Although this animal does not appear to be as assailed as his counterpart on Pluto, he is utterly isolated. And the alarming redness spreading right across his body signifies that he might well be covered in blood.

Even more poignant is a painting whose title pays tribute to the poetry of Dylan Thomas: *Don't Go Gently Into That Good Night* (p. 207). Bailey unleashes a terrifying apocalypse in this large canvas, where blazing fireballs seem to descend on some doomed rhinos as they try making their way across the bottom of the picture. This powerful painting was first displayed in March 2018, when Bailey's solo exhibition opened at Everard Read in London. It coincided with the distressing news that the world's last male northern white rhino had died in Kenya. His name was Sudan, and he played a major role in an attempt to save his species from extinction after decades of ruthless hunting by poachers.

Bailey is in no doubt about the imminent dangers confronting our world. Although he gave his London exhibition the affirmative title *Light Beyond the Dark*, visitors found themselves surrounded by images that alerted them to the uncertainties of existence. Plenty of vitality can be found in *Rainbow Race* (p. 213), where naked slender men run across an empty terrain. But the truth is that, for all their undoubted energy and competitive excitement, the heat that emanates from the red-hot rockscape beyond could easily overwhelm these blanched figures. They look almost spectral, and a related awareness of life's fundamental vulnerability runs through Bailey's images of dancing. Several spirited copperplate etchings focus on subjects as joyful as *Freedom Dance* and *Cha Cha Cha* (pp. 222–3). Even here, though, the performers seem on the verge of fighting, and the two main figures in a crazy painting called *21st Birthday Party* (p. 209) are so hectic that one almost seems to be reeling away from a blow struck by her wild companion.

As we have seen, Bailey's involvement with sculpture is equally intense, and a bronze *Bowie Dancer* (p. 133) shows just how poised a performer can be even when thrusting one bright blue leg high in the air. Yet this dancer's attenuated body could easily topple over and end in the position assumed by the upside-down figure in *Fallen Angel*. Even a sculpture as commanding as *Walking Tall*, which appears to celebrate the decisive commitment of a man/woman striding through space, looks almost as thin as a Giacometti figure; and the bronze *Peaceman* (p. 93) who holds out a white dove in the palm of his hand, must realise how easily this little bird could tumble down from its perch. Bailey, it seems, is conscious at all times of life's precariousness.

A similar fate might well await the dramatically silhouetted animal in a painting titled *Cat on a Hot Tin Roof*. Although its tail still curls up in the air, this creature appears to be assaulted from all sides by blistering heat. The canvas is very small, but Bailey fills every inch with marks evoking the turbulence of a nation afflicted by too much sun. The Western Cape has recently been suffering from a severe drought, and in another tiny painting called *Dry Season*, Bailey shows how parched and stricken this water-starved land can become. No wonder he devotes one of his largest recent paintings to a theme as redemptive as *The Resurrection of Mammiwatti* (p. 211). It refers to a water deity venerated in West, Central and Southern Africa. Bailey shows her emerging from a reassuringly blue expanse of sea, looking like a mermaid. She is accompanied by other pale figures, and their mythological potency cannot be doubted.

All the same, there is more than a hint of ghostliness about this painting. Like so many of Bailey's images, it haunts our imagination. Indeed, *The Resurrection of Mammiwatti* remains a fantasy, rather than an event capable of saving a country from its beleaguered condition. Bailey is far too aware of our planetary disorders to offer any facile consolation in his art. He aims, instead, at exploring the human predicament, and his determination is as forthright as the near-naked man in *Midnight Walker* (p. 194). Scarcely visible, he nevertheless fills his limbs with defiant energy while striding through the darkness, thrusting one arm out in front of him. Bailey's work is animated by the same undaunted resolve, and we can gain immense nourishment from his adventurous insistence on probing our bewildered world with such impulsive flair.

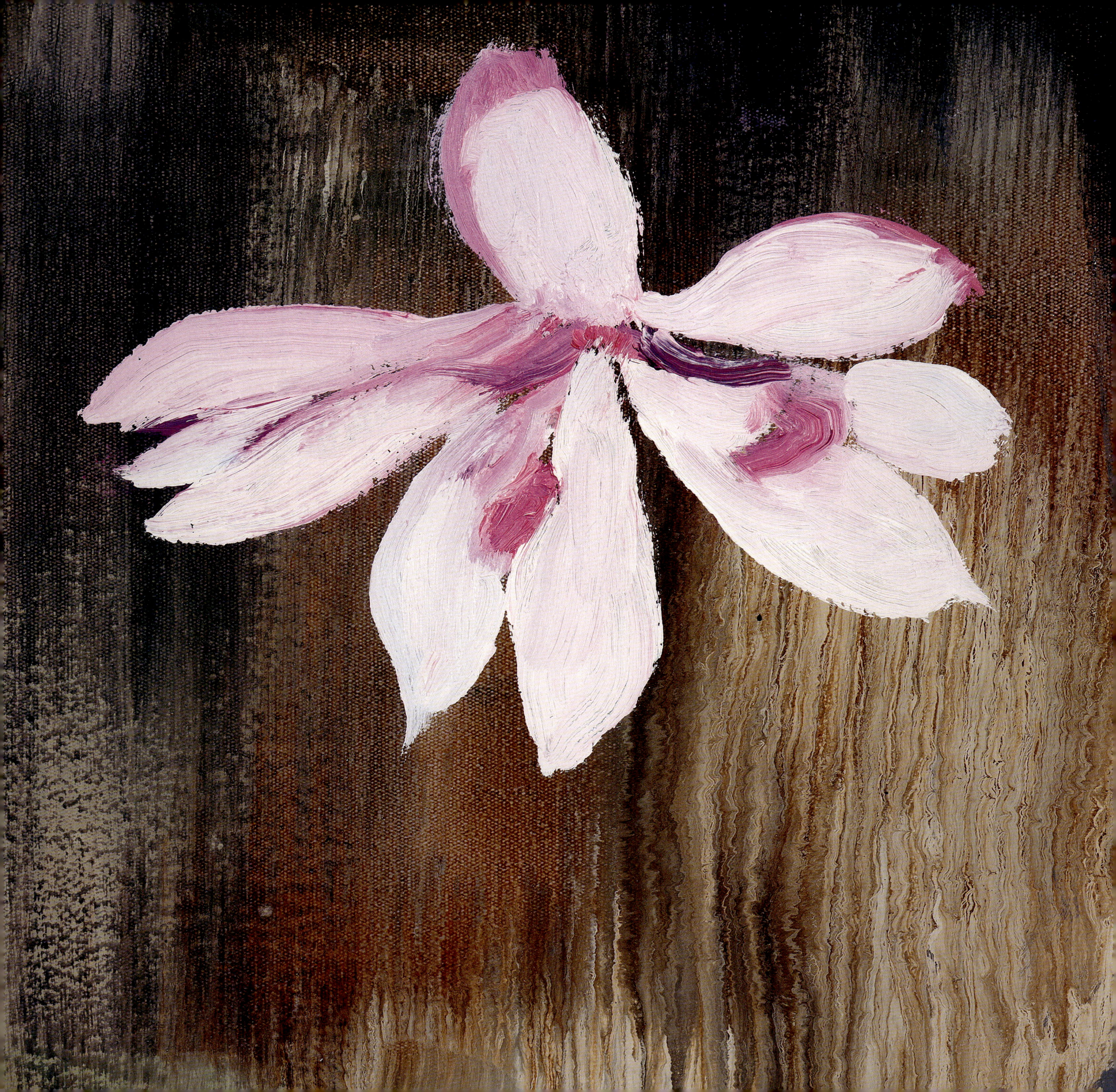

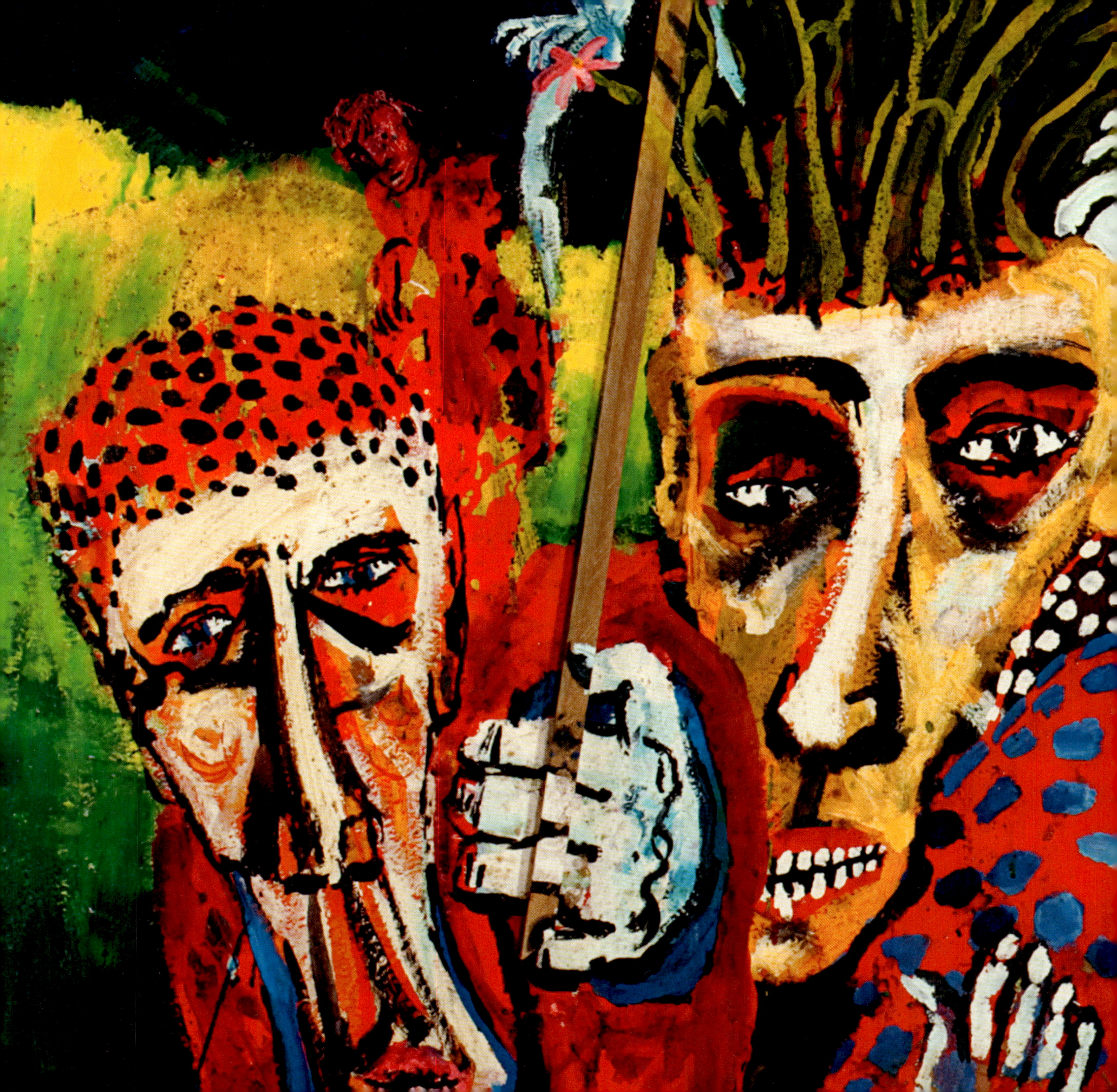

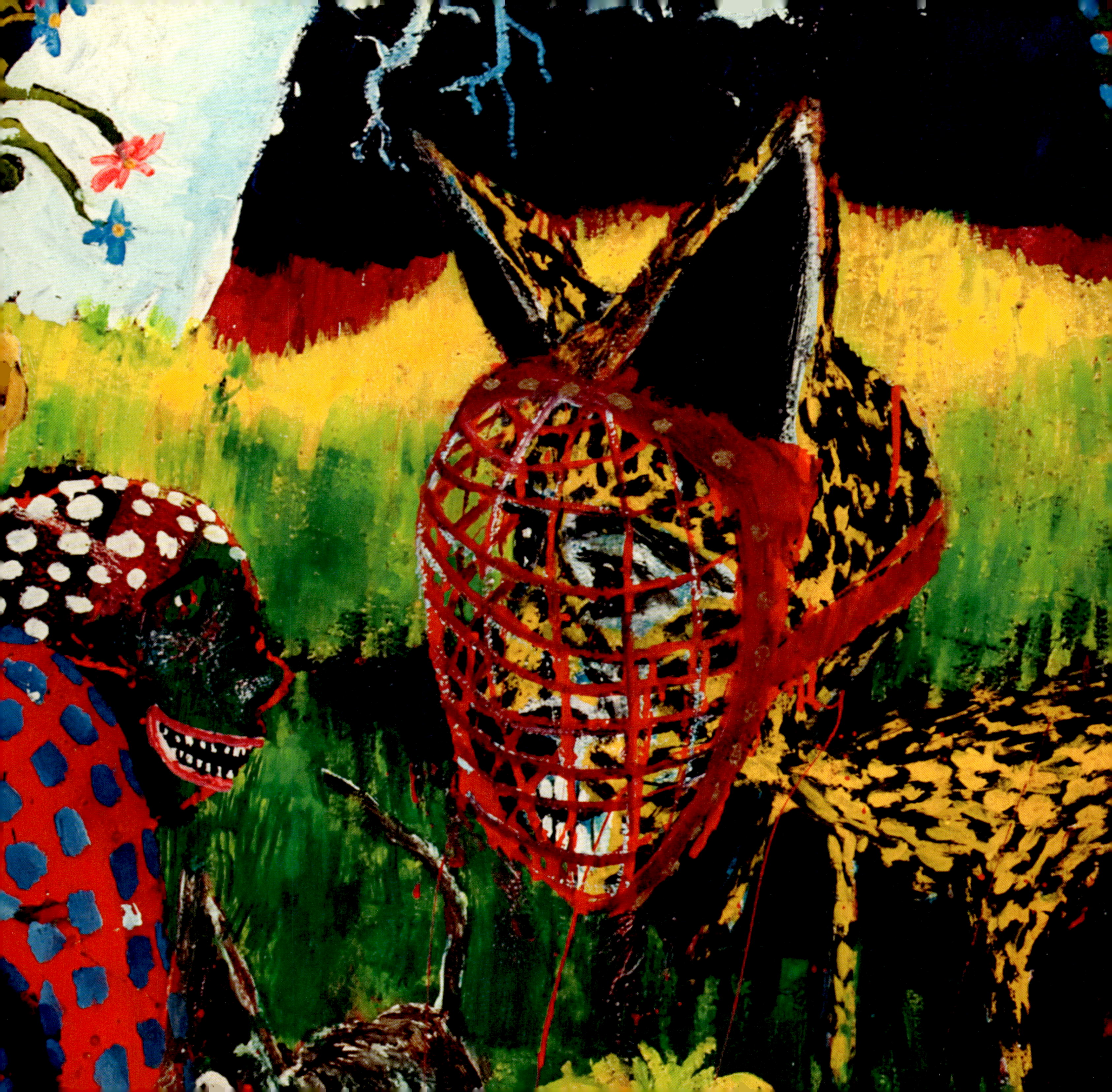

THE ARMS DEALER 2002 Patinated bronze with oil paint 104 × 20 × 18cm

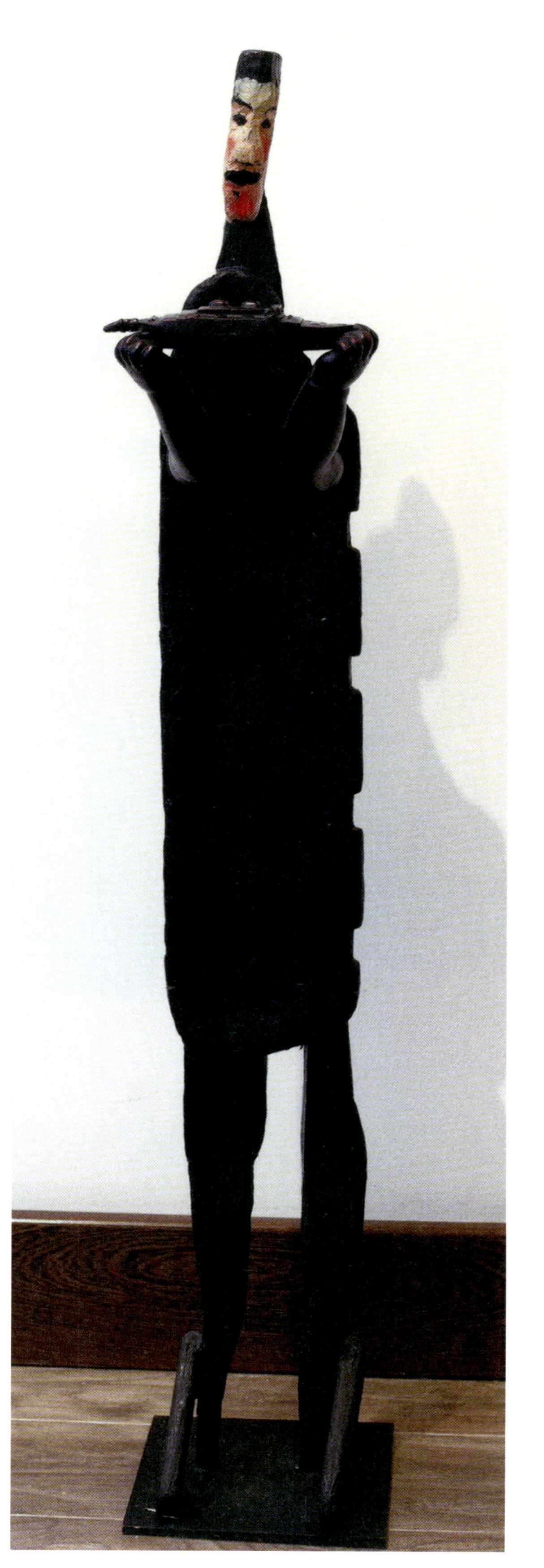

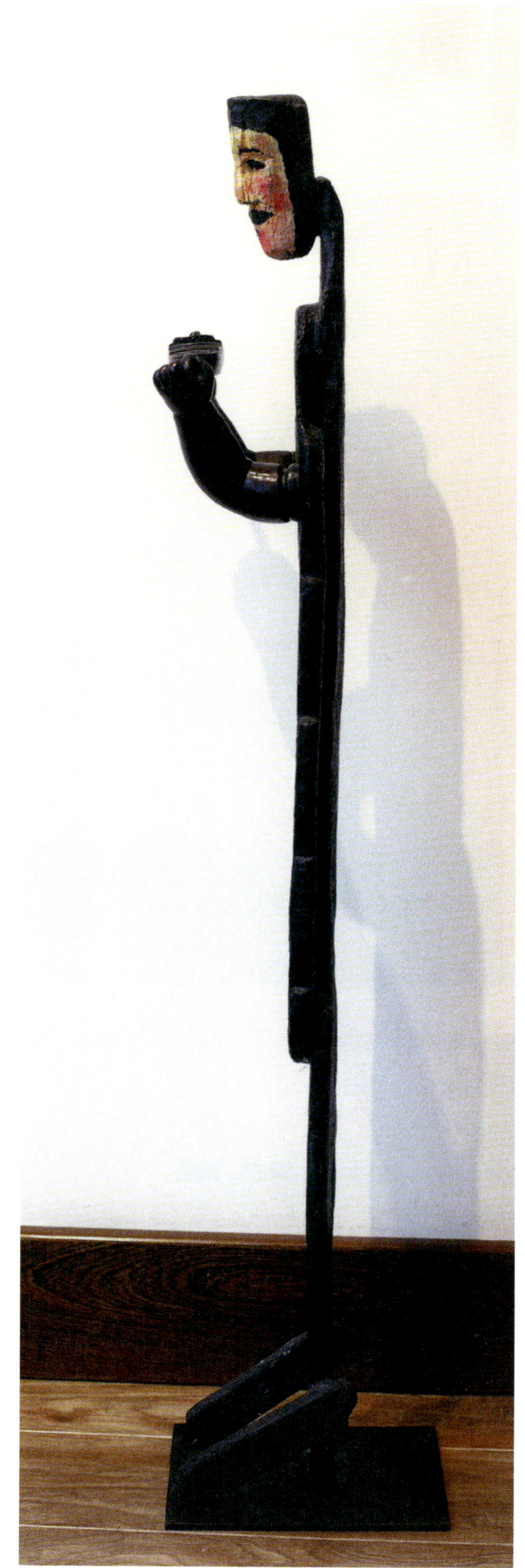

SOLDIER HEADS 1999 Painted carved wood with nails 69 × 18cm and 54 × 25cm

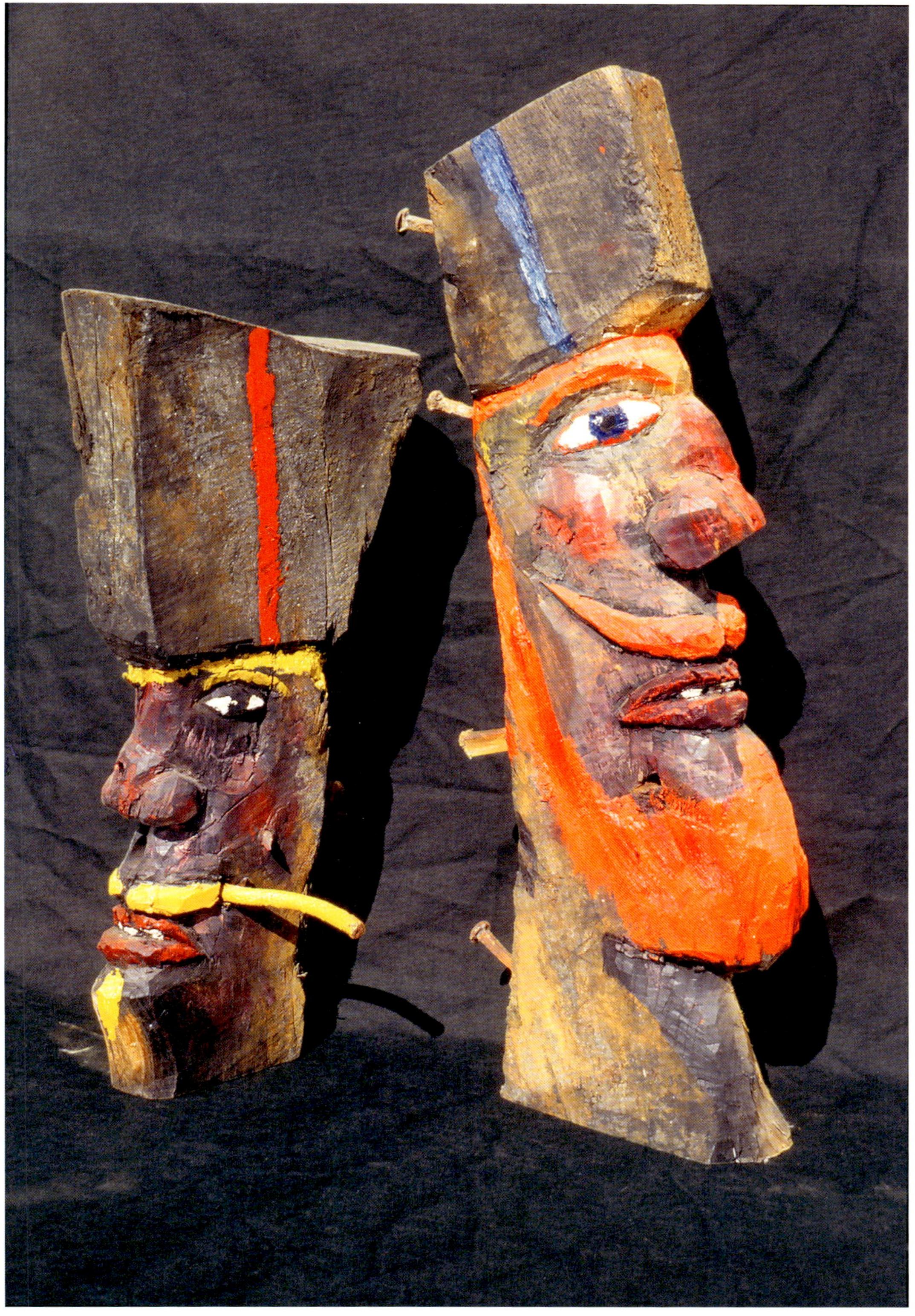

LEARNING TO FLY AGAIN 1999 Silkscreen and gold leaf on Masonite 133 × 107cm

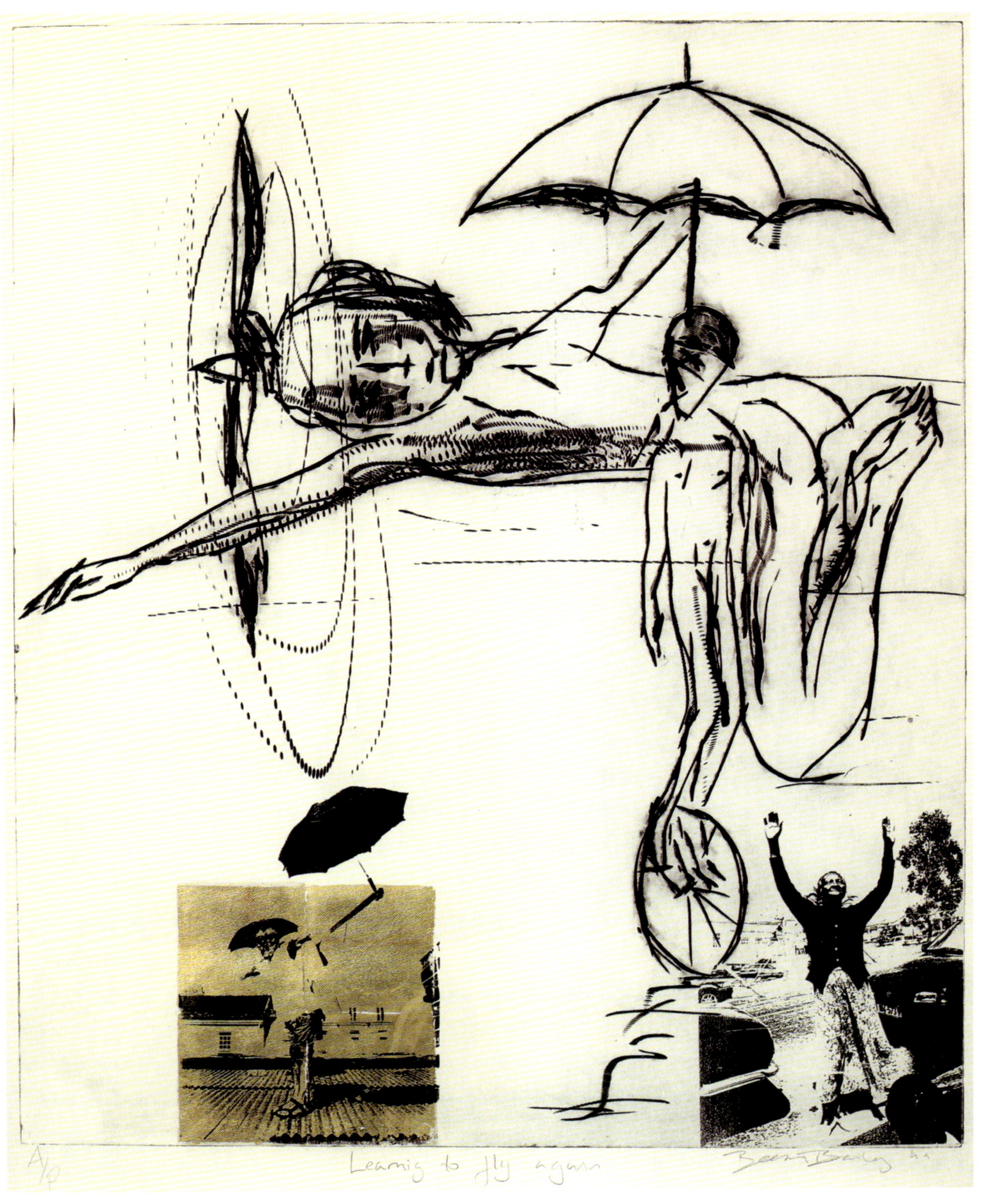
A/P
Learnig to fly again

CLOWN ELLIOT IN DOVER 1988 Oil and charcoal on canvas 152 × 152cm

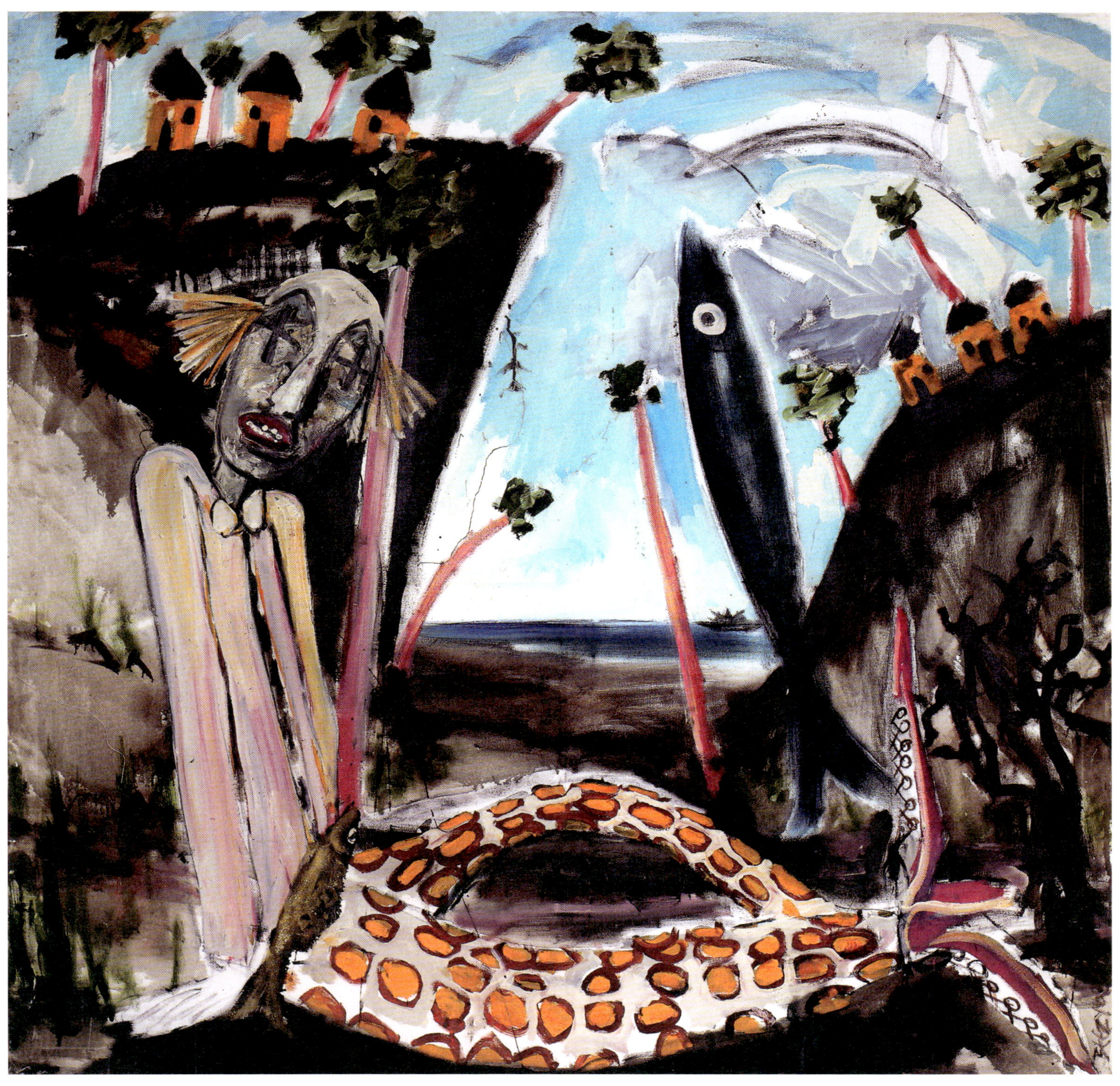

TAKE OFF 2002 Angle-grinder print (hand coloured) 107 × 134cm

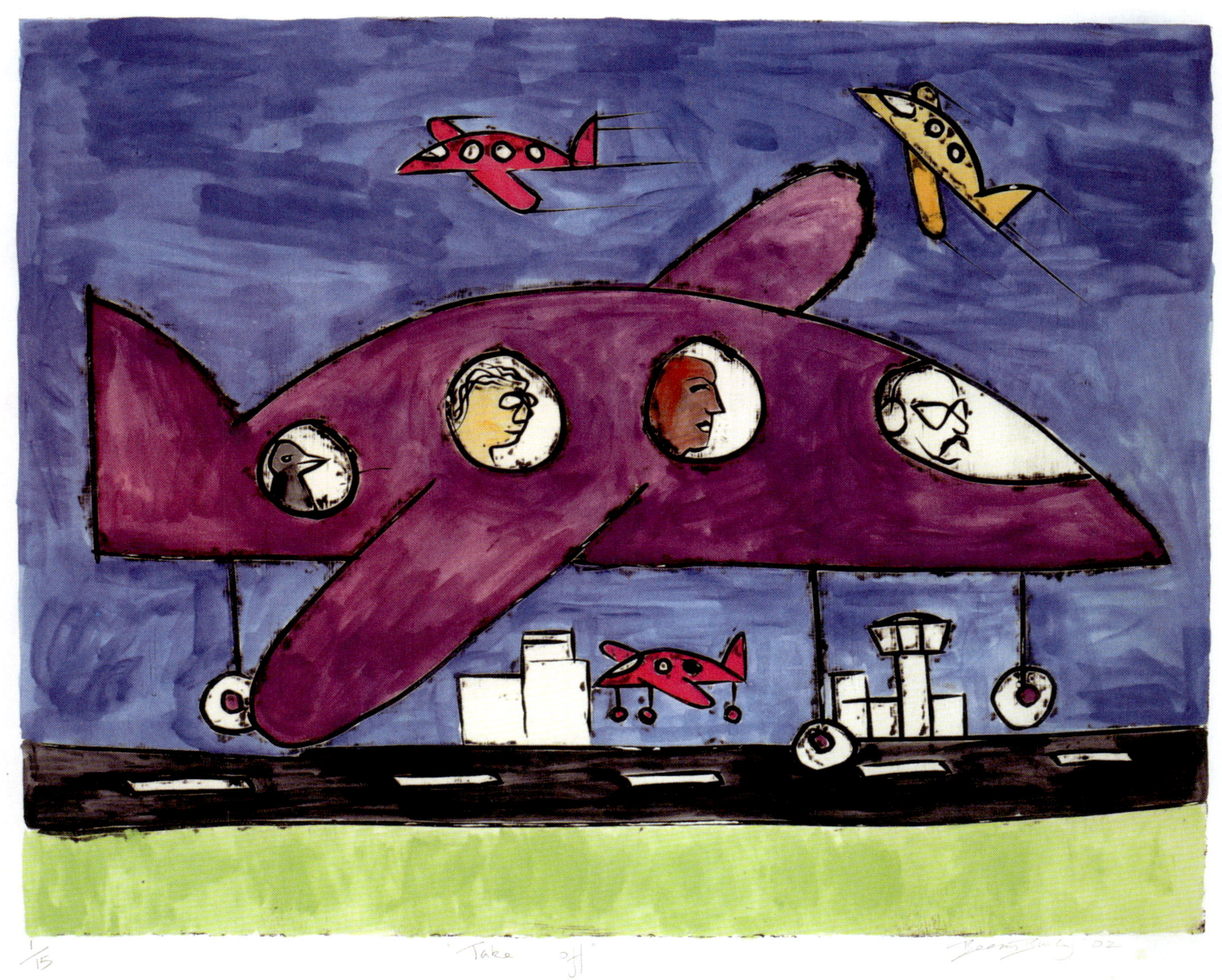
1/15
'Take off'

RUNNING FROM ROME 1987 Oil and bitumen on canvas 104.5 × 77cm

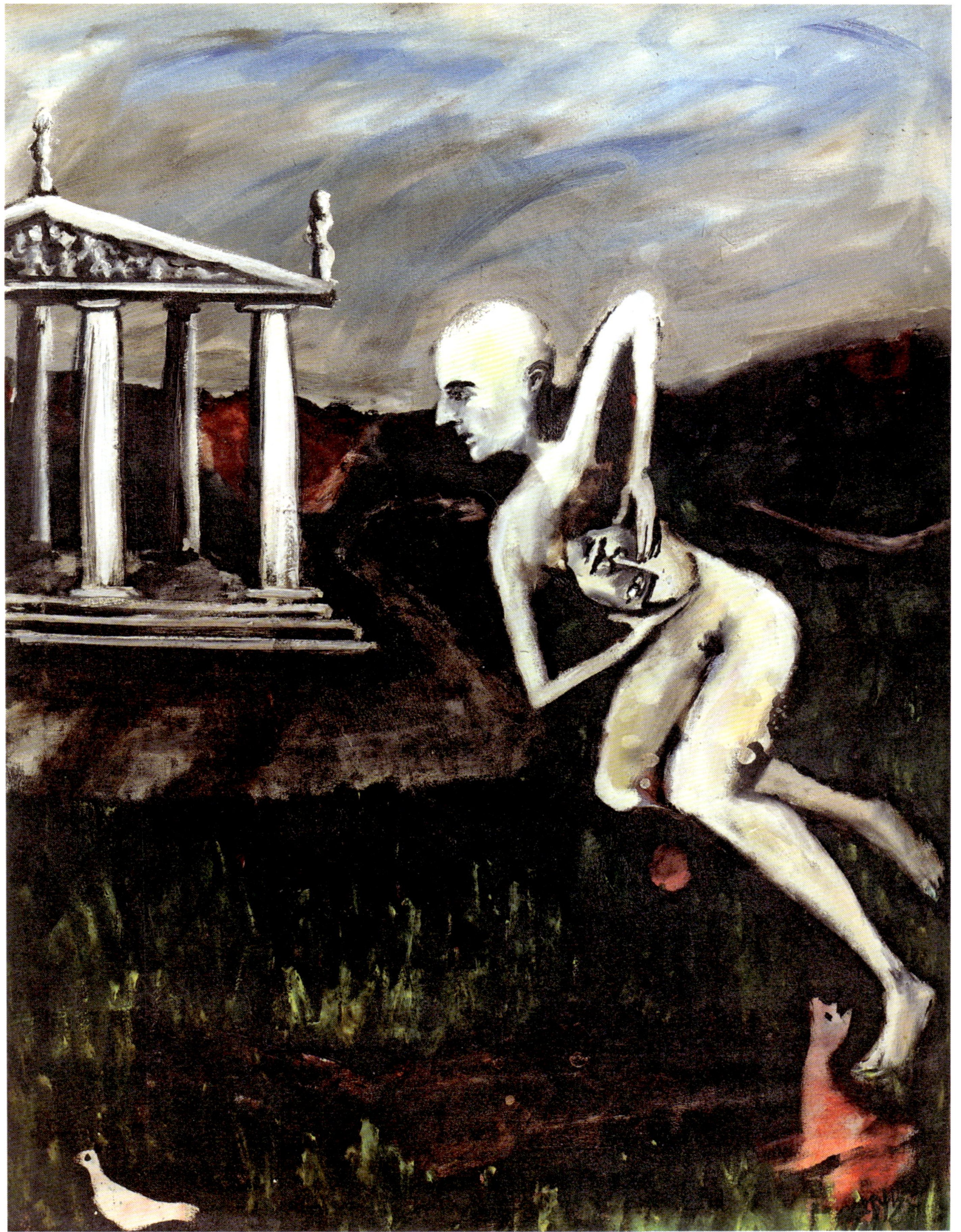

TRANSCONTINENTAL LOVE 1987 Oil on canvas with sand 121.5 × 241cm

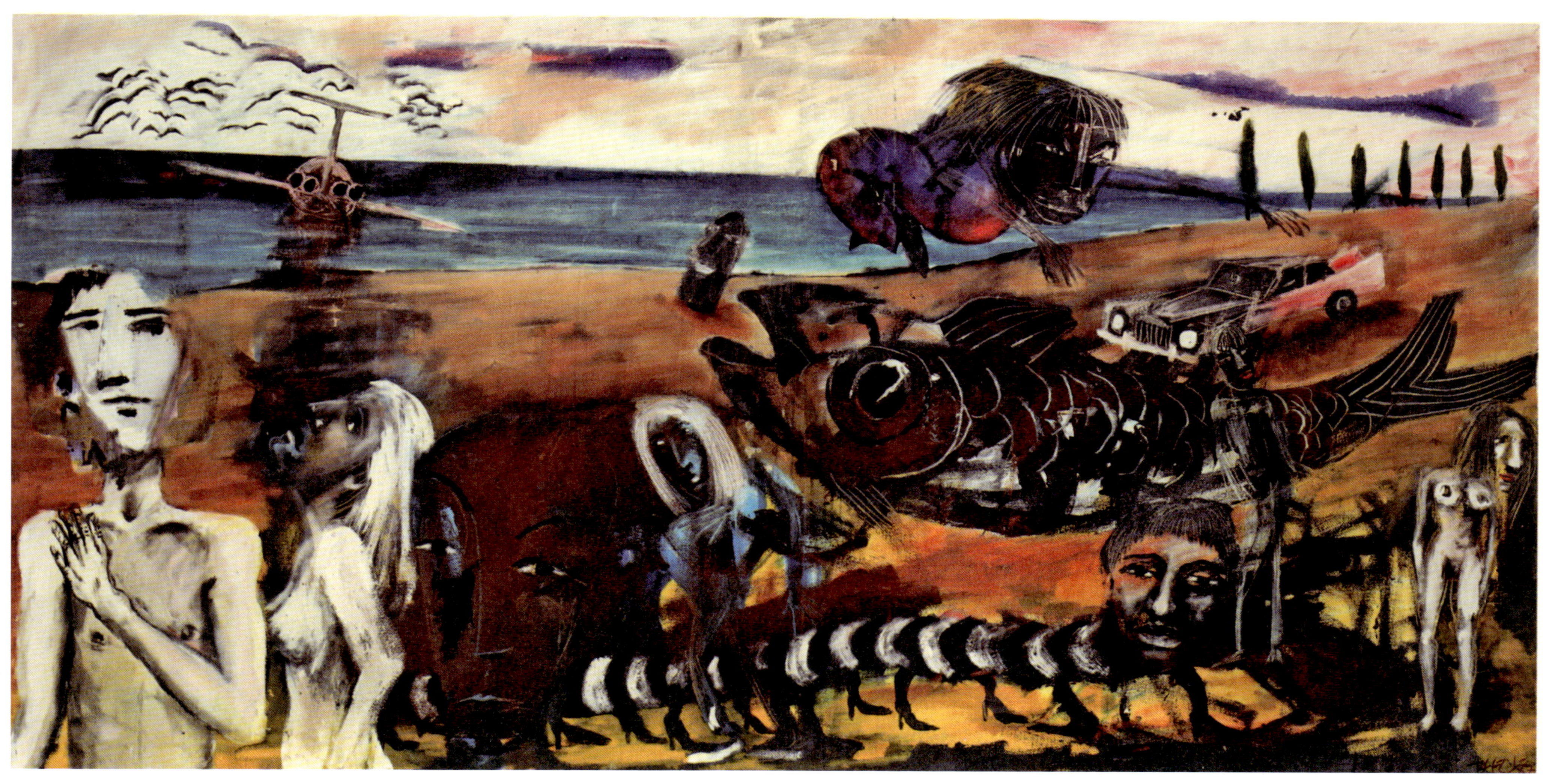

THE DEATH OF NELSON MAKUBA 1987 Enamel and oil on canvas with wood 181 × 259cm

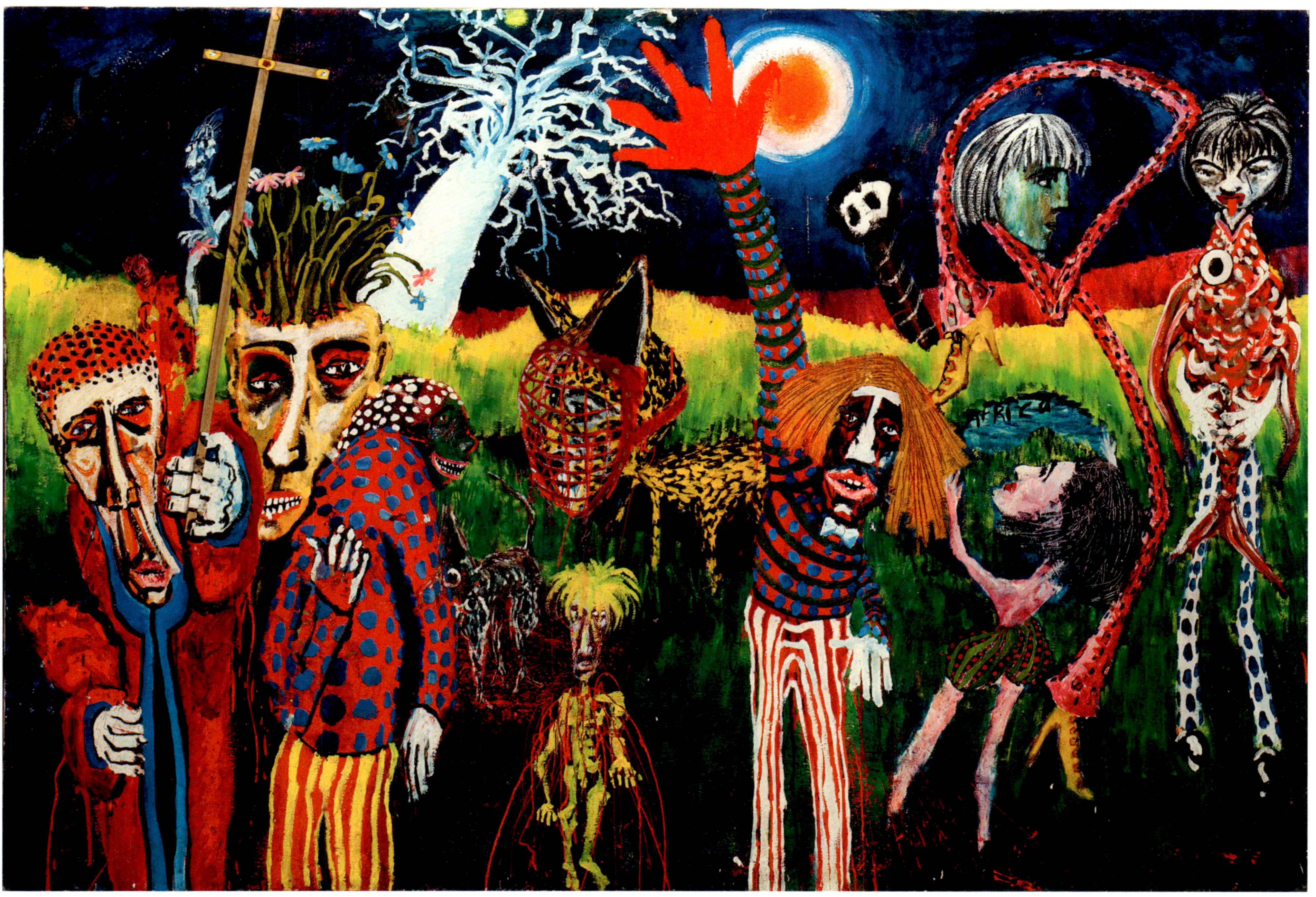
AFRICA

THE TANTRUM GIRL 2005 Oil on canvas 250 × 170cm

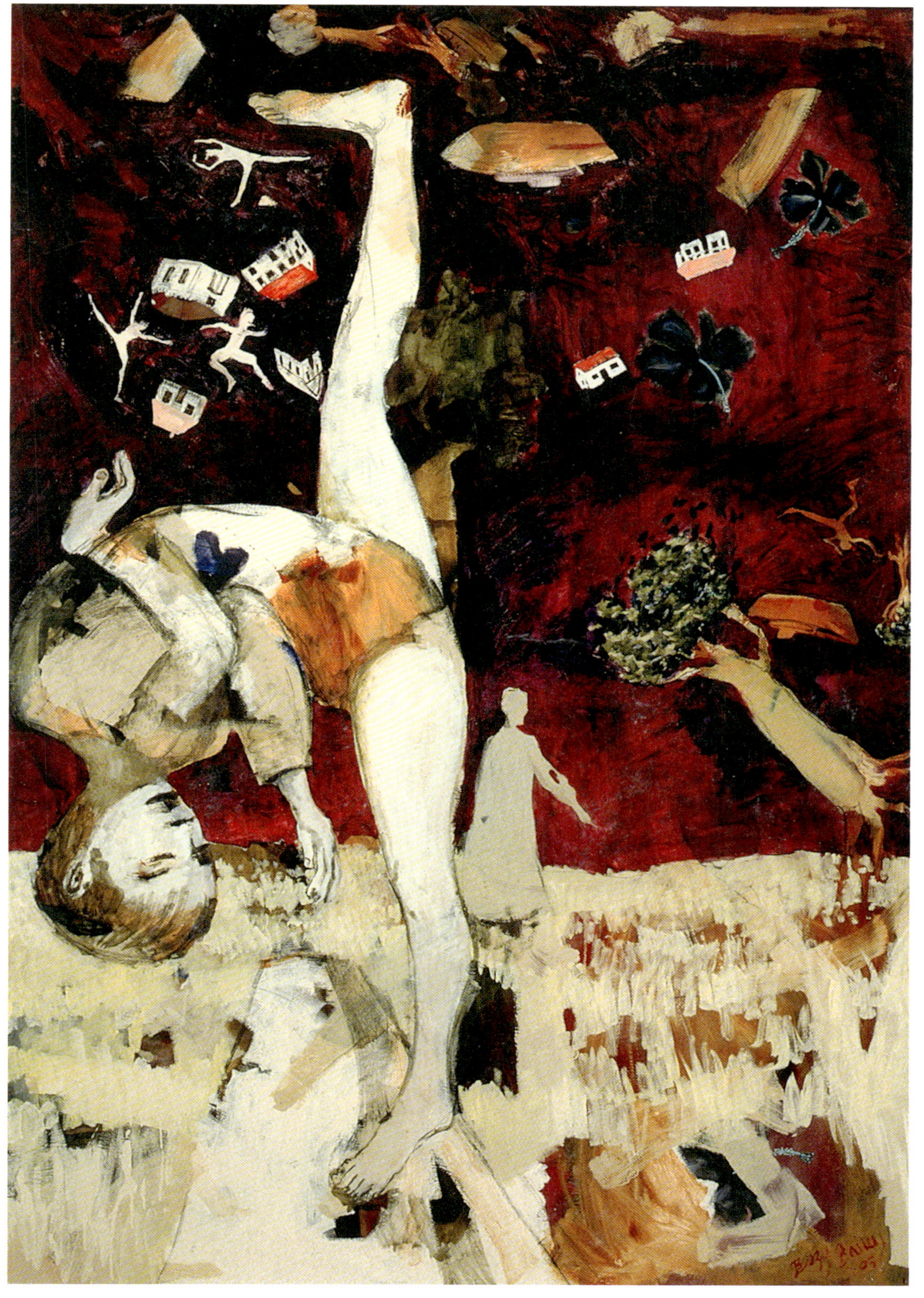

LIFE DANCE 1990 Angle-grinder-on-steel etching 75 × 56cm

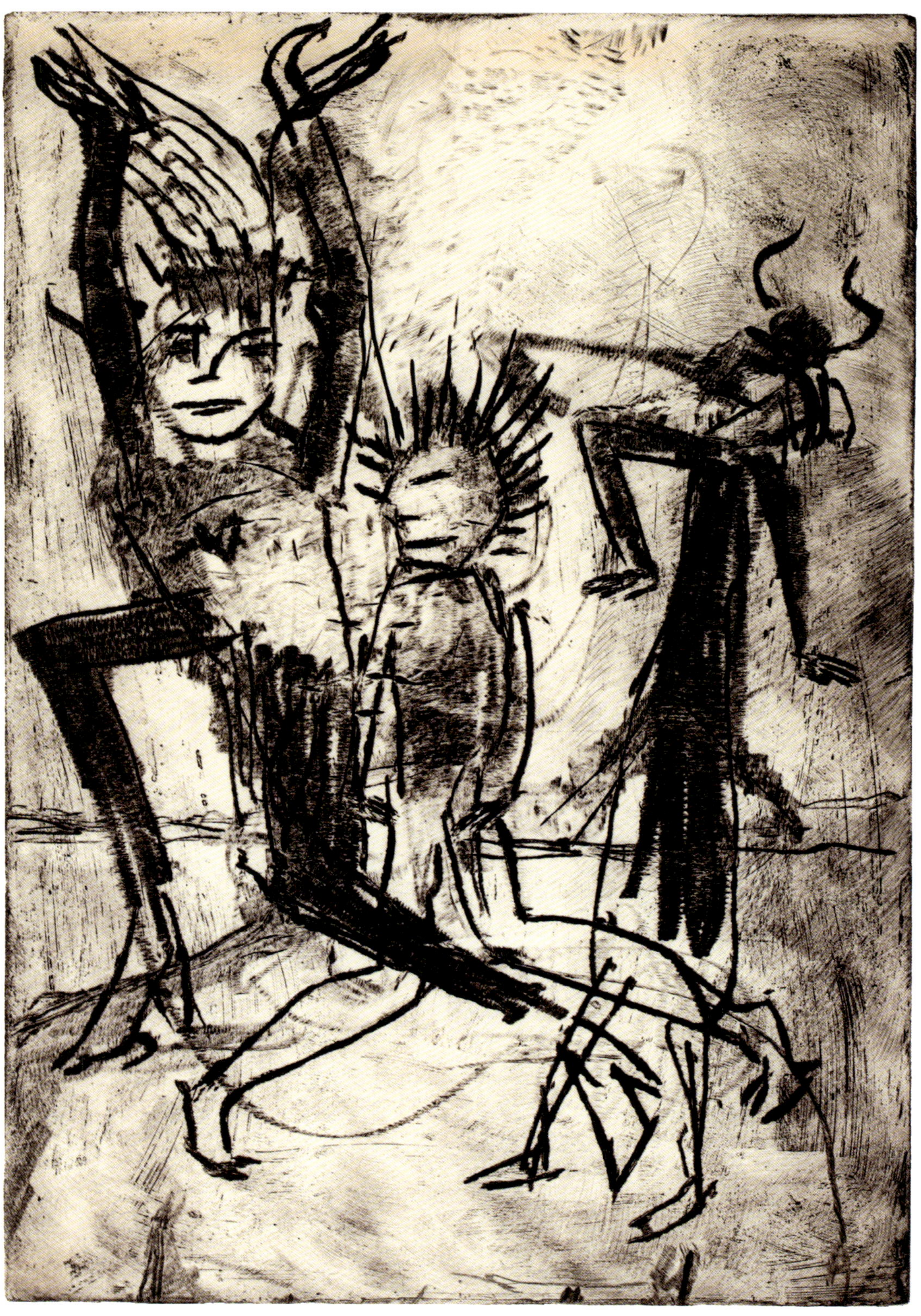

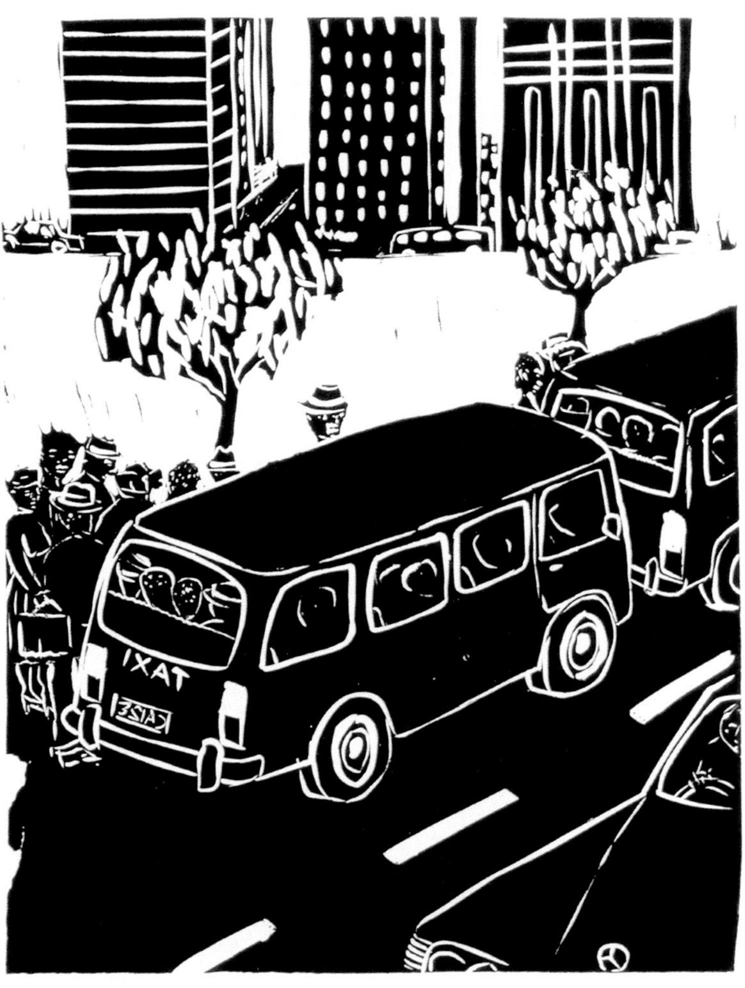

GO HOME (Joyce Ntobe) 1991 Linocut 46 × 32cm

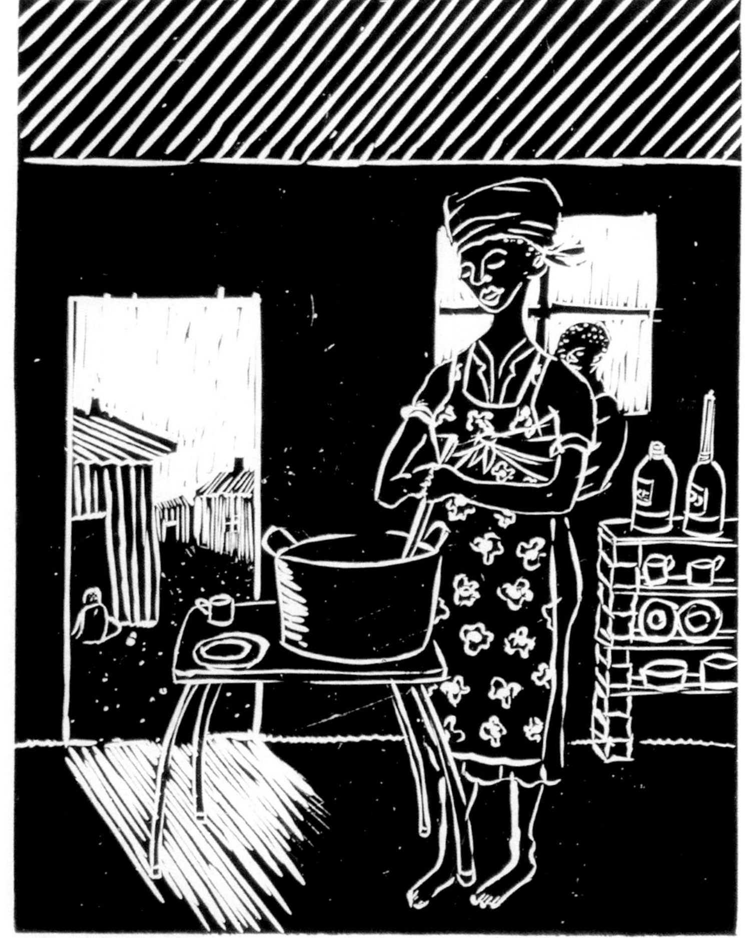

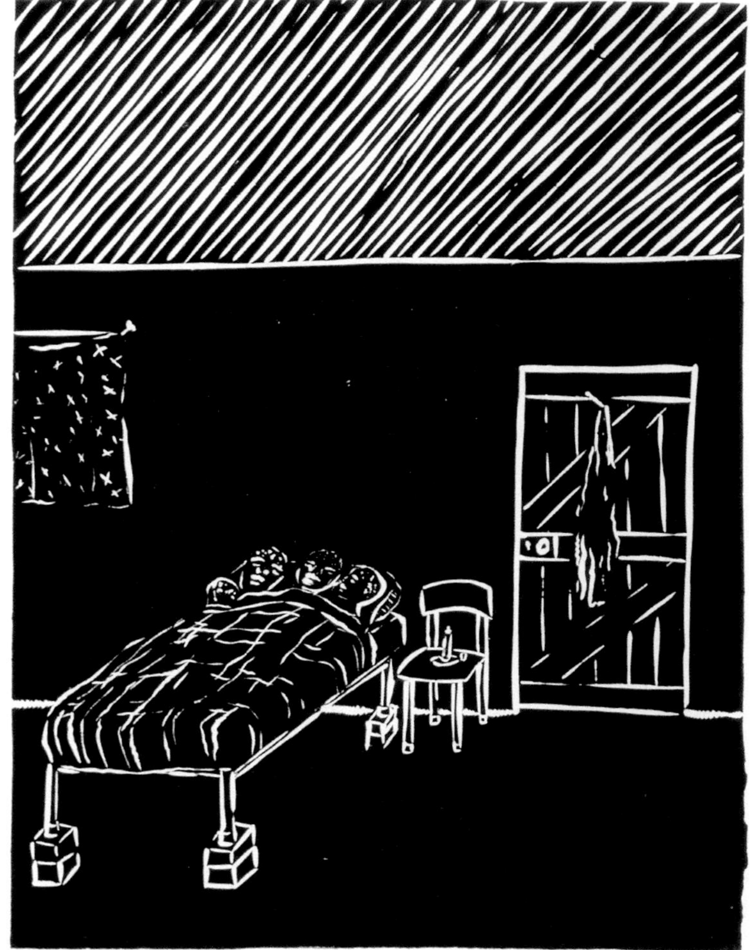

MAKE SUPPER (Joyce Ntobe) 1991 Linocut 46 × 32cm

GO TO SLEEP (Joyce Ntobe) 1991 Linocut 46 × 32cm

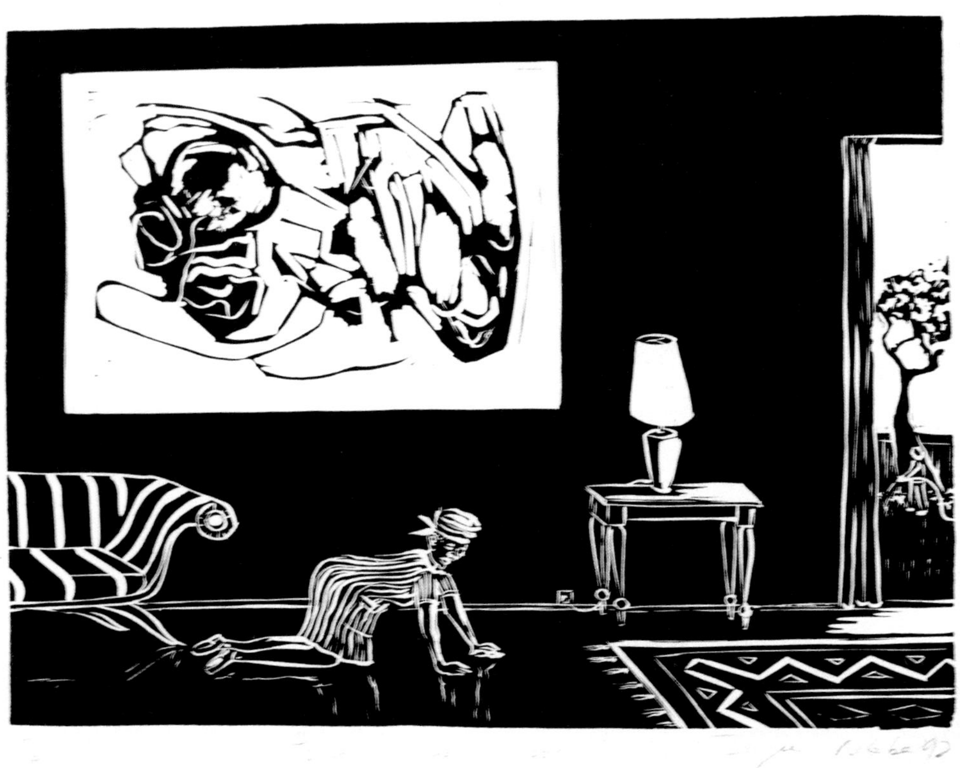

POLISHING THE FLOOR (Joyce Ntobe) 1992 Linocut 32 × 46cm

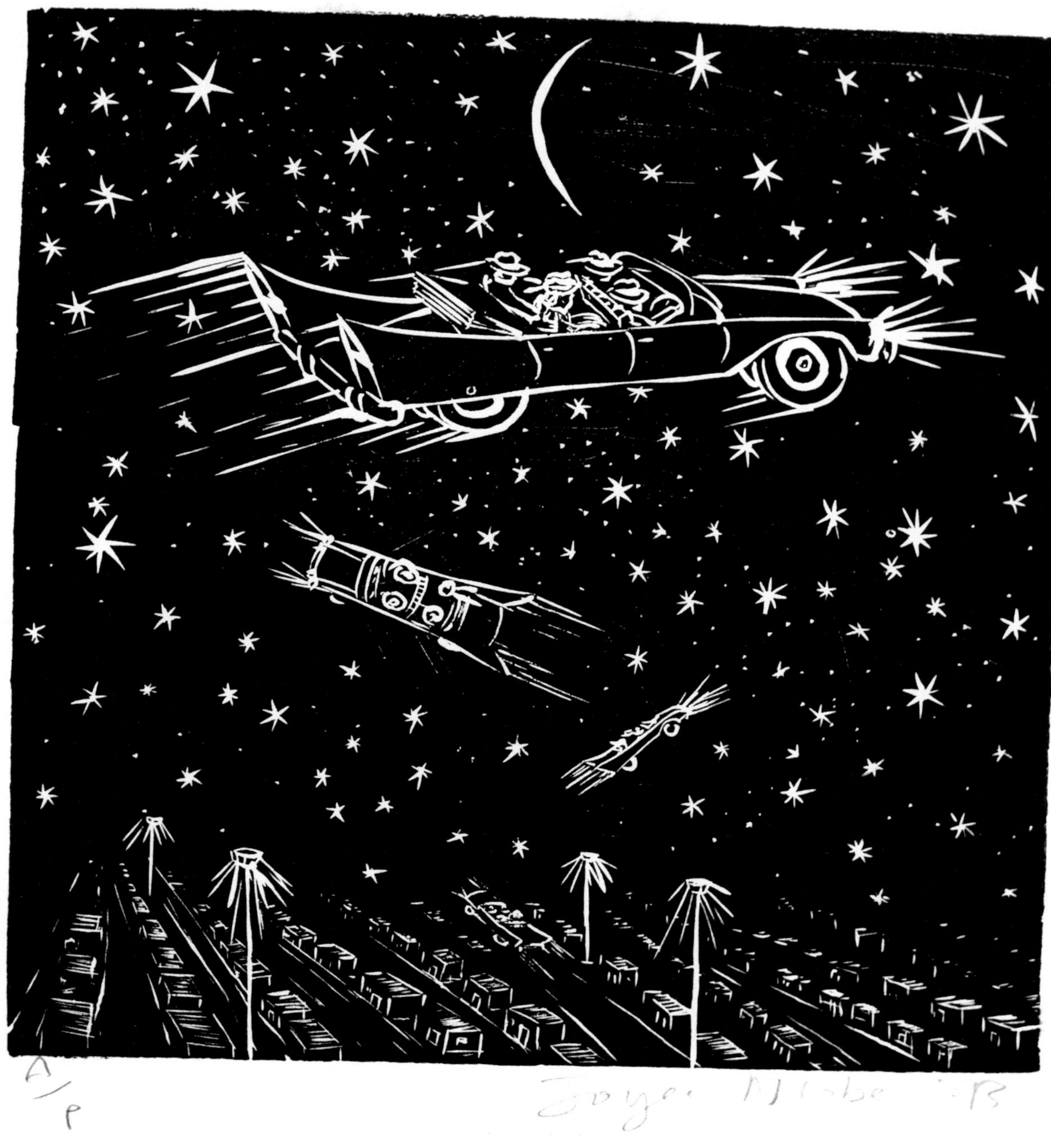

I DREAMT I FLEW AWAY WITH THE AMERICANS IN THEIR CADILLAC (Joyce Ntobe) 1993 Linocut 60 × 56cm

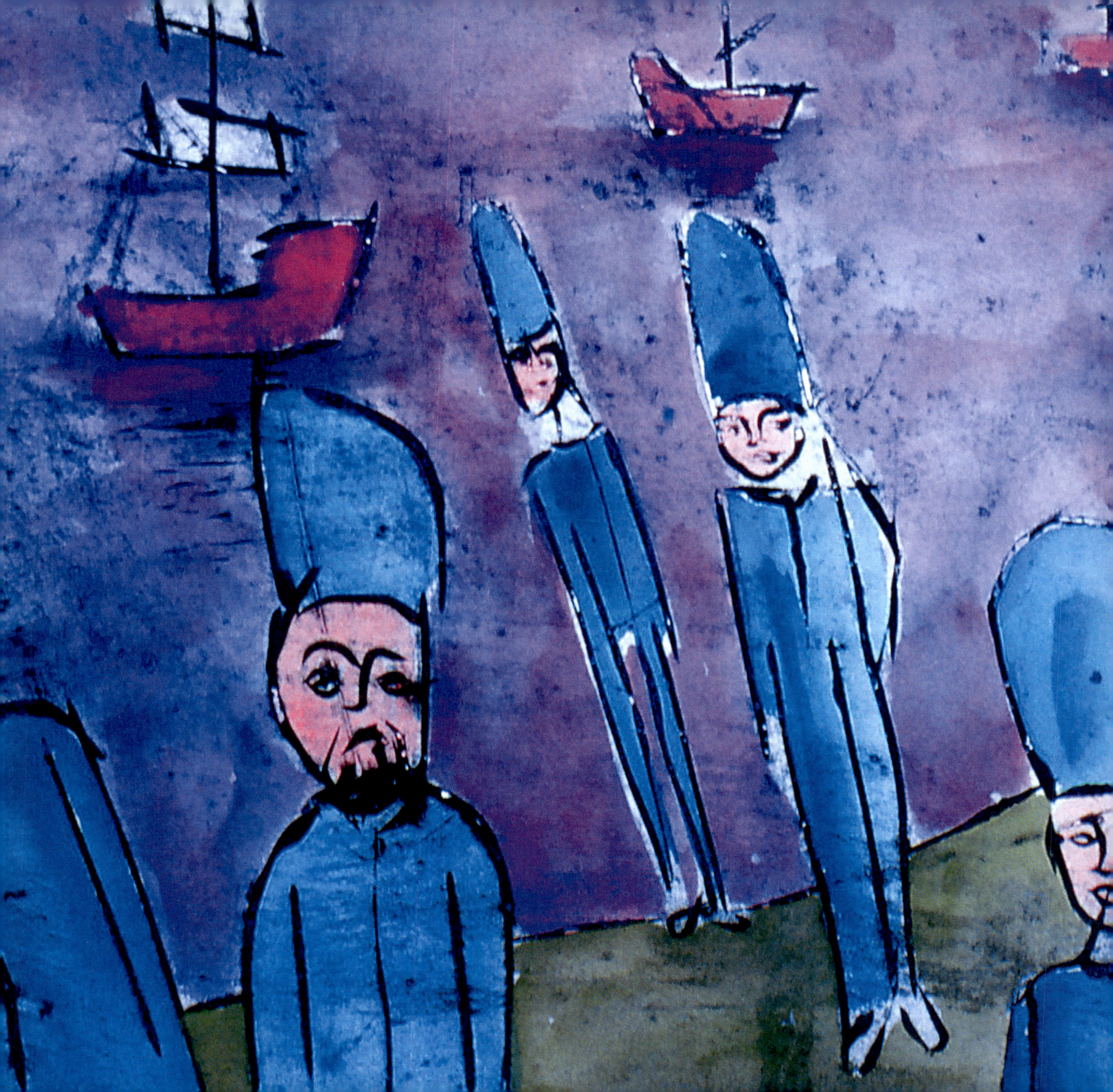

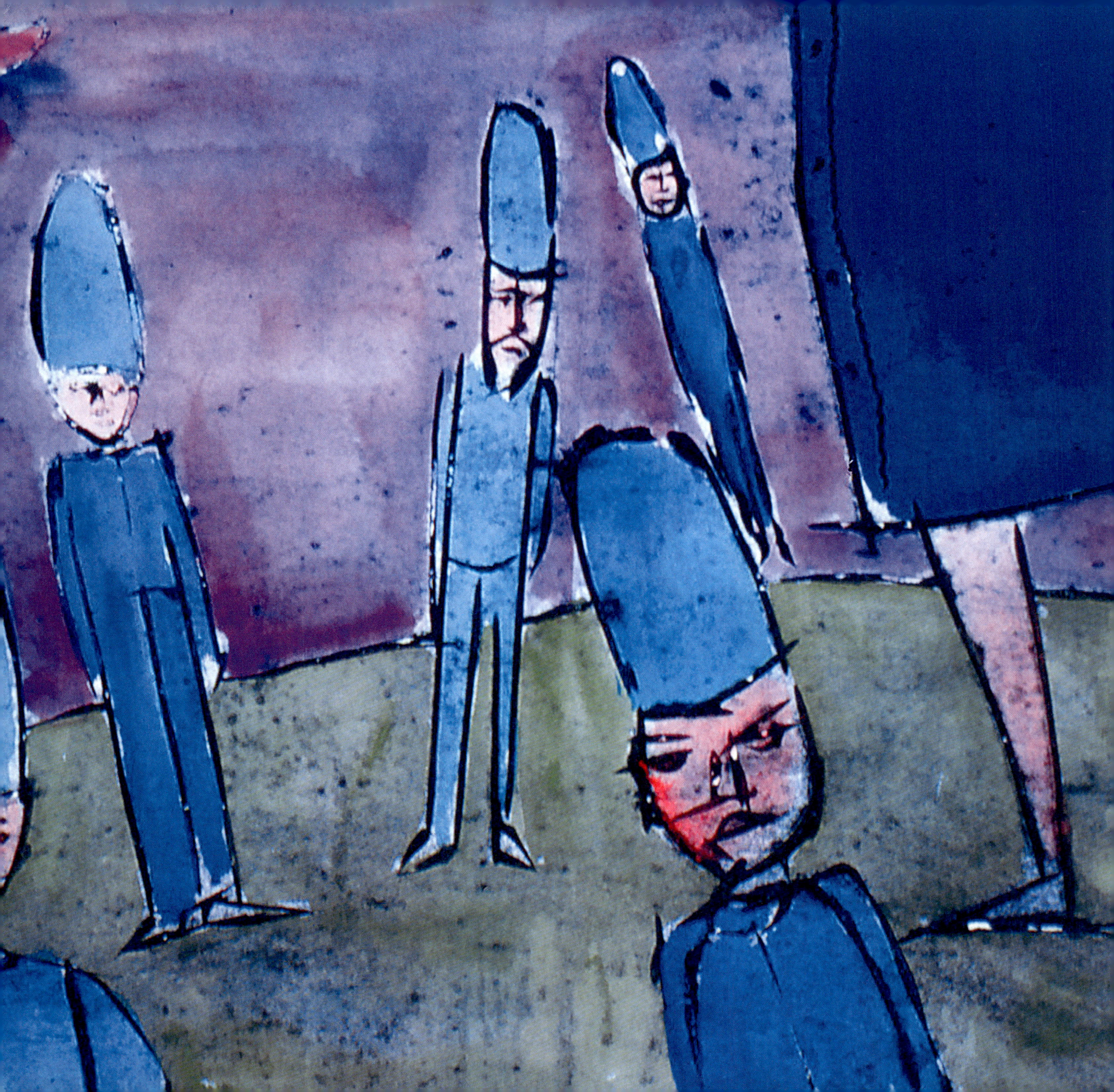

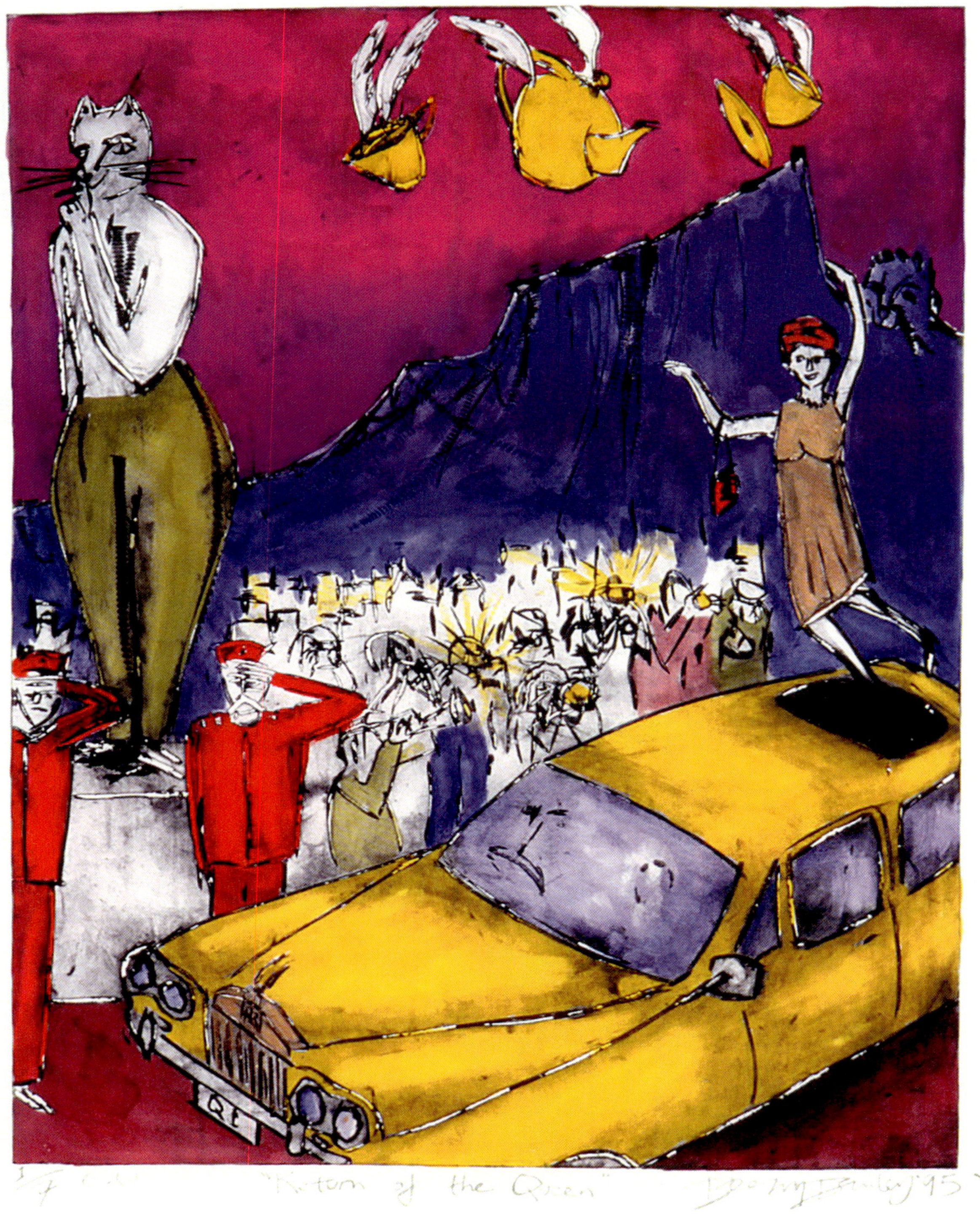

RETURN OF THE QUEEN 1994 Angle-grinder print (hand coloured) 121 × 100cm

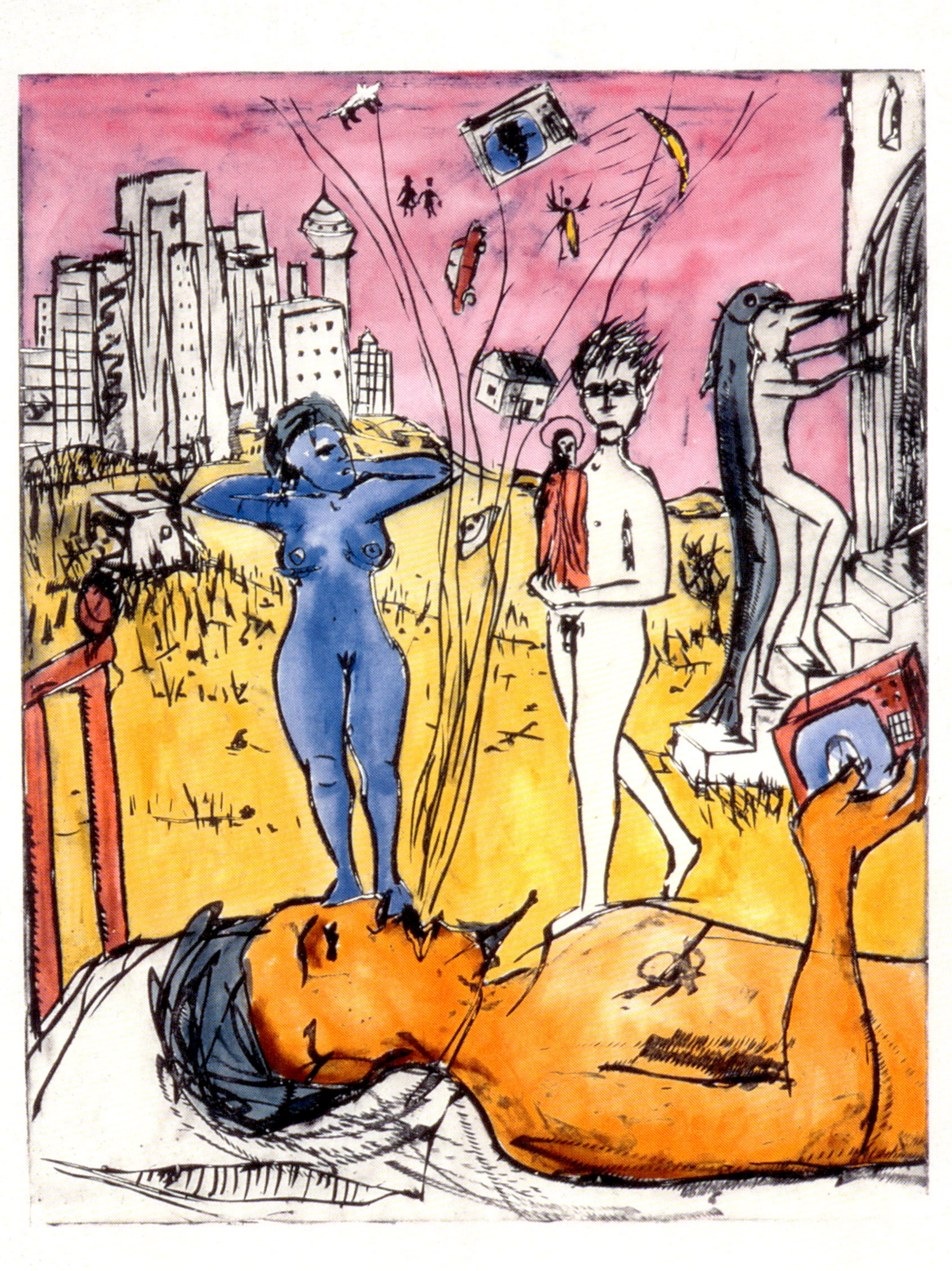

THE DYING MAN SPOKE OF MANY THINGS 1998 Angle-grinder print (hand coloured) 121 × 100cm

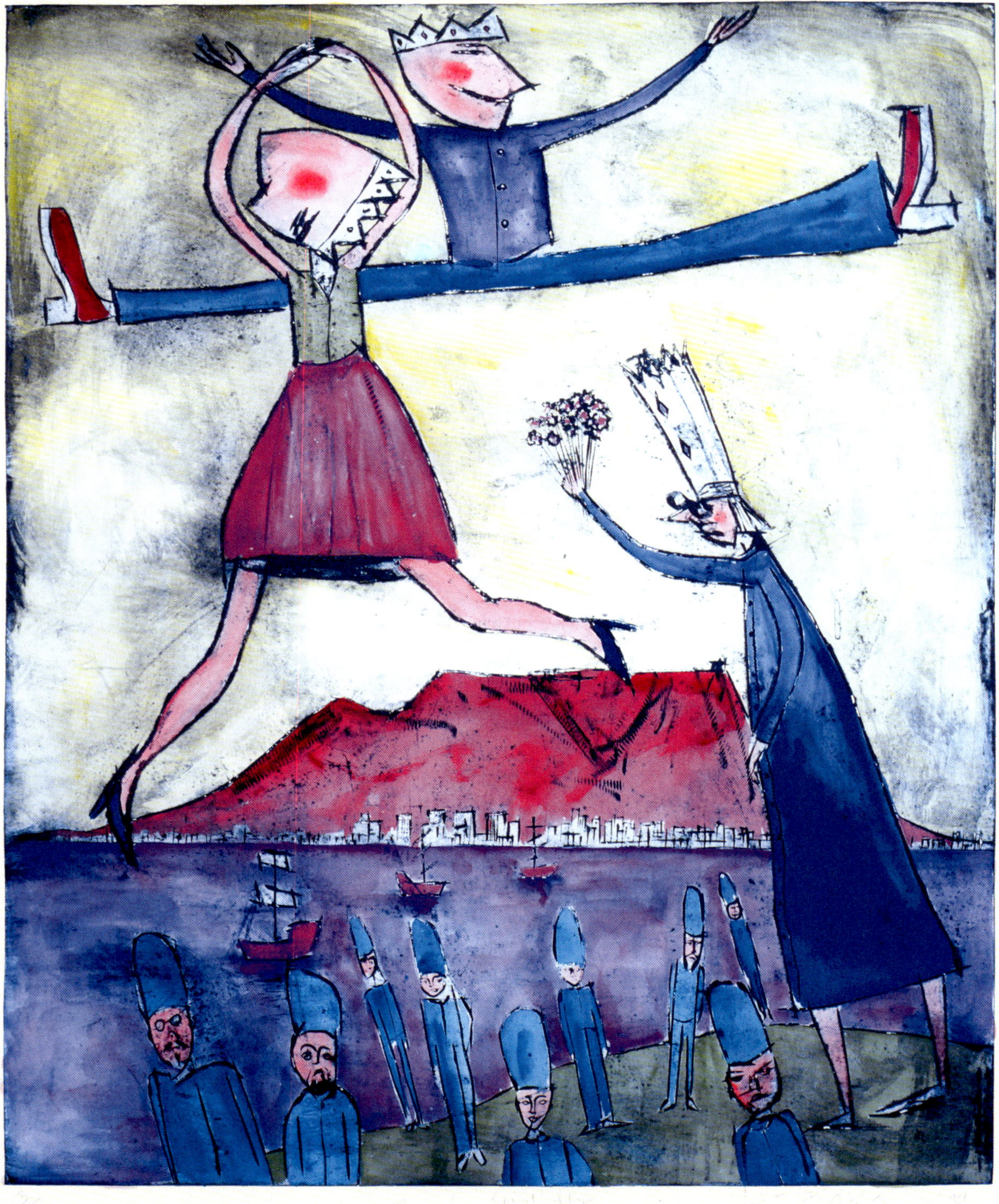

DANCING SOLDIERS I 2015 Angle-grinder print (hand coloured) 121 × 100cm

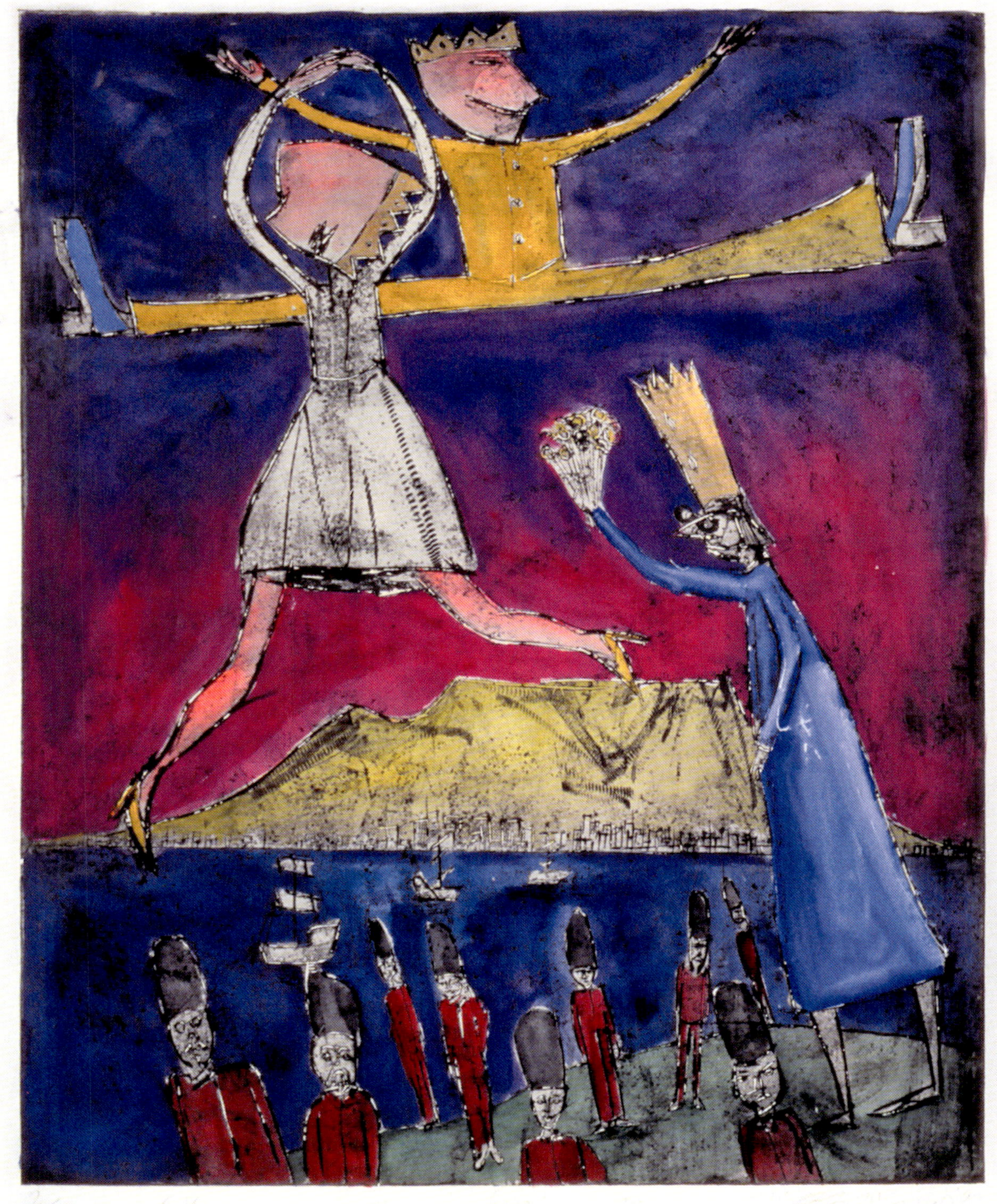

DANCING SOLDIERS II 2015 Angle-grinder print (hand coloured) 121 × 100cm

LEE PING ZING GOES TO SCHOOL 1996 Silkscreen 75.5 × 56cm

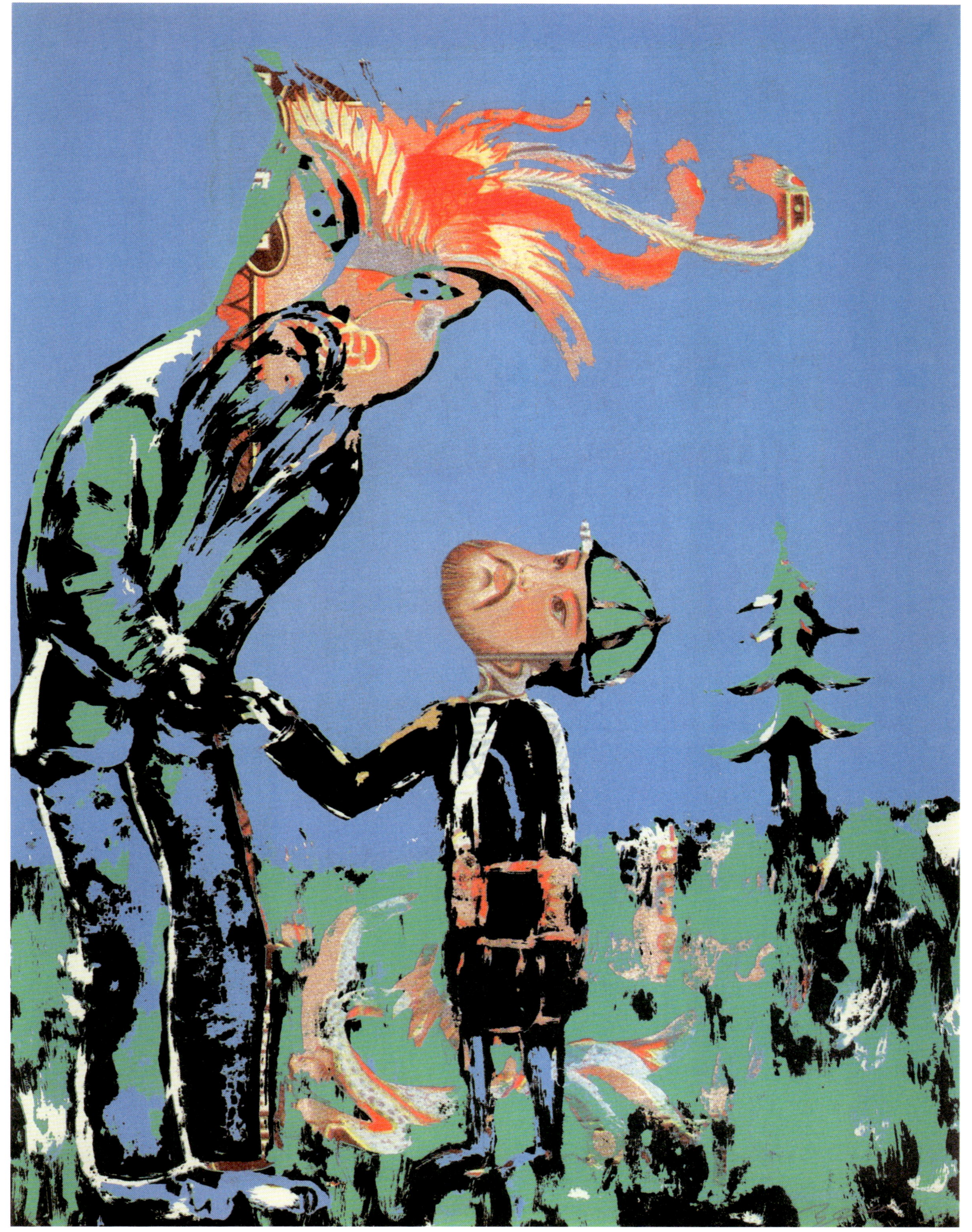

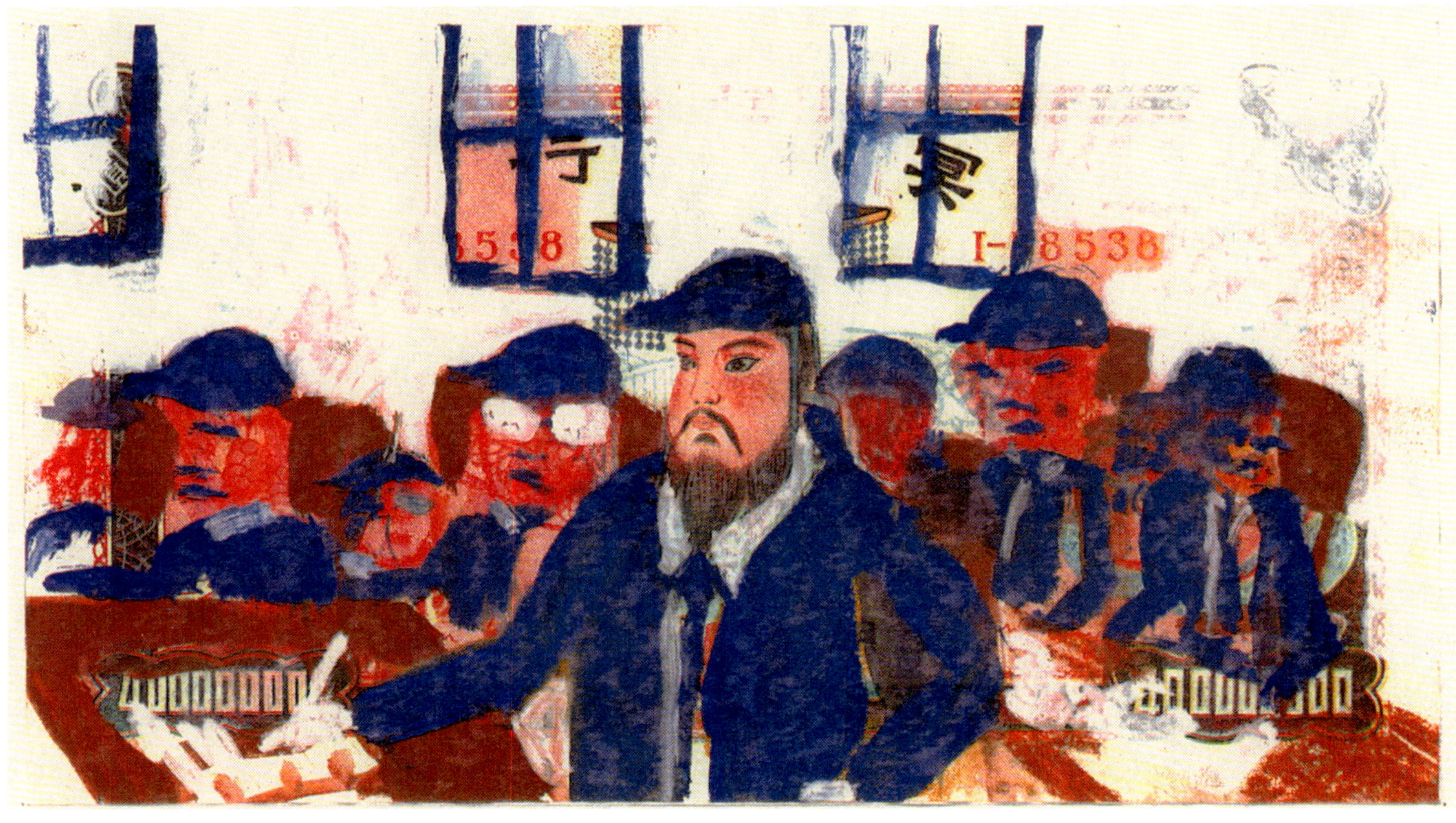

THE CLASSES AT SCHOOL WERE BORING AND HE OFTEN LOOKED OUT OF THE WINDOW AND DREAMED 1995
From Lee Ping Zing series Gouache and pastel on paper 10 × 18.5cm

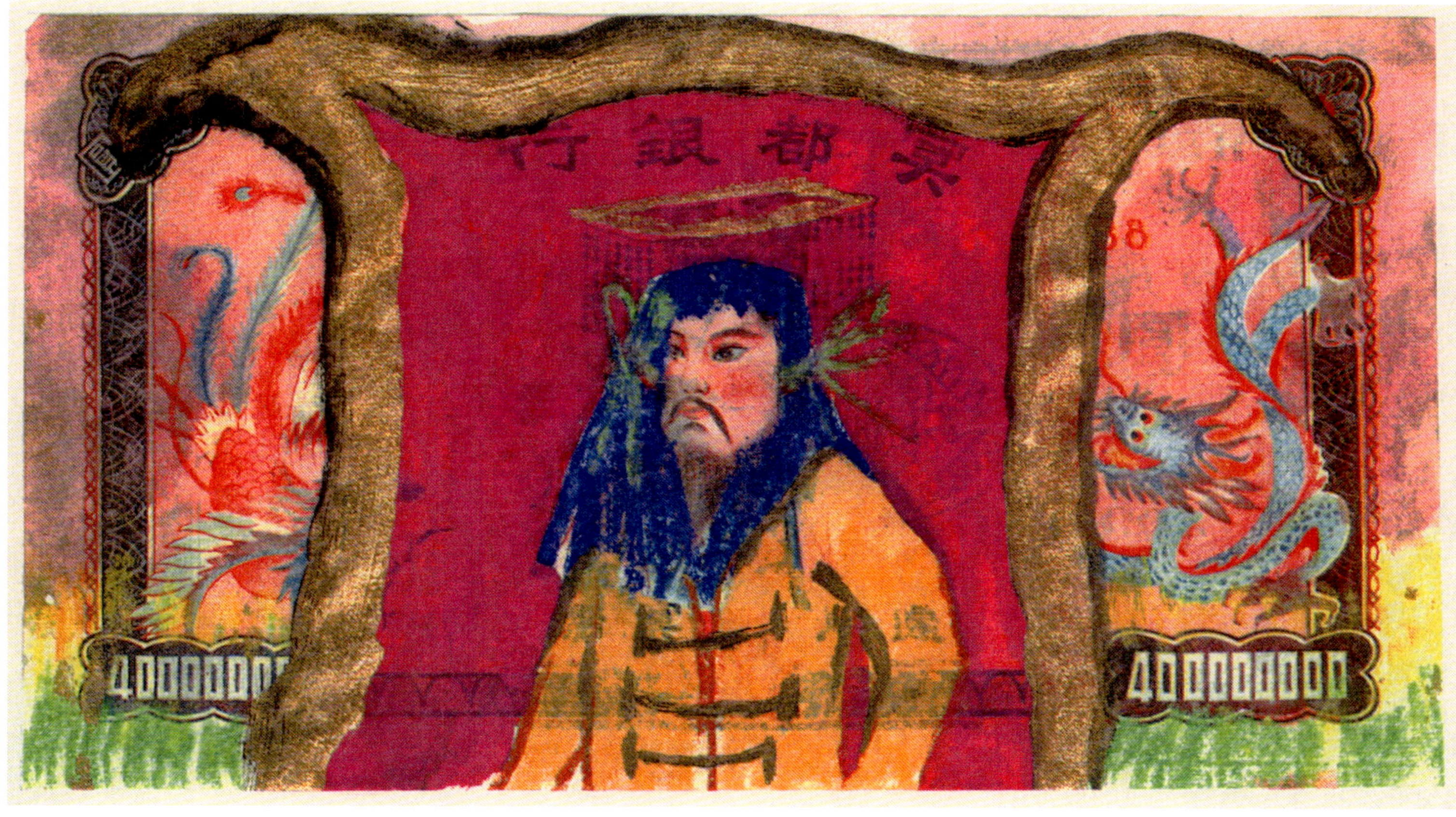

LEE PING LIKED THE IDEA OF A GIANT THRONE, SO ALTHOUGH HE WAS NOT A REAL KING, HE FELT LIKE ONE,
AND NOT 3EING A KING, HE WAS FREE TO DO AND BE WHATEVER HE WISHED, SO HE DIDN'T HURT ANYONE 1995
From Lee Ping Zing series Gouache and pastel on paper 10 × 18.5cm

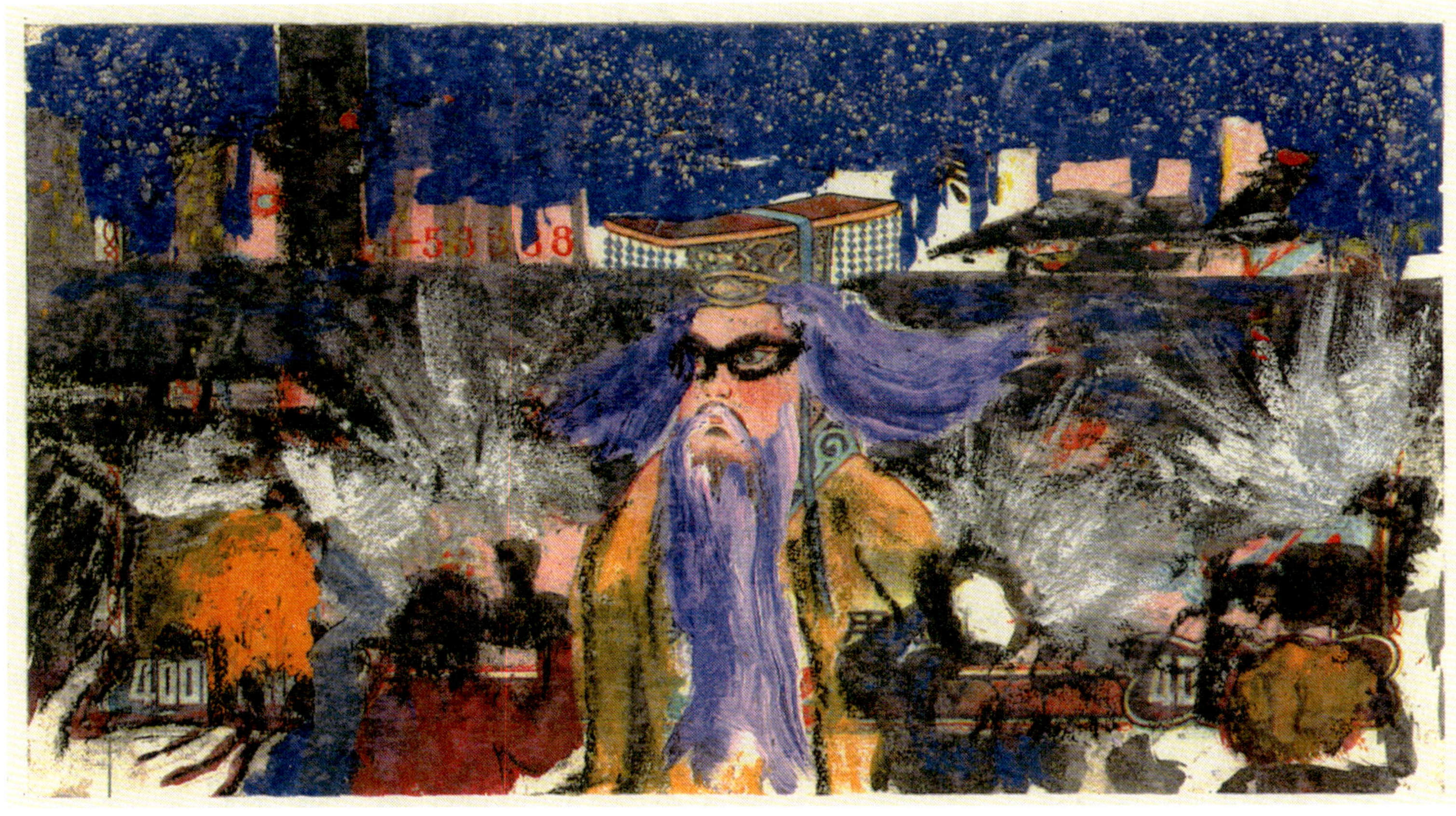

FROM BEHIND HIS GLASSES THE WORLD FLASHED BY, STARS AND CAMERAS CLICKED AND SNAPPED AND HE FELT HAPPY AND SAD AT THE SAME TIME 1995 From Lee Ping Zing series Gouache and pastel on paper 10 × 18.5cm

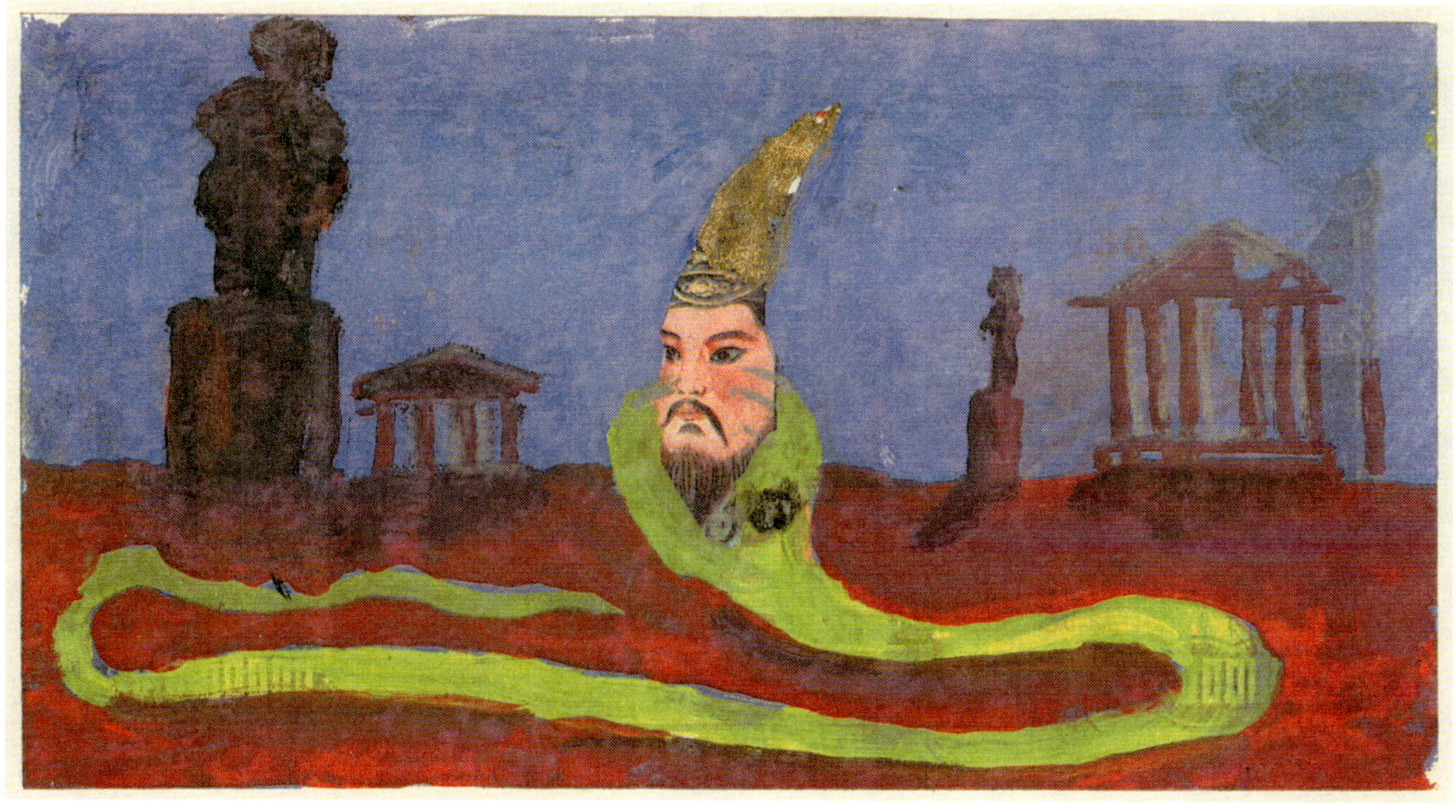

HE FELT LIKE THE SNAKE OF ROME WAS SWALLOWING HIM 1995
From Lee Ping Zing series Gouache and pastel on paper 10 × 18.5cm

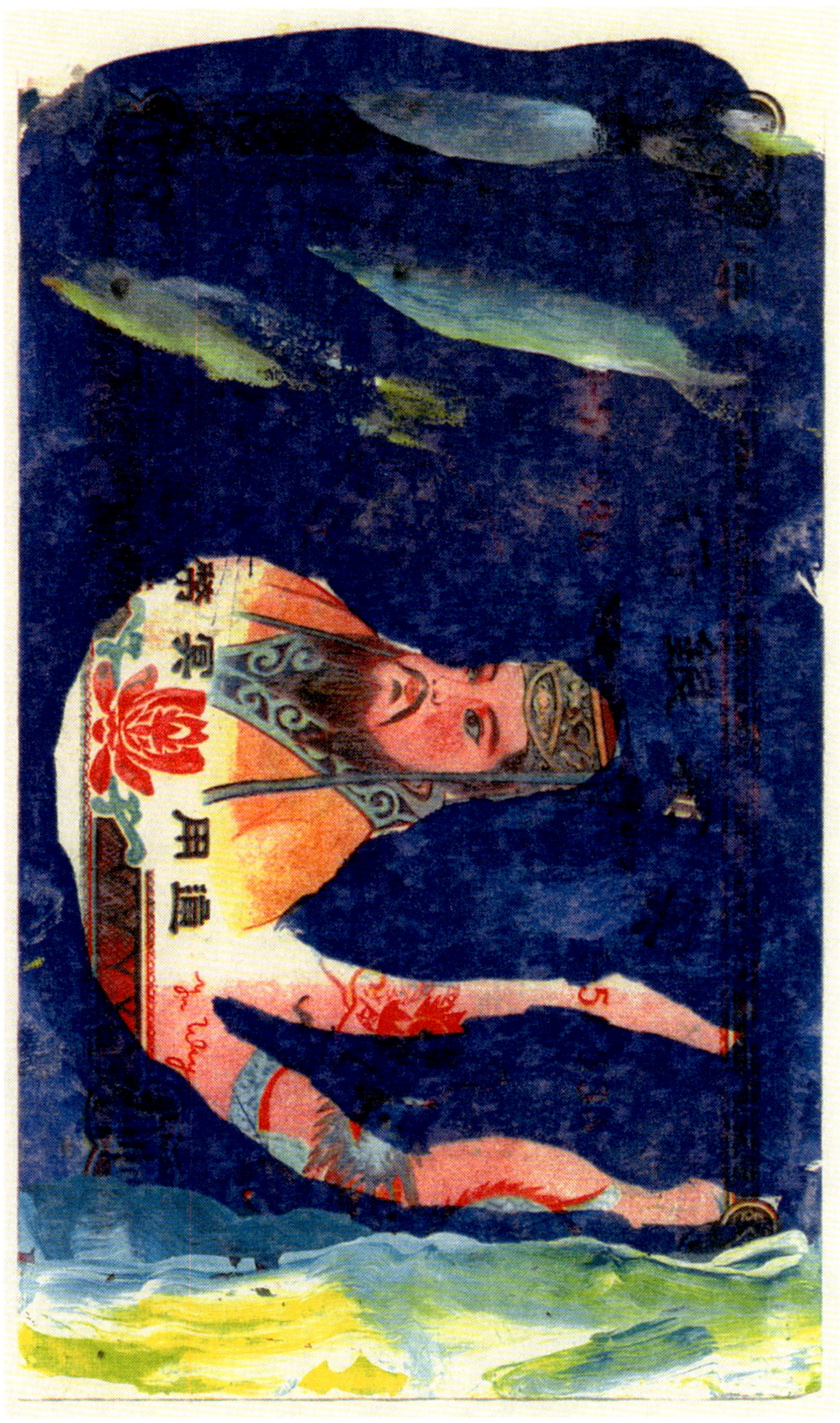

AND HE SWAM WITH THE FISHES THAT PRETENDED TO BE SPACESHIPS 1995
From Lee Ping Zing series Gouache and pastel on paper 10 × 18.5cm

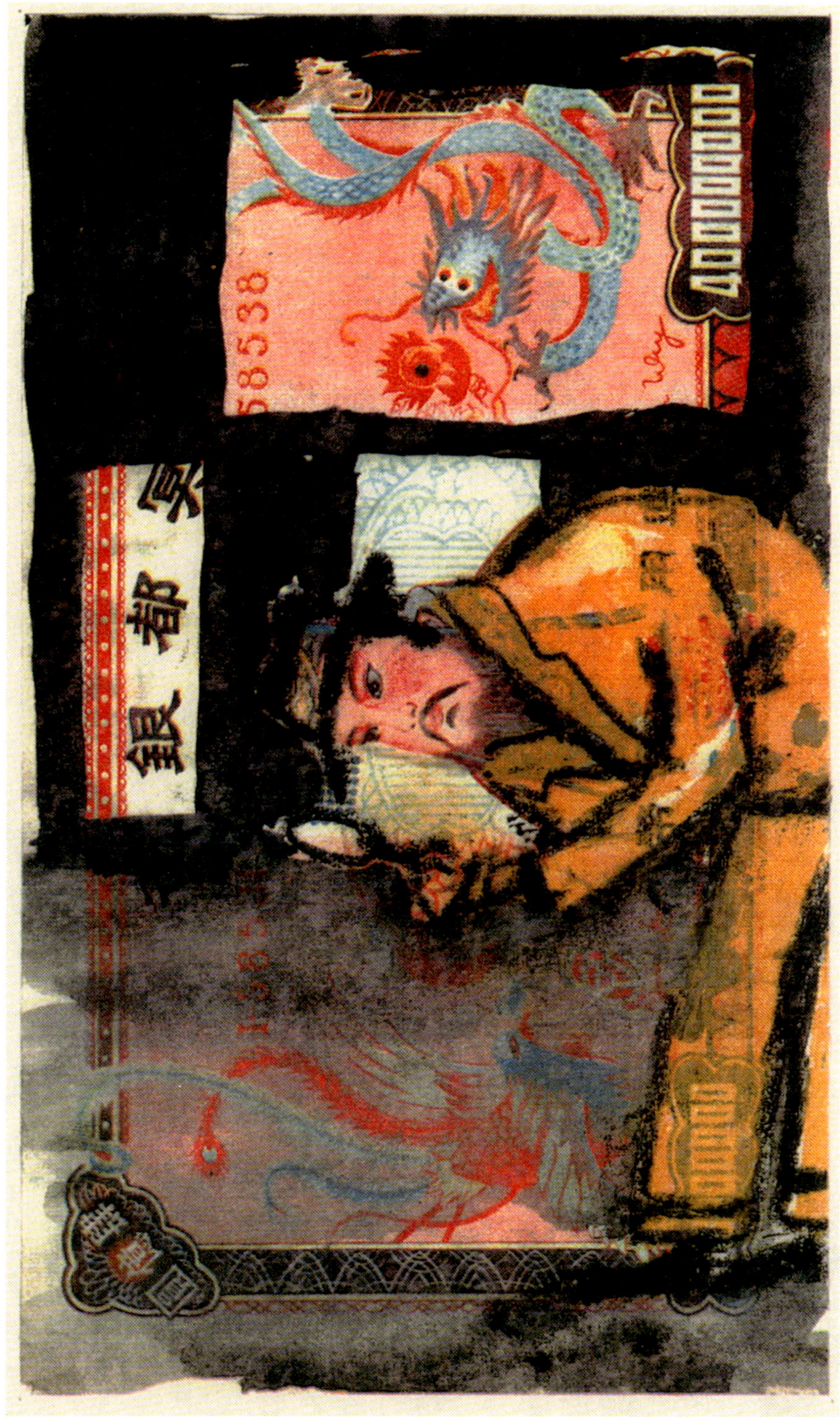

MAYBE HE COULD BECOME A DETECTIVE SO HE COULD SNOOP OUT BAD PEOPLE 1995
From Lee Ping Zing series Gouache and pastel on paper 18.5 × 10cm

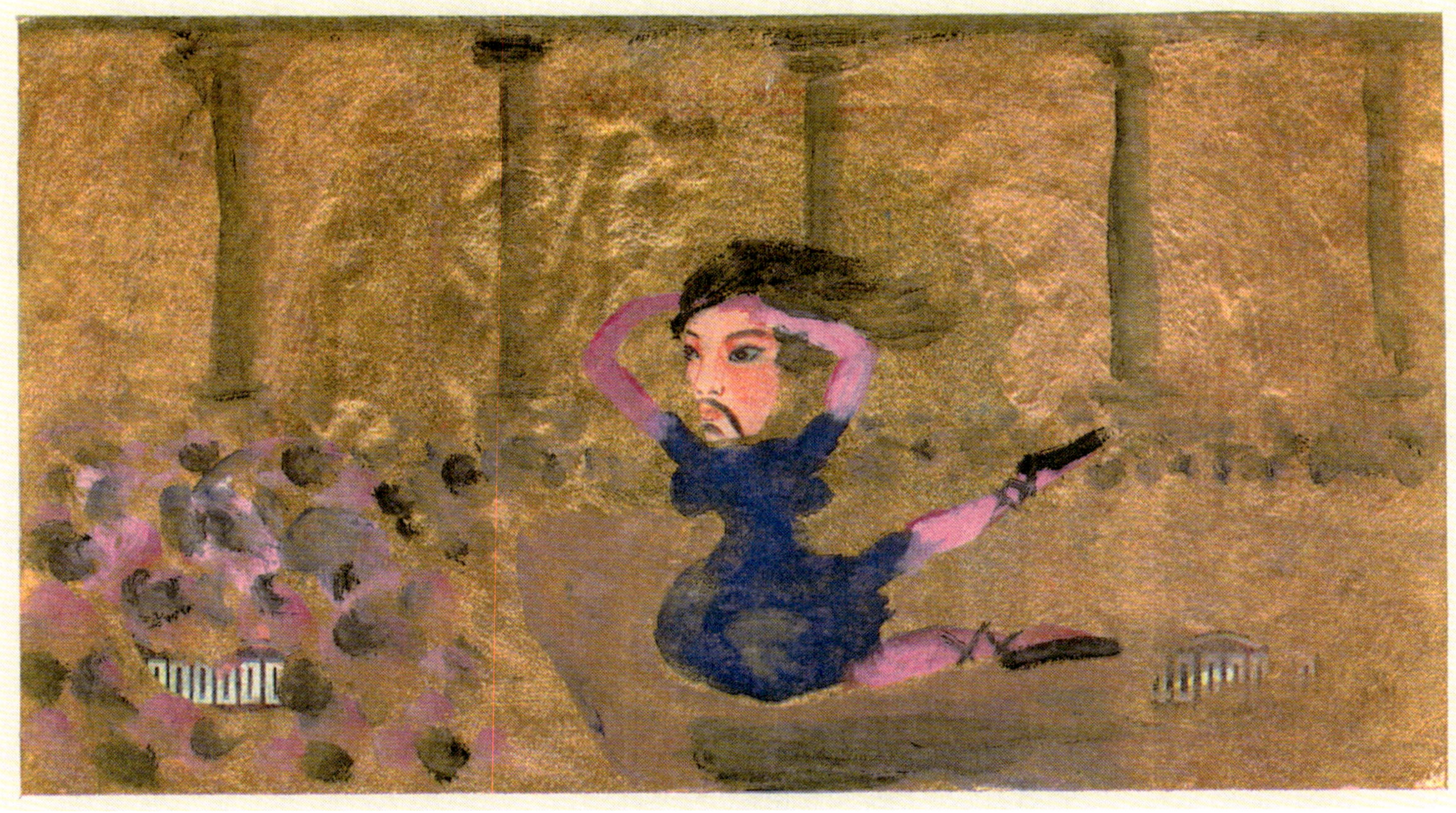

OR A FAMOUS BALLET DANCER WHO COULD PERFORM BEFORE THOUSANDS IN RUSSIA 1995
From Lee Ping Zing series Gouache and pastel on paper 10 × 18.5cm

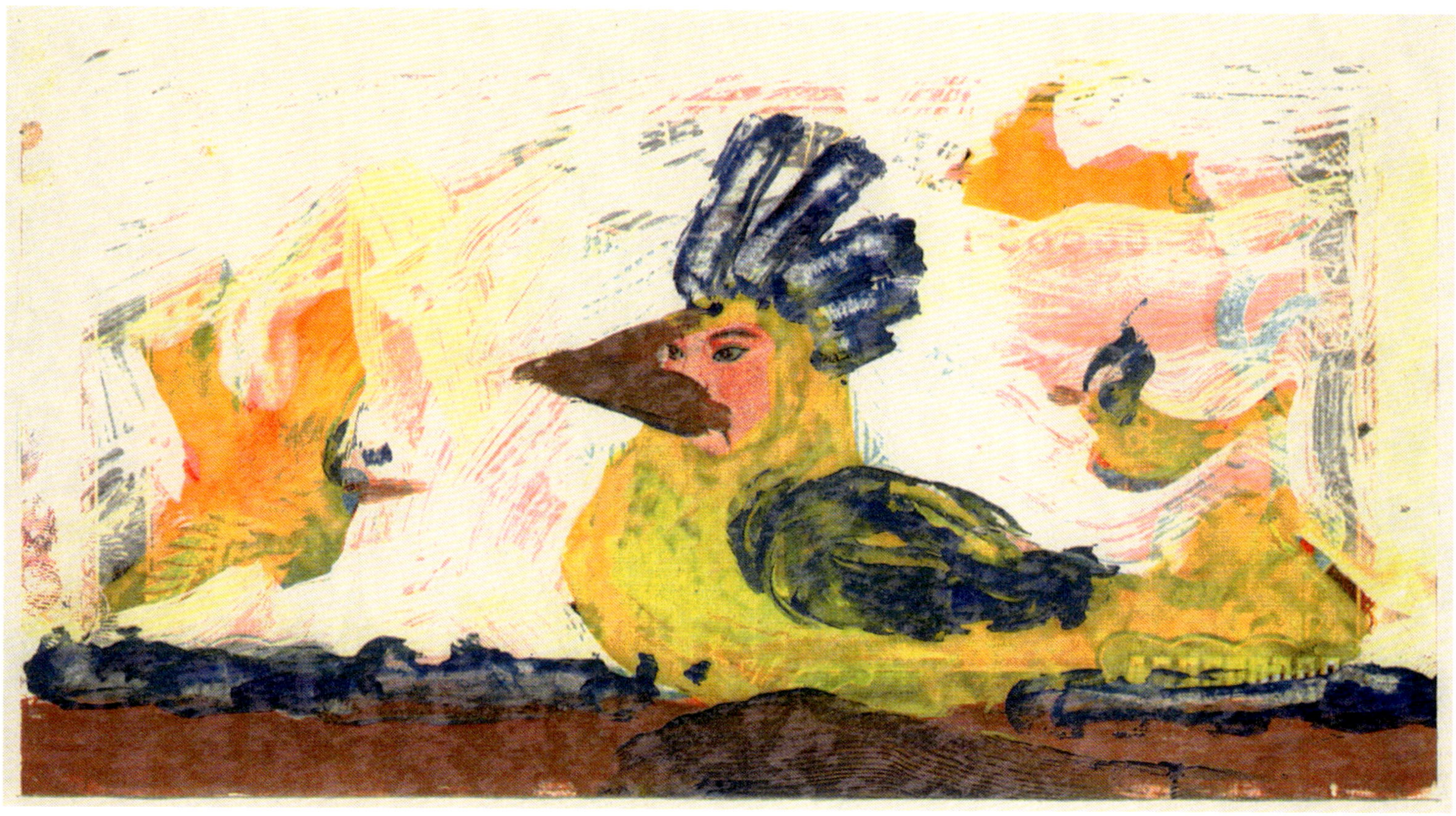

HE POPPED UP TO THE SURFACE AND BECAME A GREEN DUCK, SO THAT THE OTHER DUCKS THOUGHT HE WAS ONE OF THEM 1995 From Lee Ping Zing series Gouache and pastel on paper 10 × 18.5cm

ONE DAY, LEE PING ZING WAS RUNNING AROUND PRETENDING TO BE AN AEROPLANE WHEN THE SKY WENT DARK 1995 From Lee Ping Zing series Gouache and pastel on paper 18.5 × 10cm

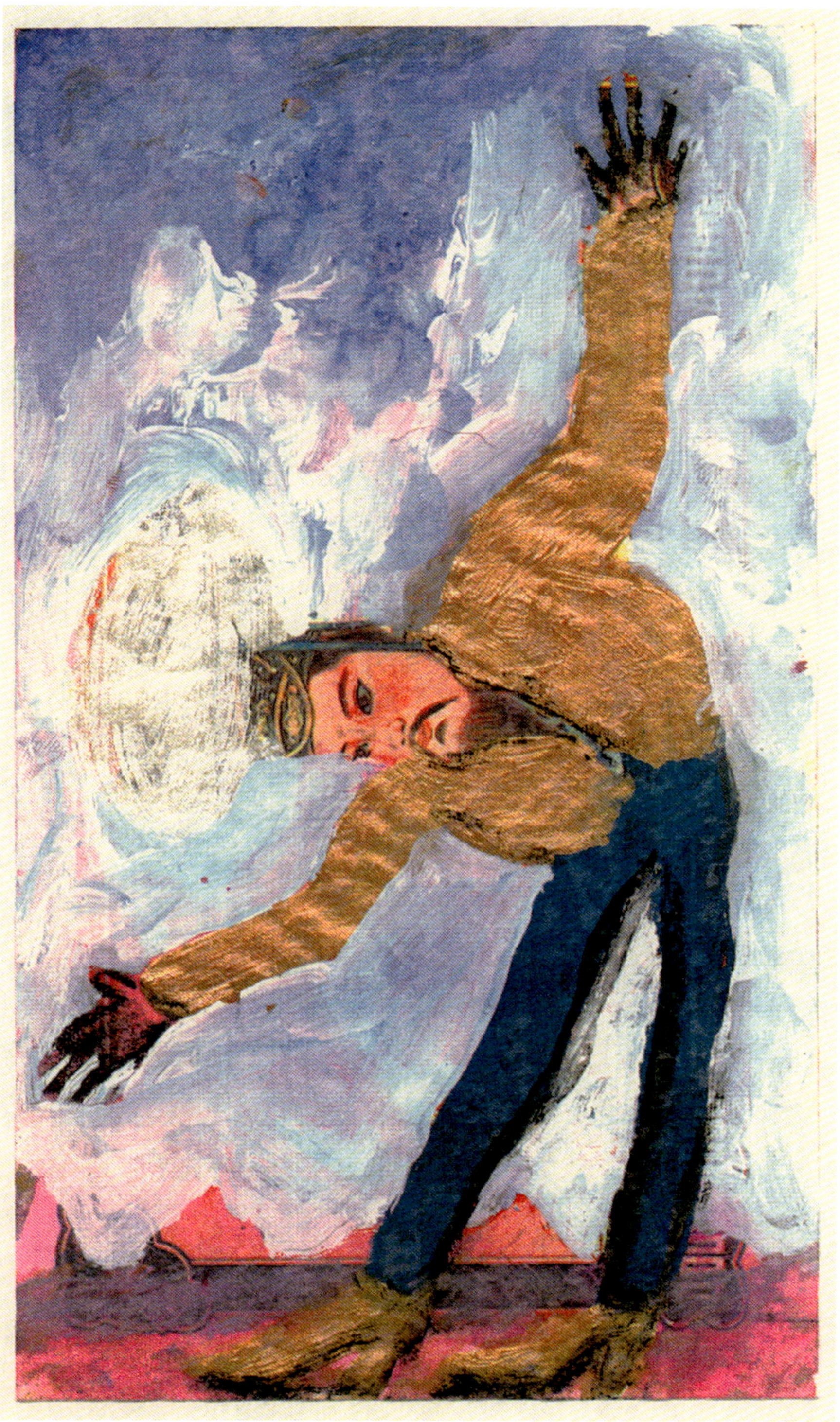

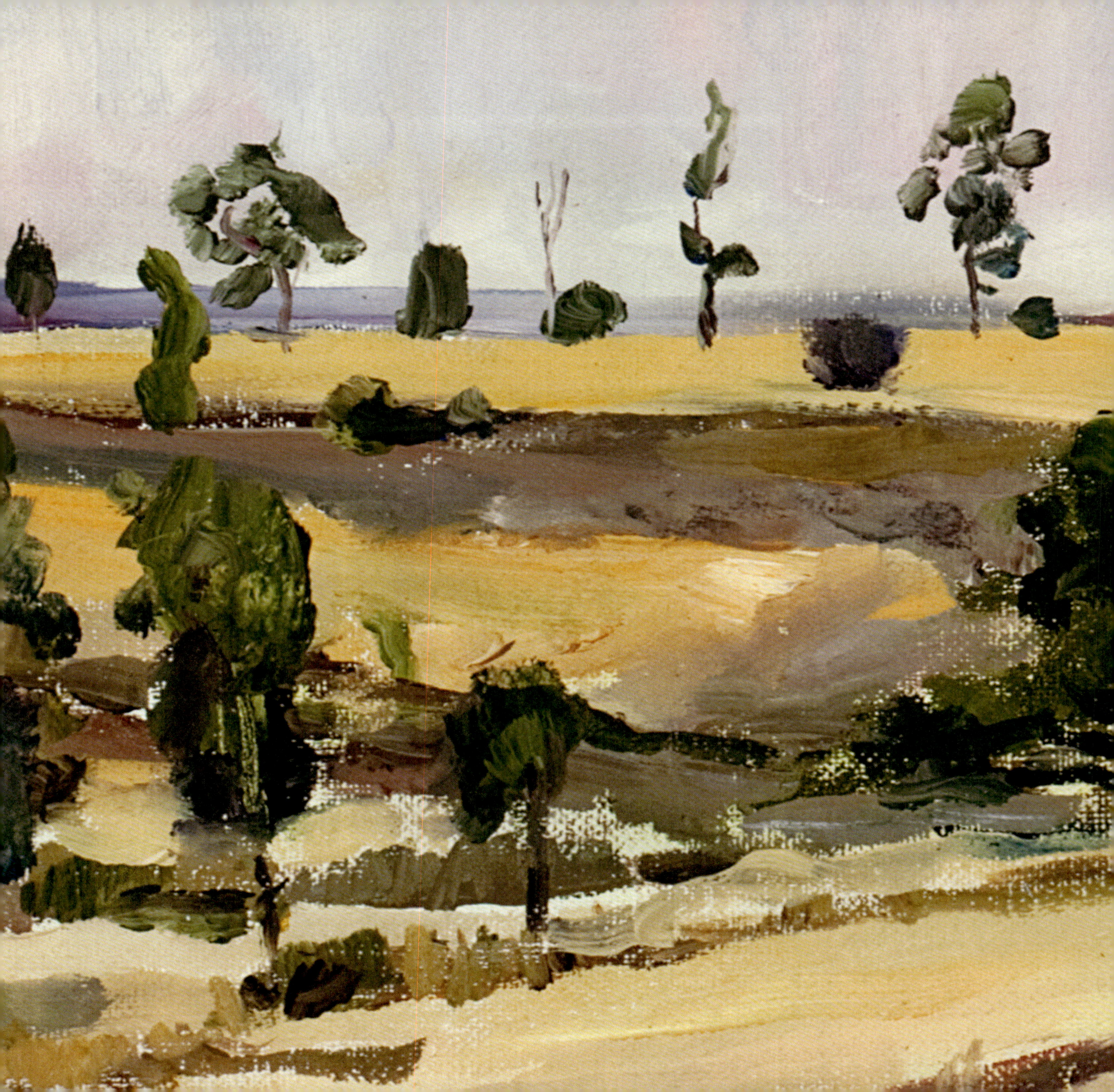

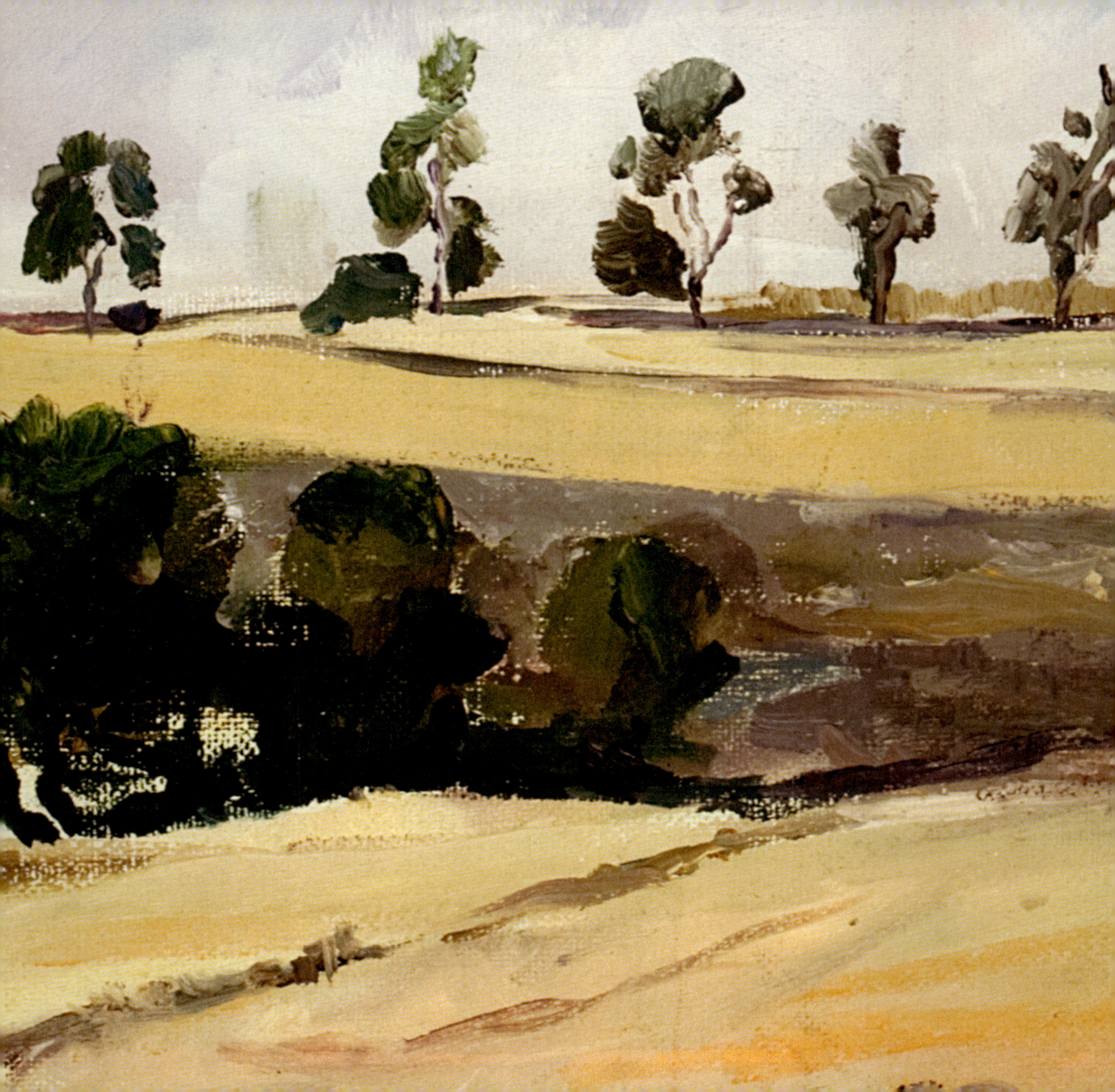

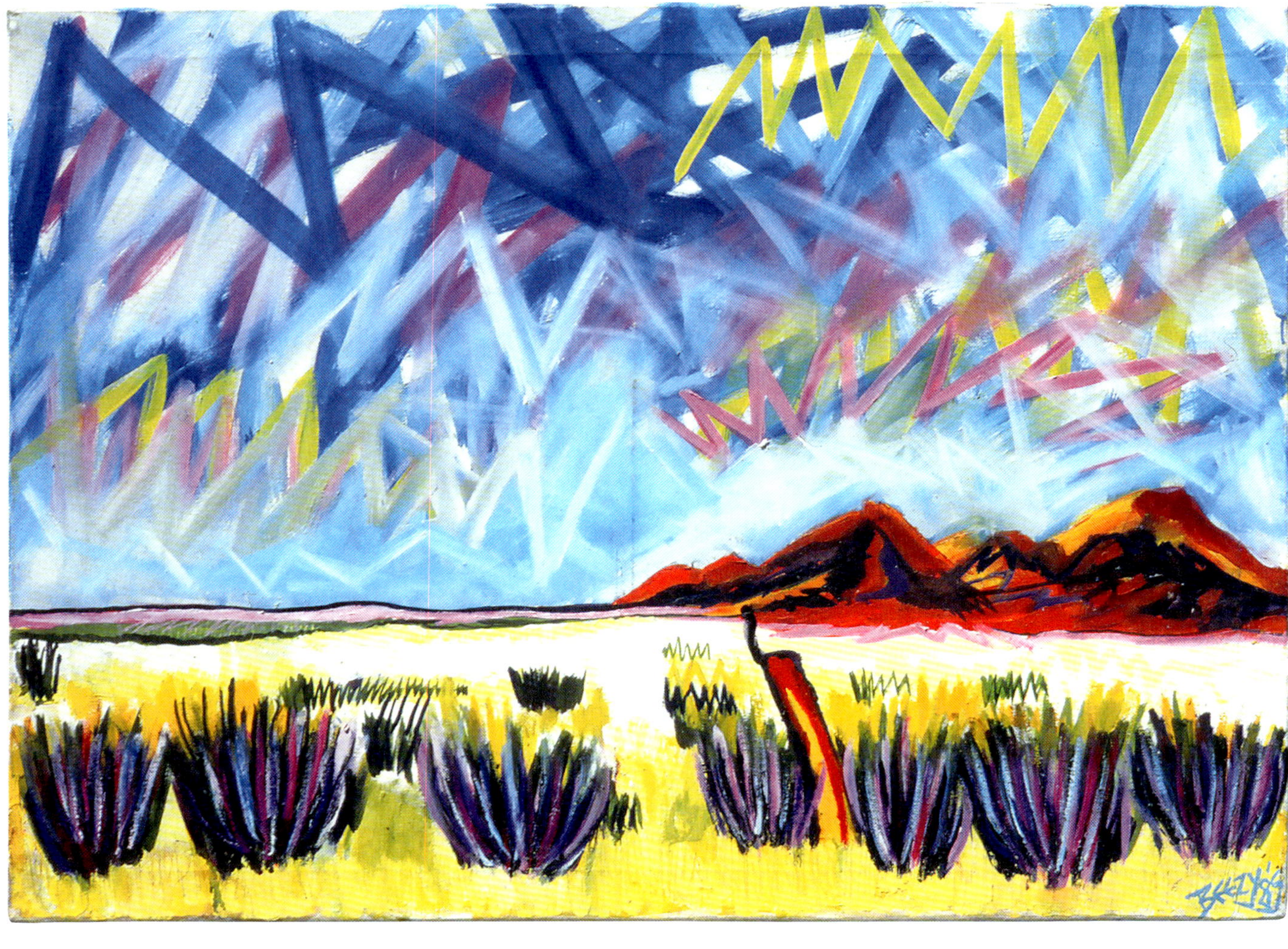

NAMIBIAN LANDSCAPE 1988 Oil on canvas 82 × 109cm

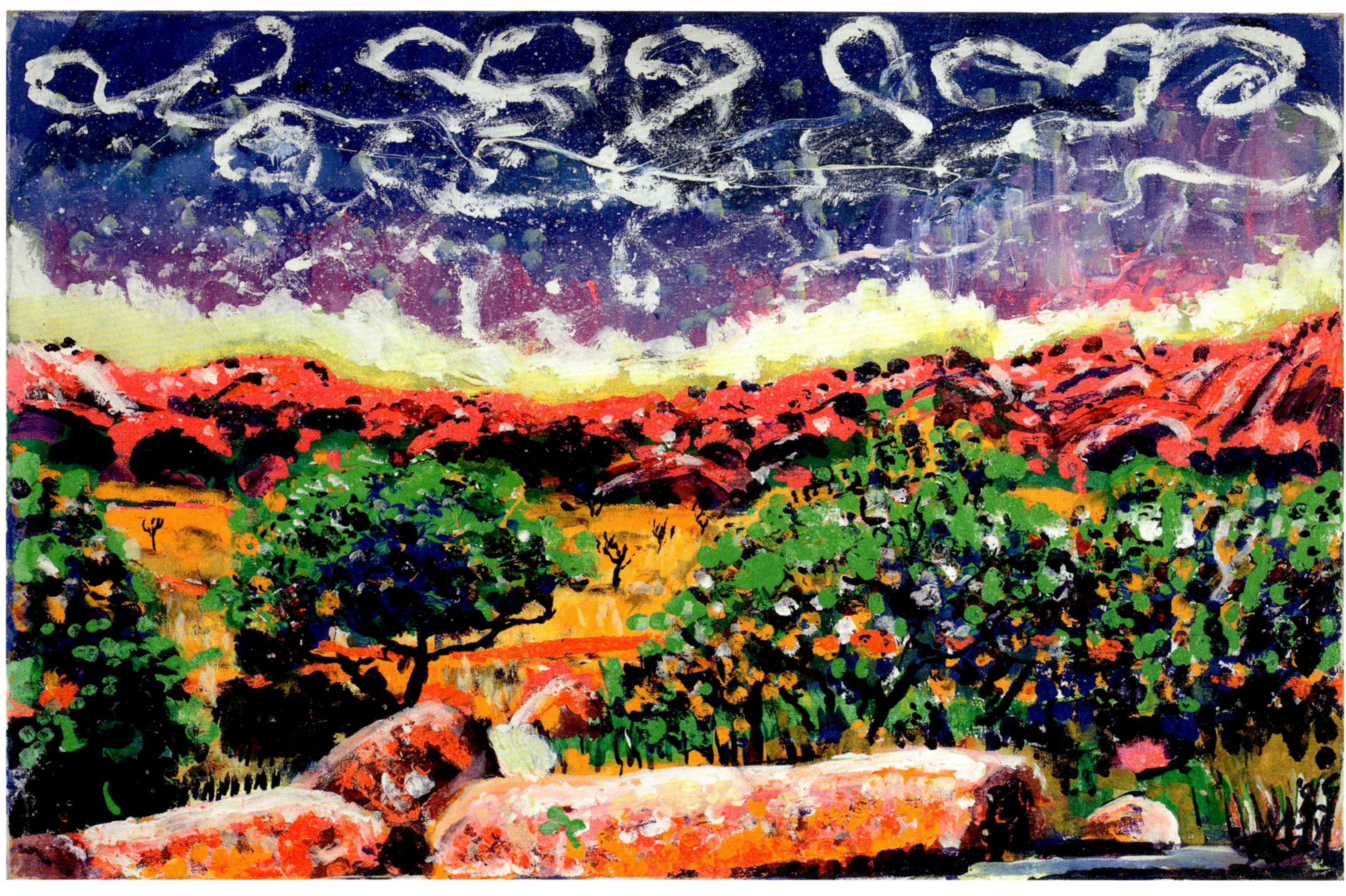

OUTSIDE MBABANE – SWAZILAND 1985 Acrylic on canvas 60 × 90cm

HAMPSTEAD HEATH 1989 Oil on board 36 × 30cm

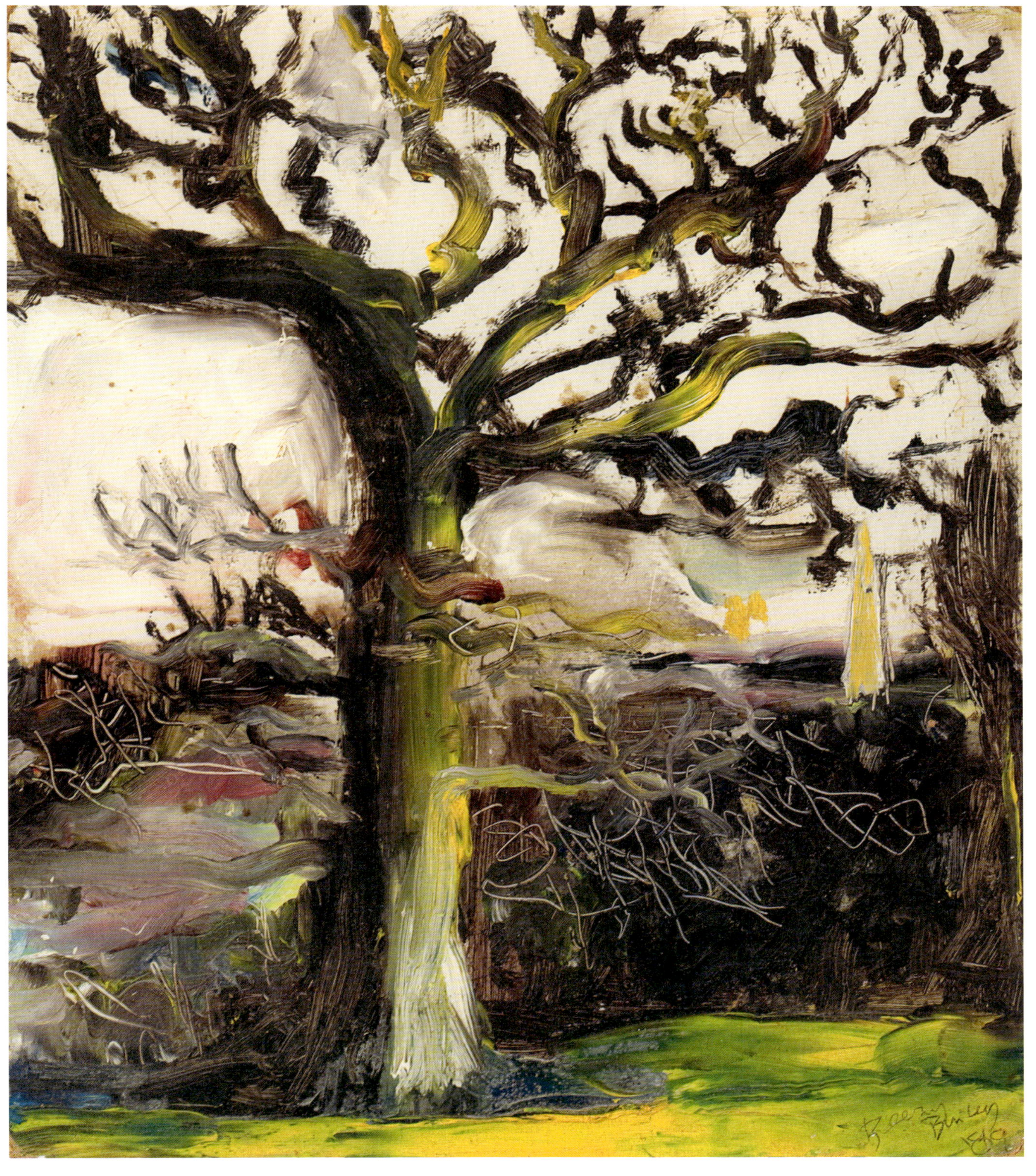

HOTTENTOTS MOUNTAIN 1993 Oil on canvas 49 × 74cm

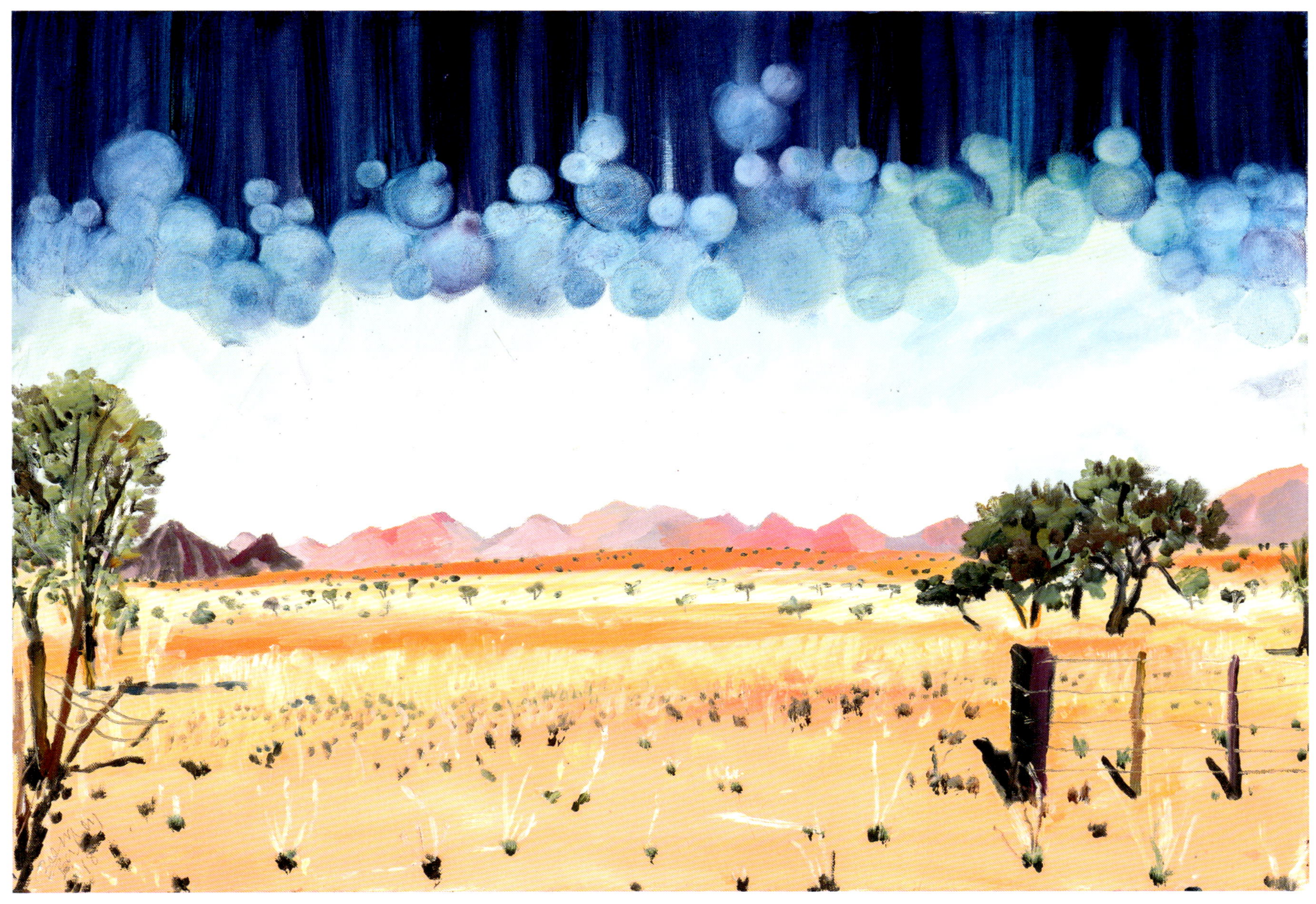

BLUE GUMS ON MONAGHAN FARM 1991 Oil on canvas 40 × 50cm

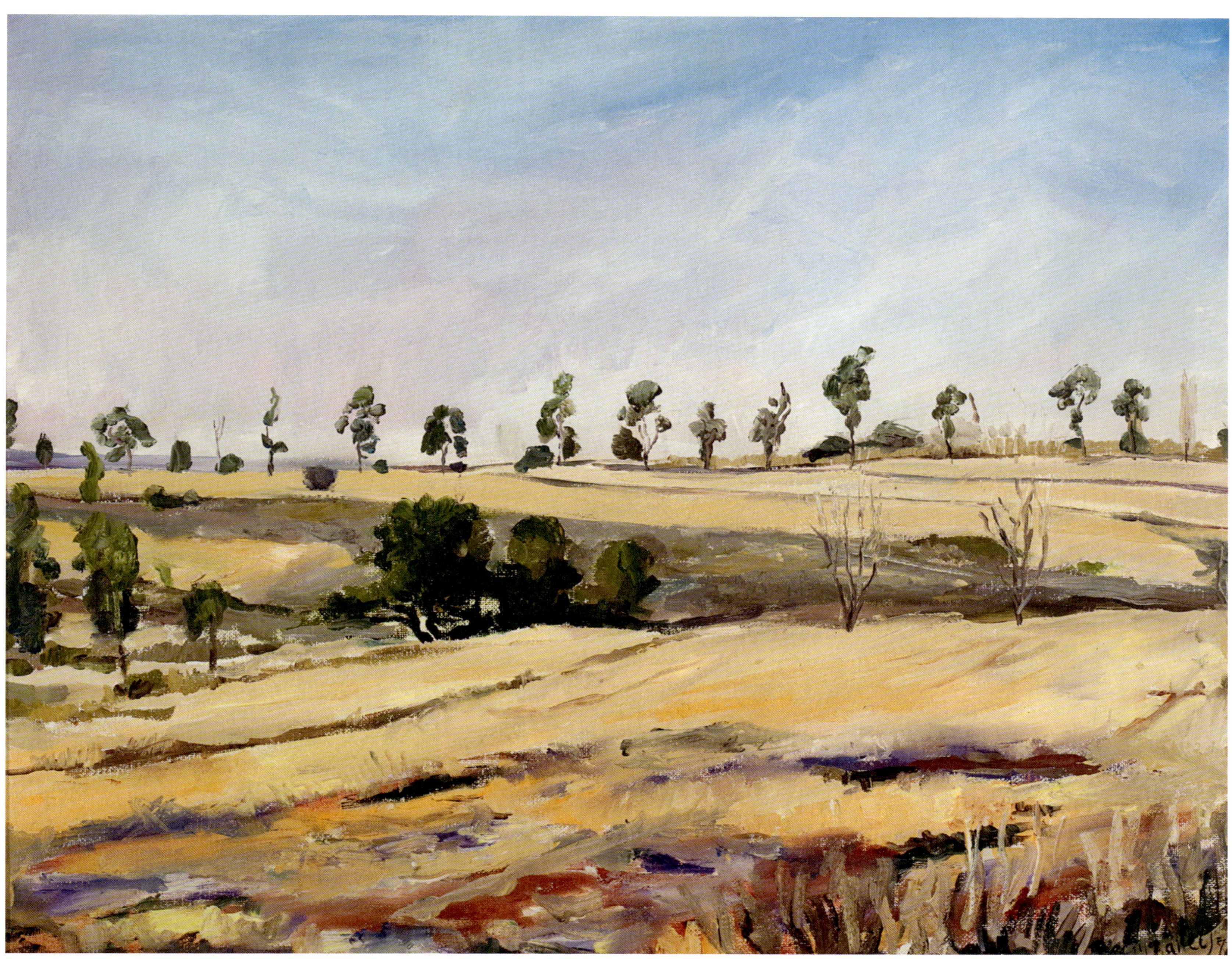

FOUR WHEEL DRIVE NAMIBIA 2005 Oil on canvas 170 × 250cm

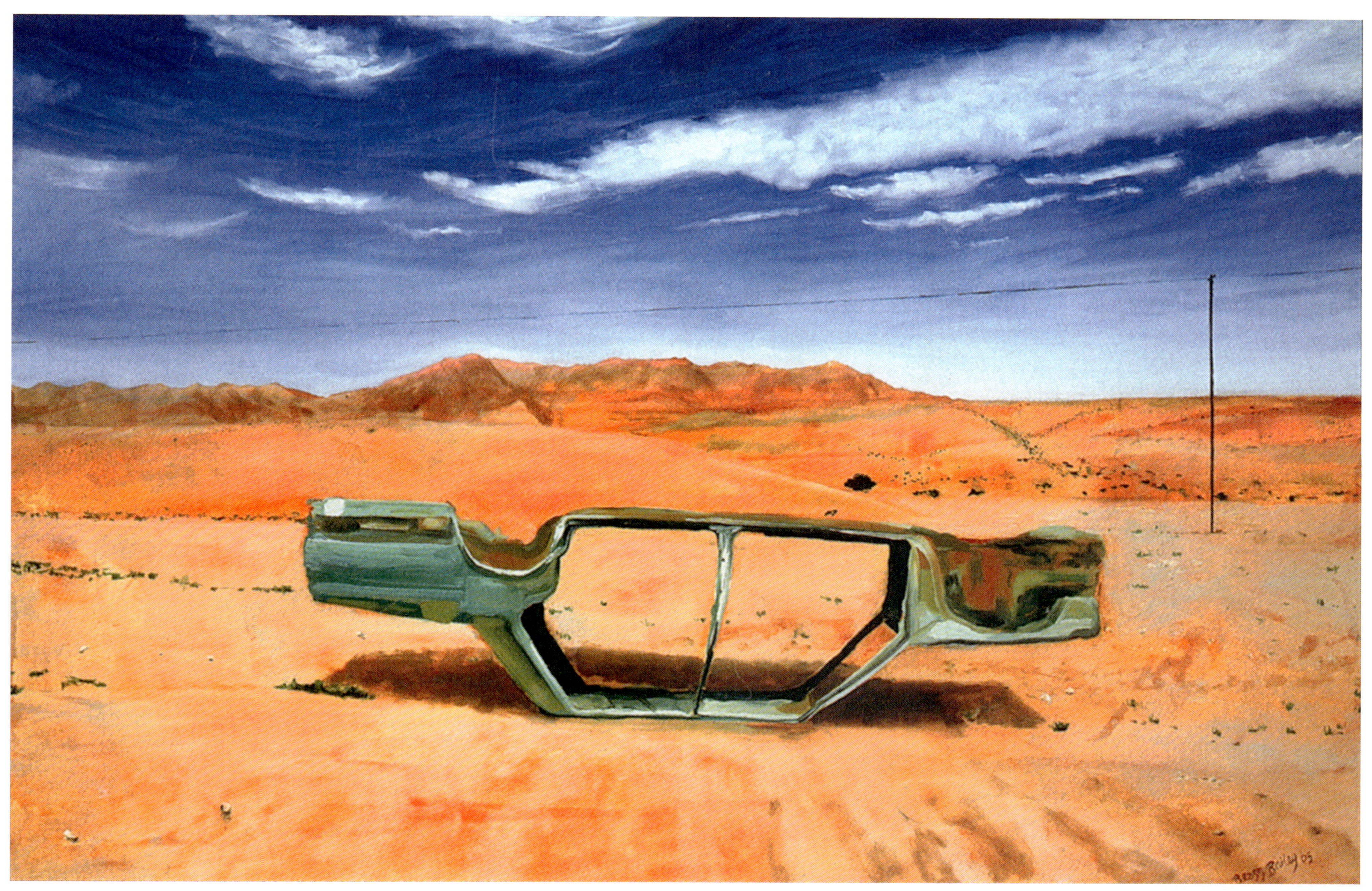

OUTSIDE UPINGTON 2015 Oil on canvas 40 × 50cm

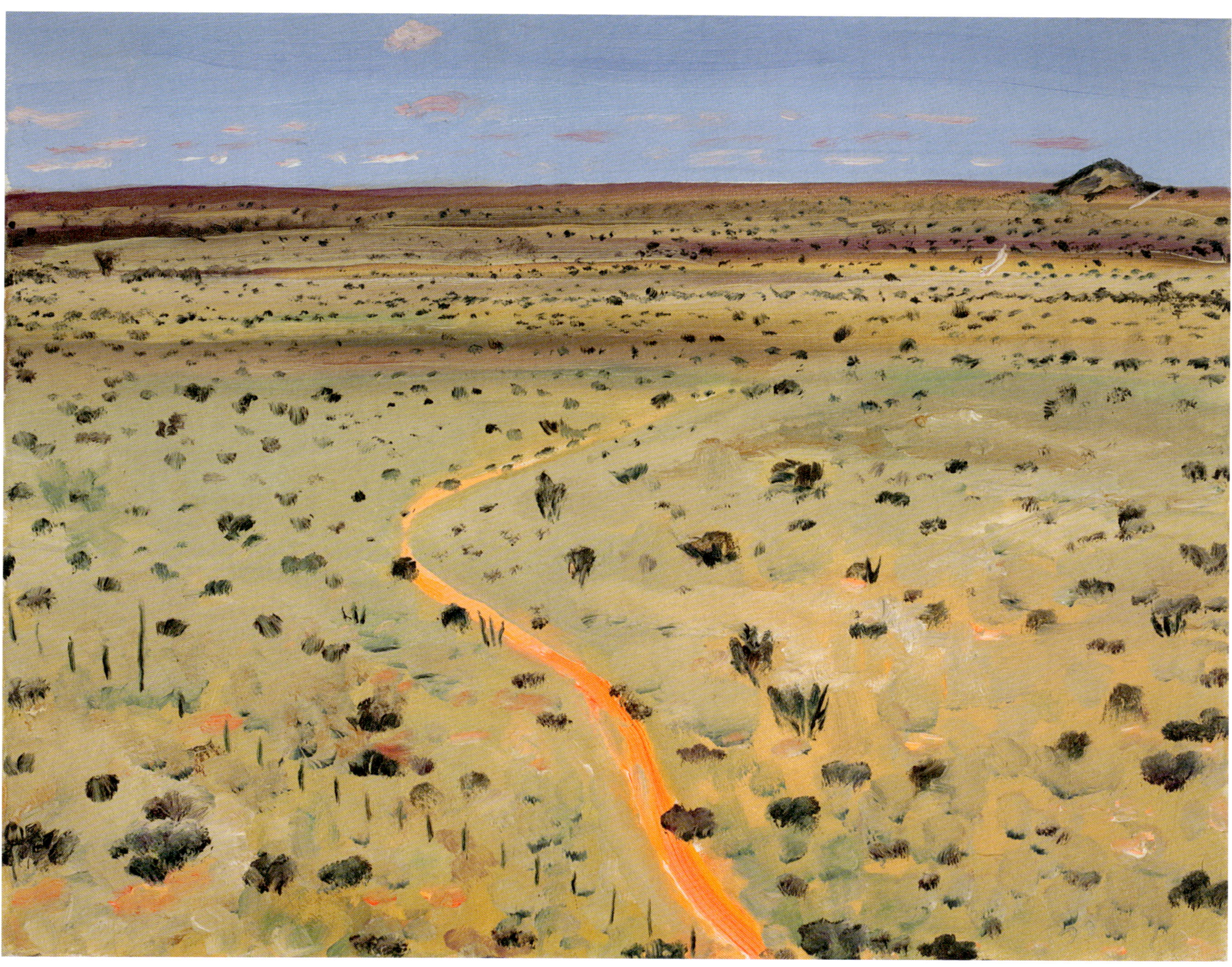

ANGEL BOATS FLYING OVER NEW YORK 2007 Pastel and charcoal on paper 121 × 100cm

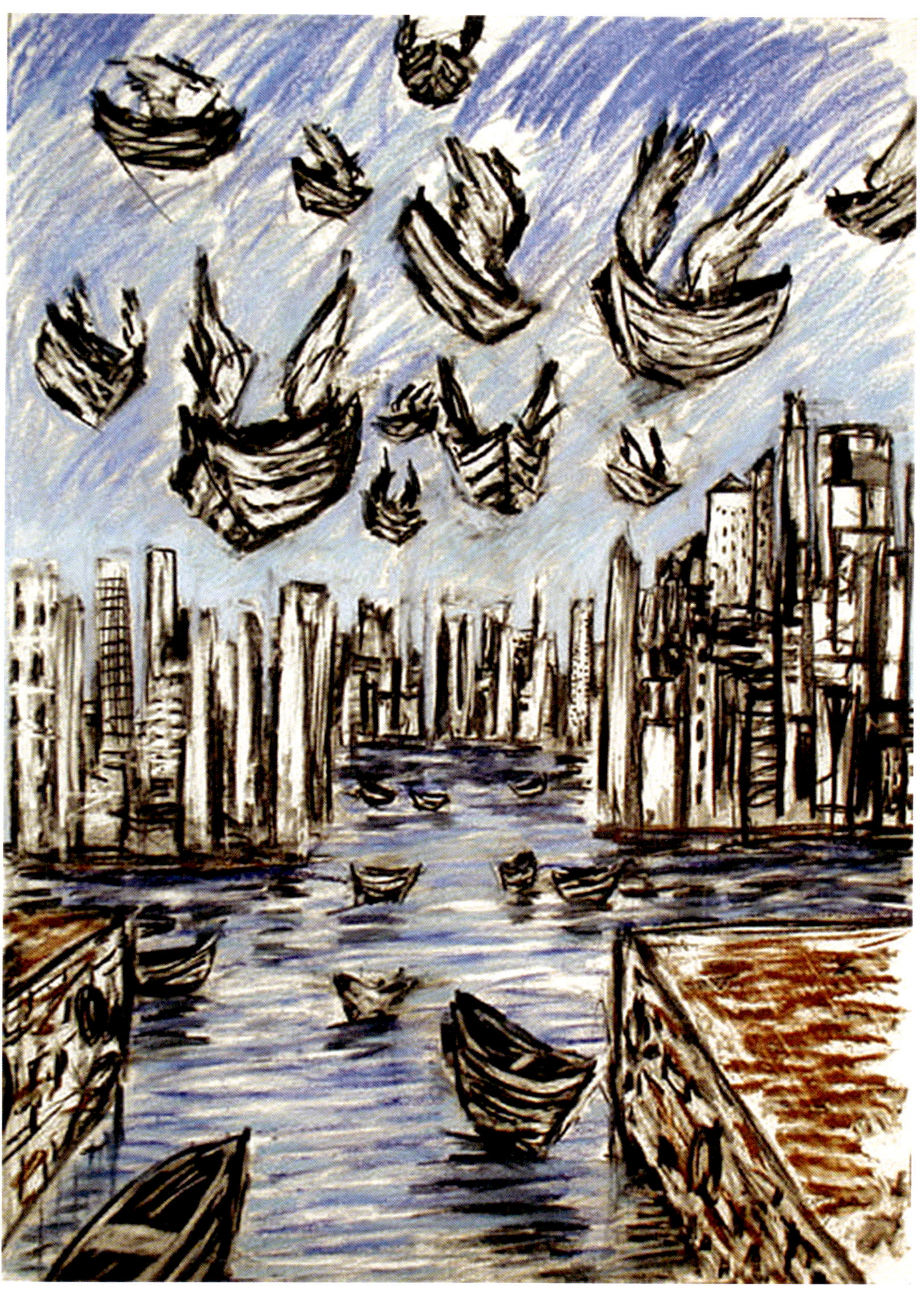

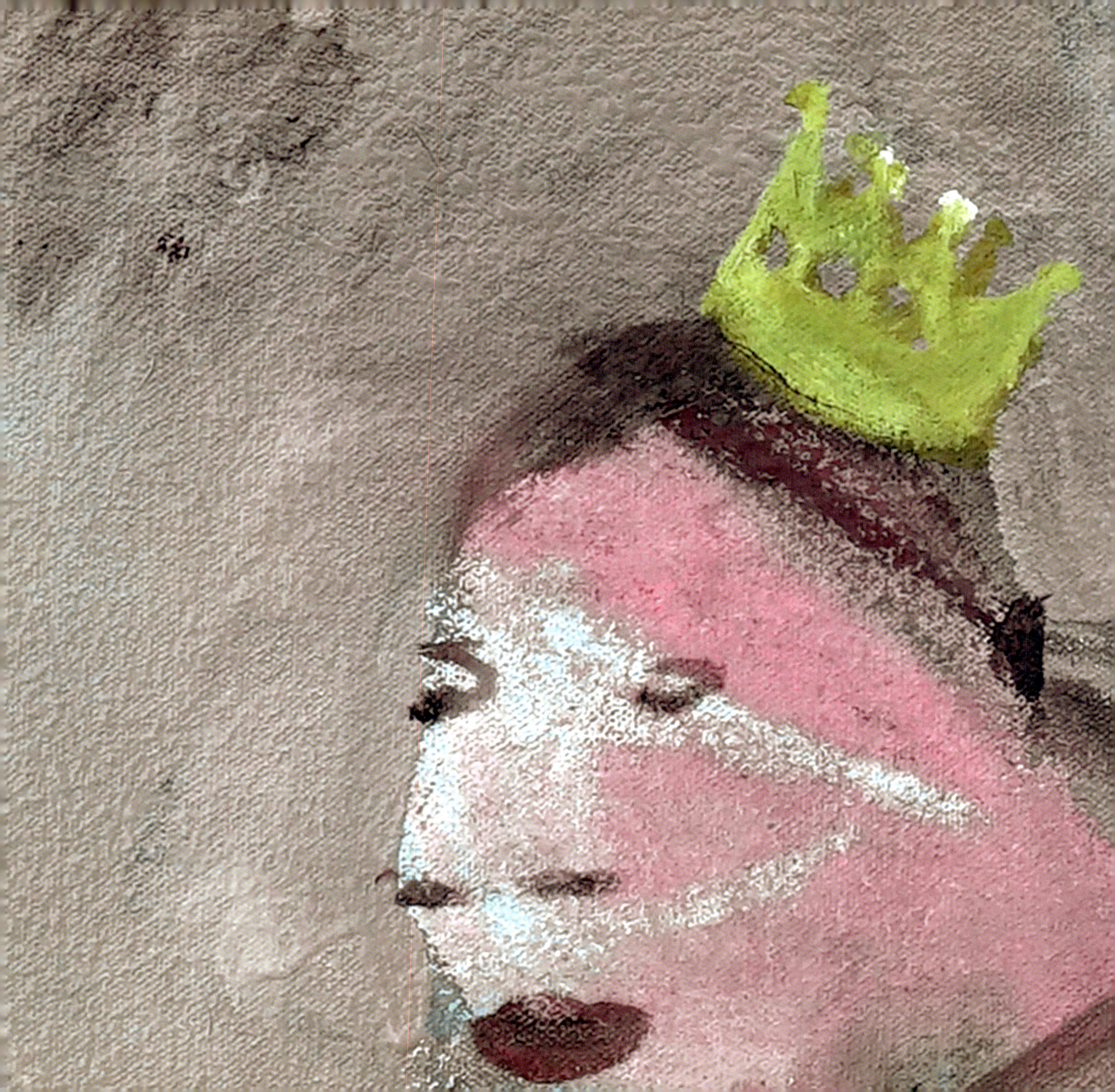

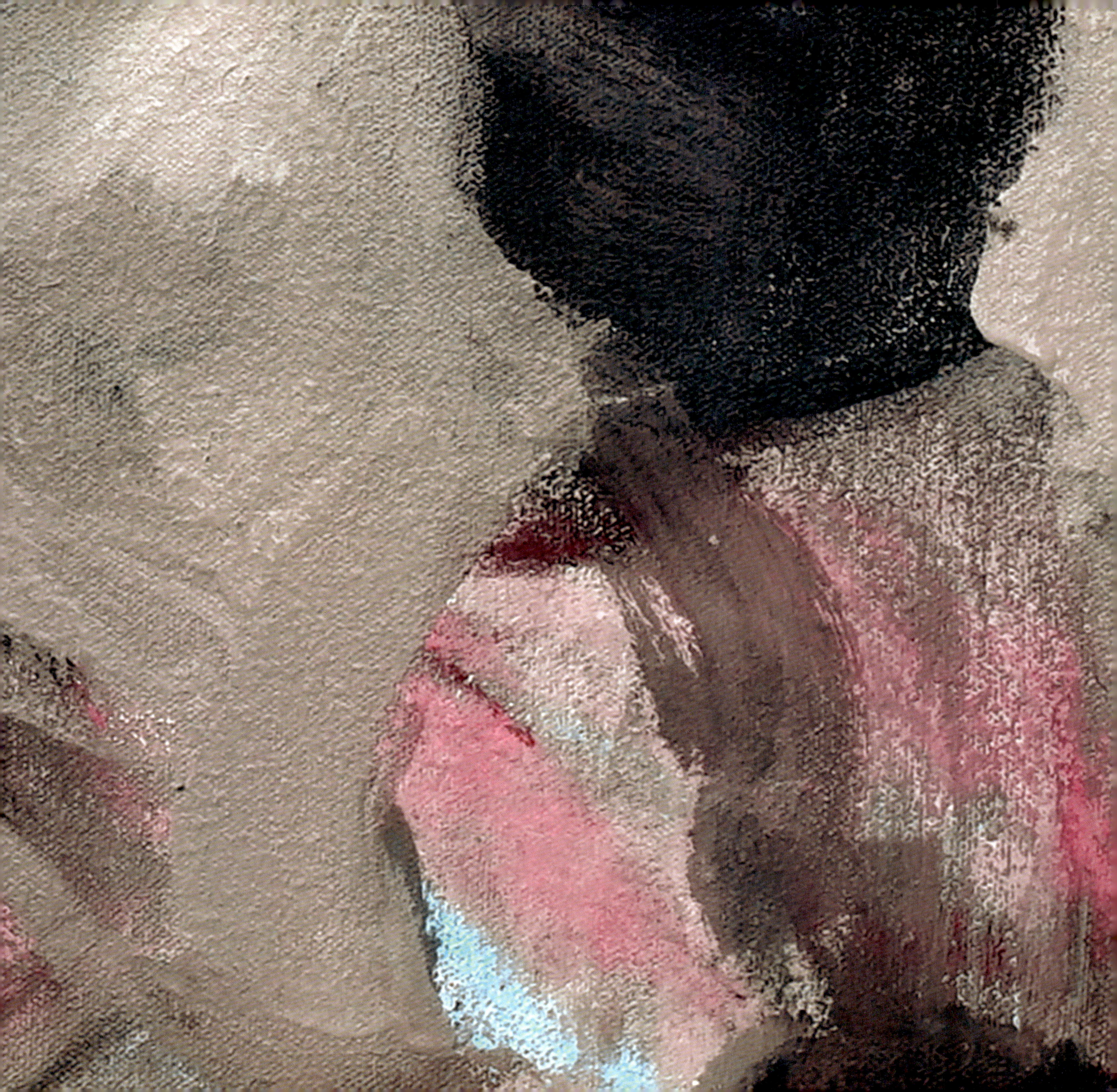

NEW YORK NEW YORK 1987 Charcoal with photographs on cotton paper 80 × 58cm

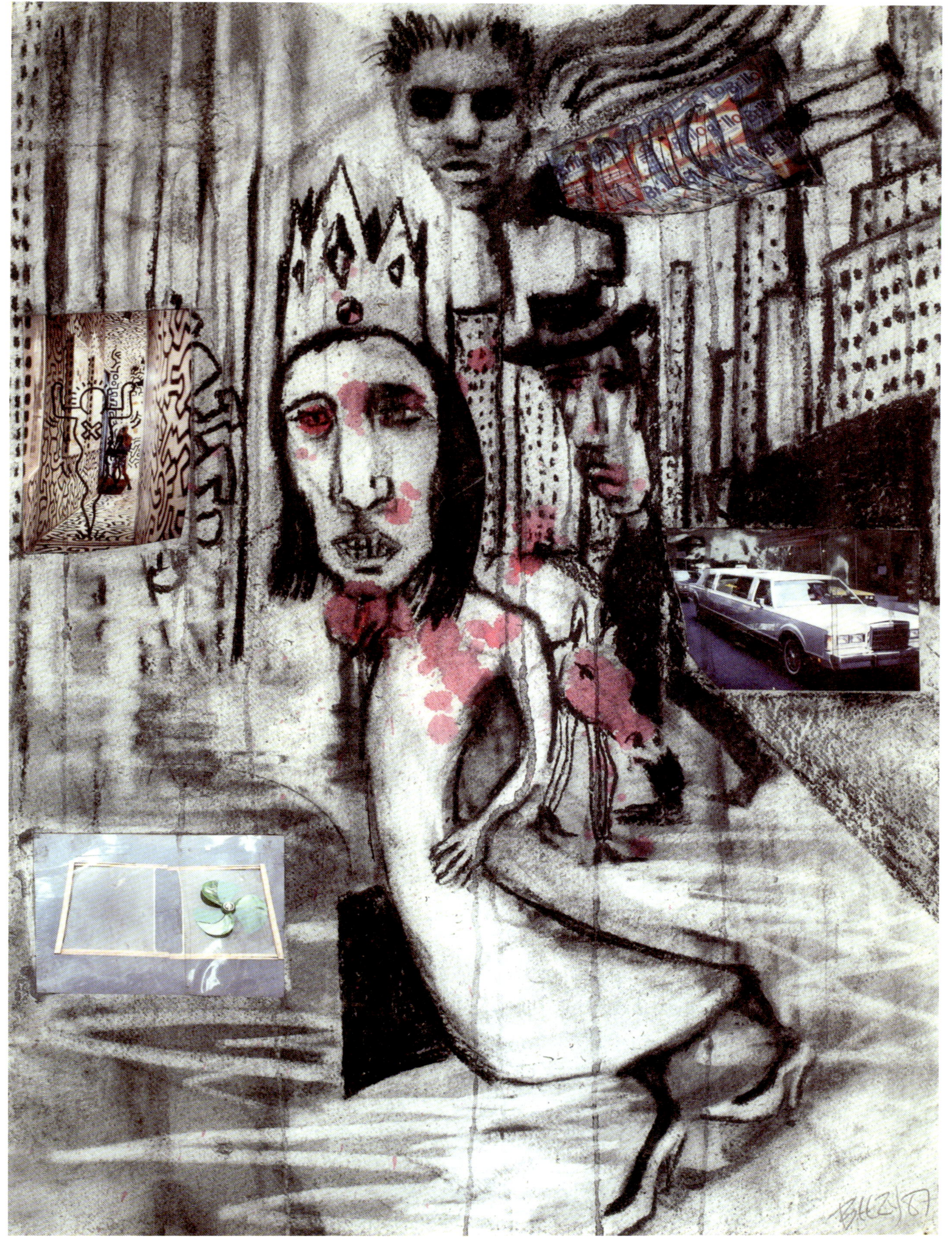

DISTRICT 6 WALKER 1995 Pastel, enamel, wood and linoleum flooring on canvas 100 × 100cm

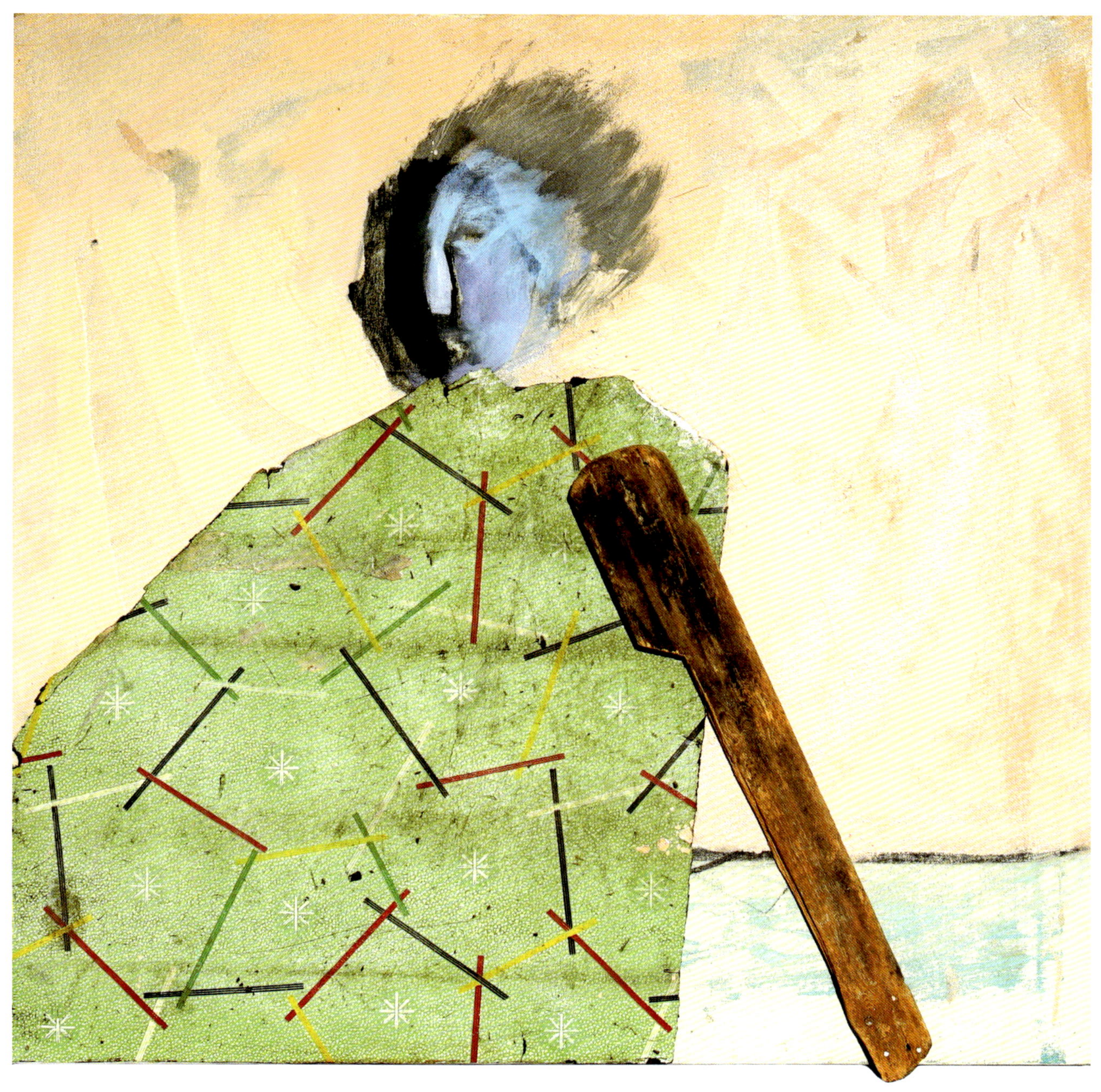

PEACEMAN 2006 Bronze 118 × 16 × 49cm

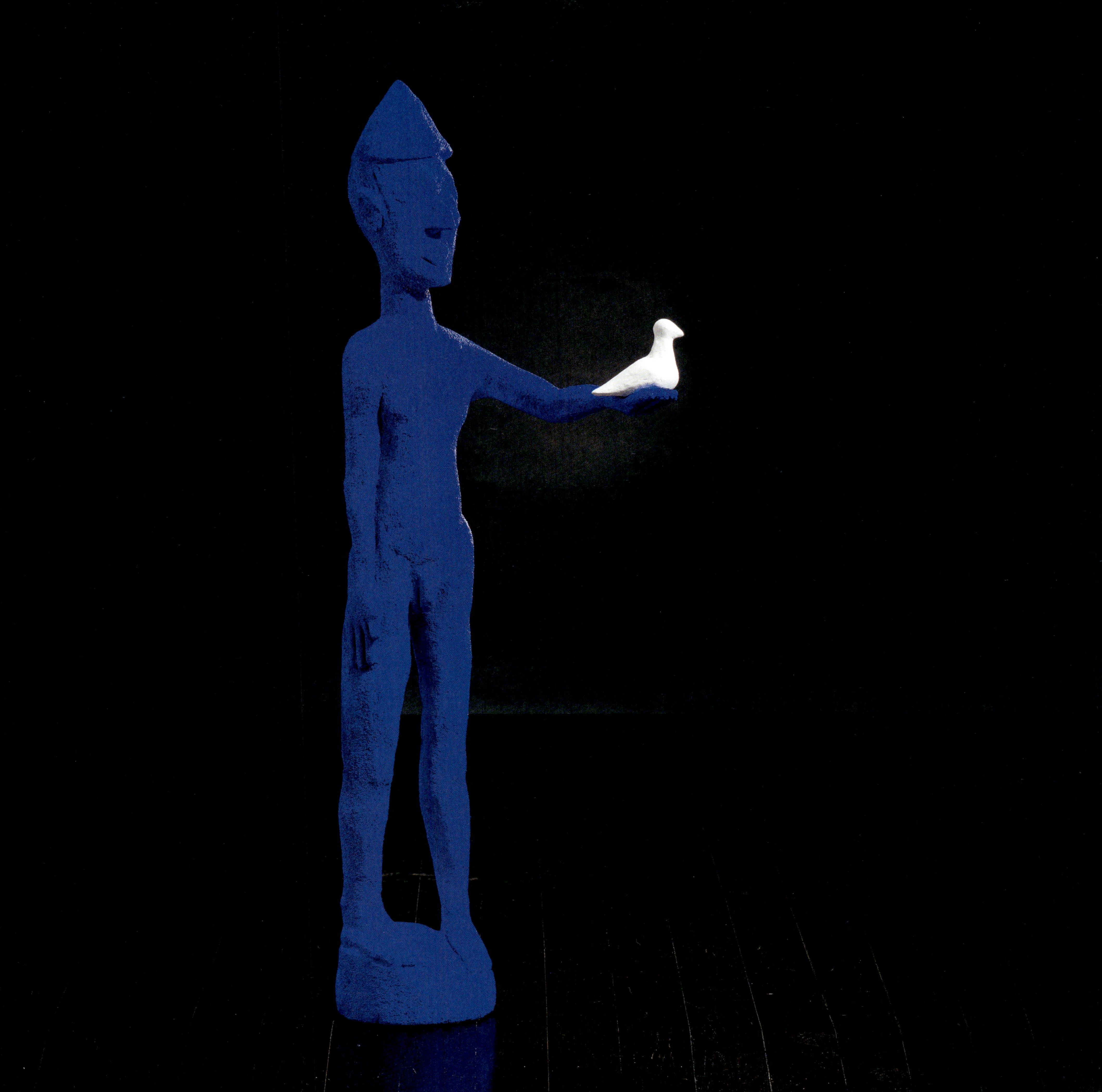

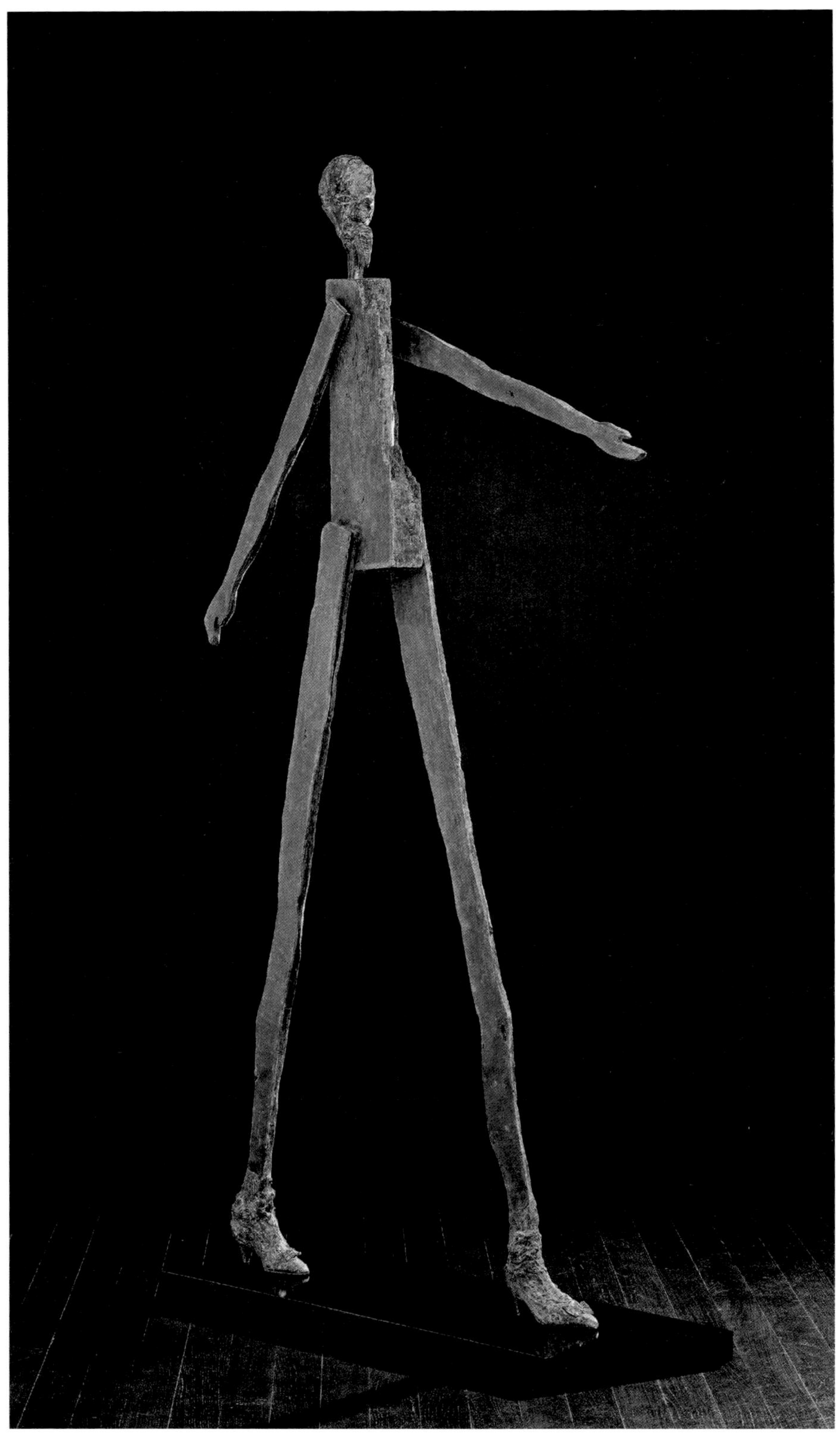

WALKING TALL 2018 Bronze 240 × 150 × 18cm

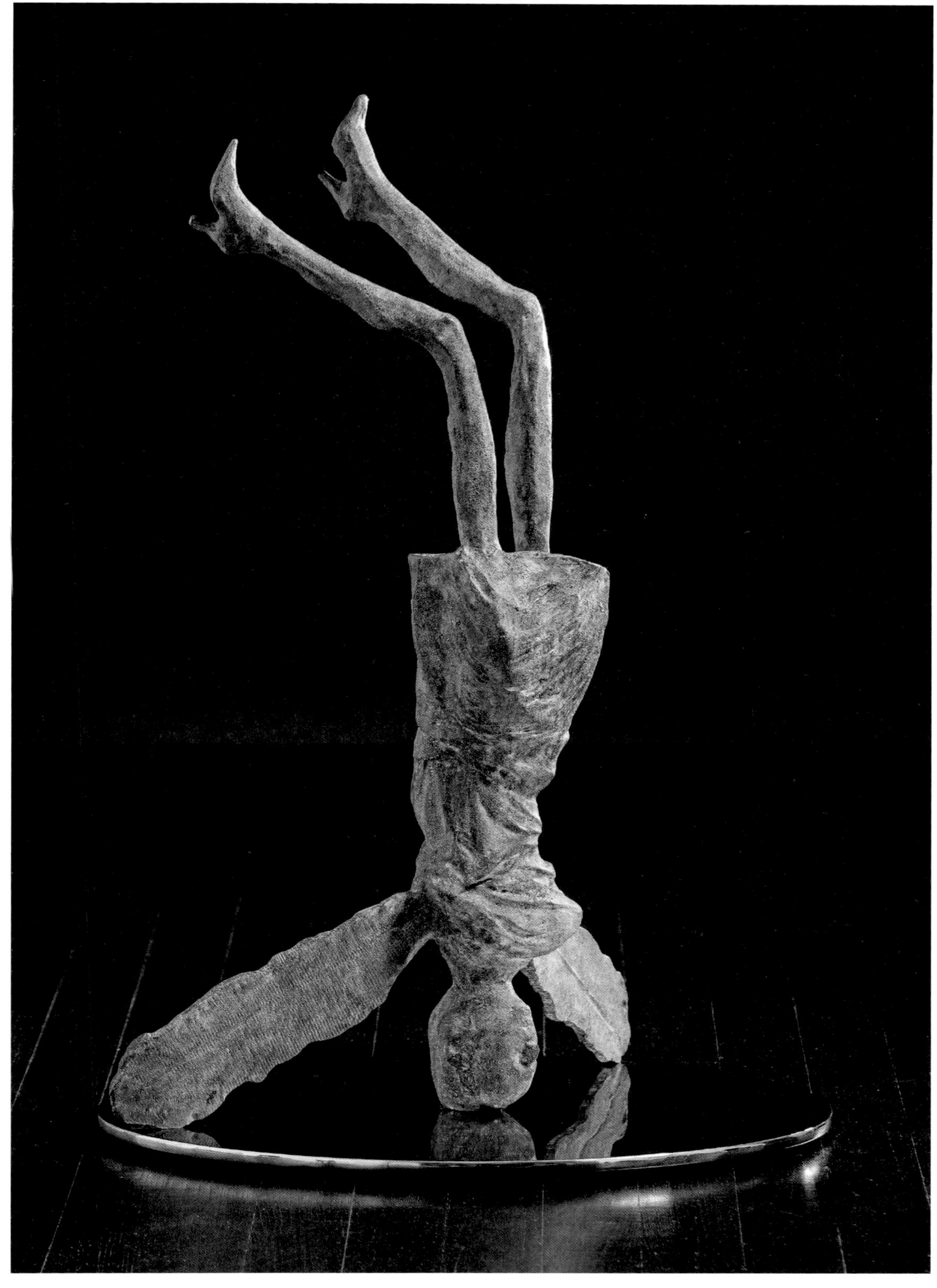

FALLEN ANGEL 2010 Bronze 100 × 70 × 15cm

MENTAL PRINCESS 2000 Oil on canvas 45 × 56cm

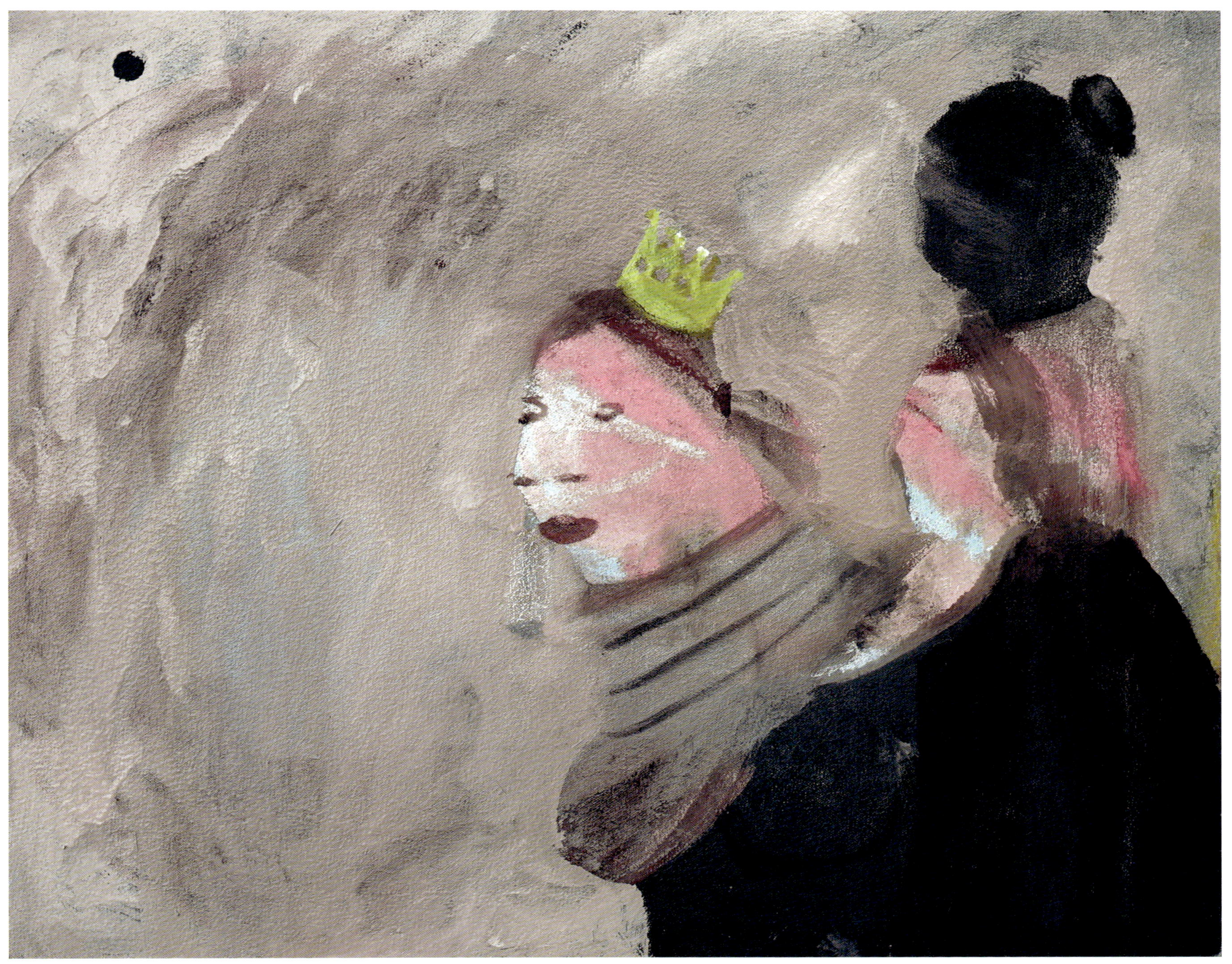

GHOSTS OF 9/11 2012 Silkscreen, oil and enamel on canvas 92 × 120cm

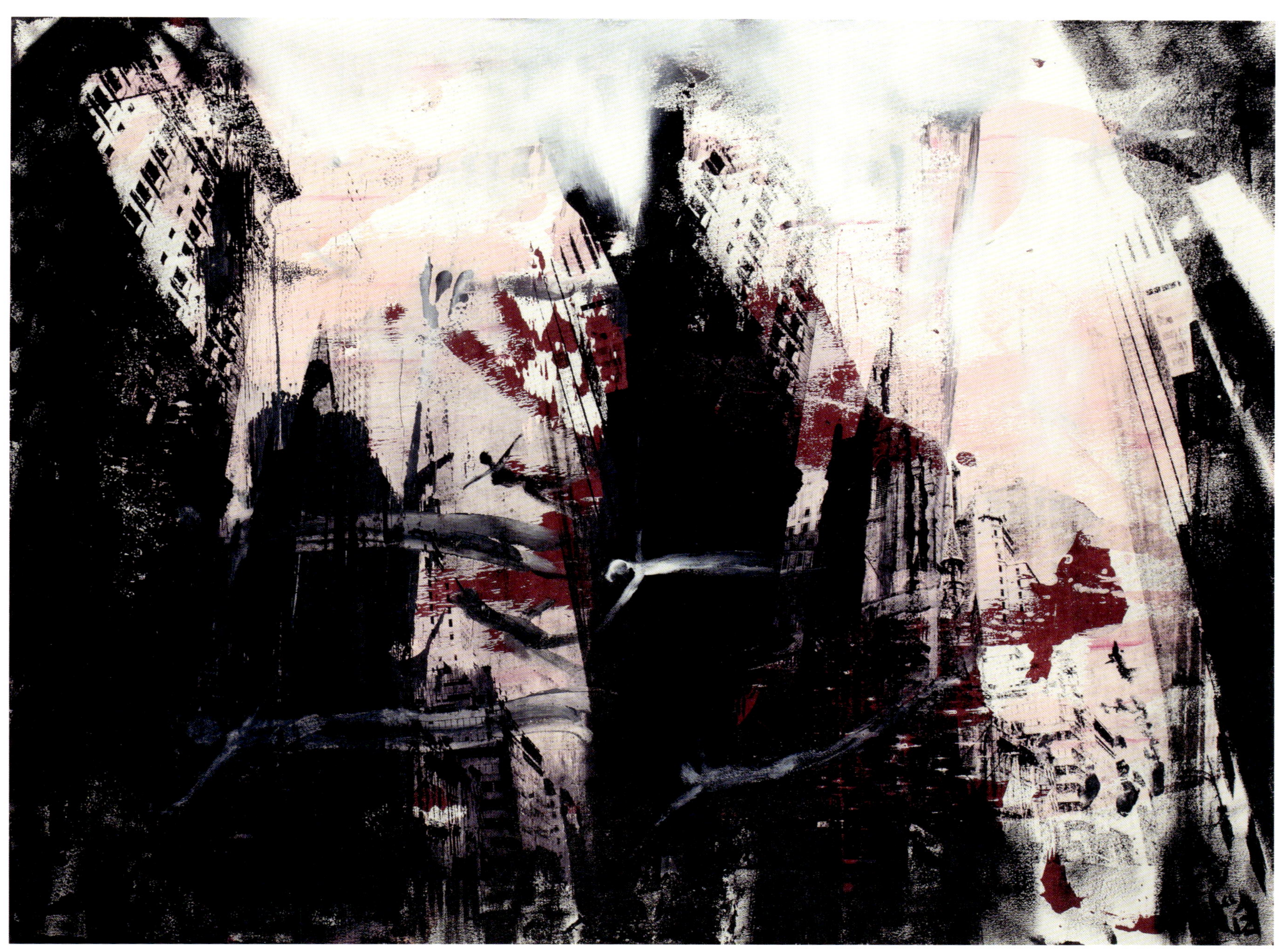

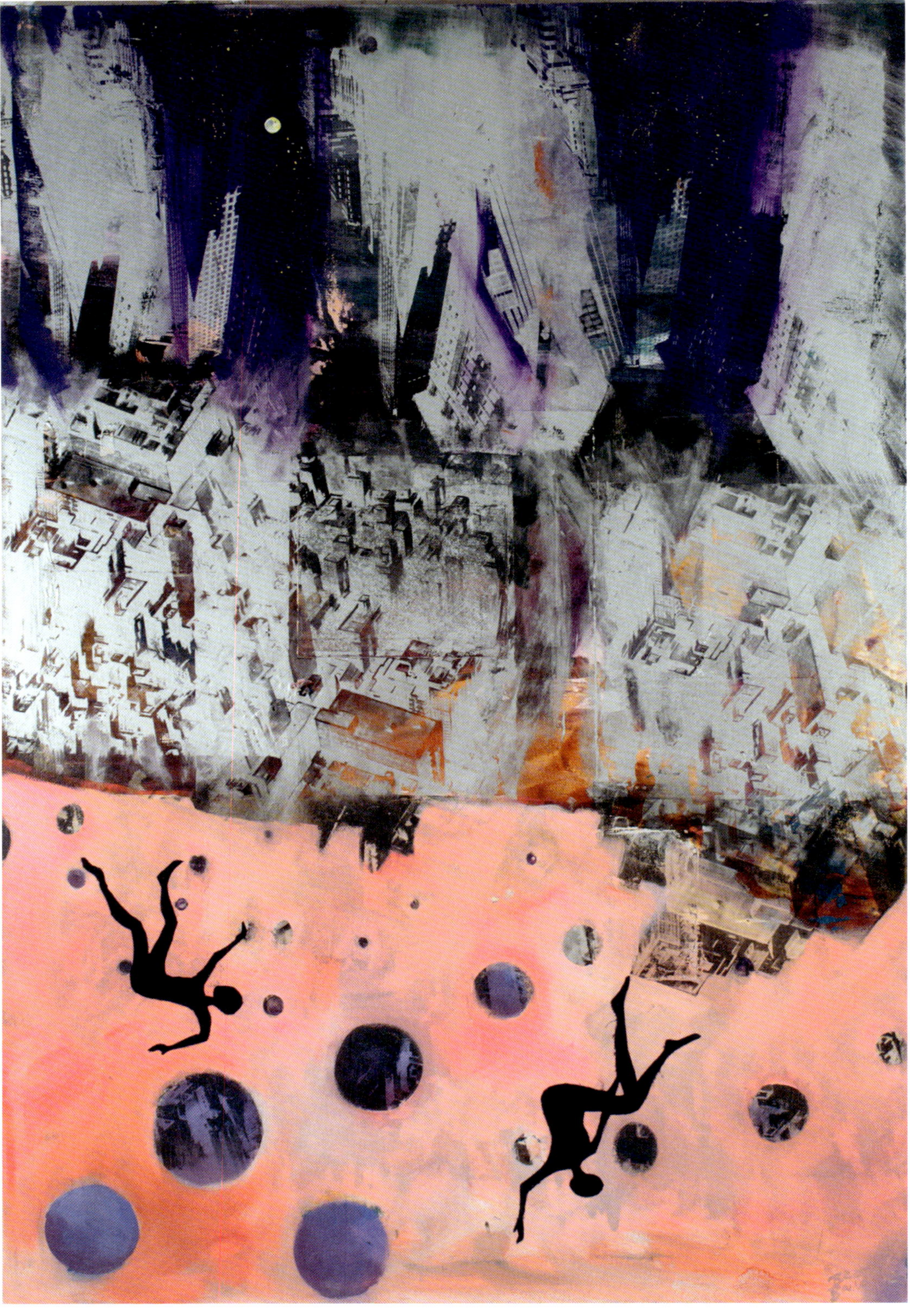

FALLING OFF THE EDGE OF THE EARTH 2008 Oil, silkscreen with velvet cut out on canvas 250 × 170cm

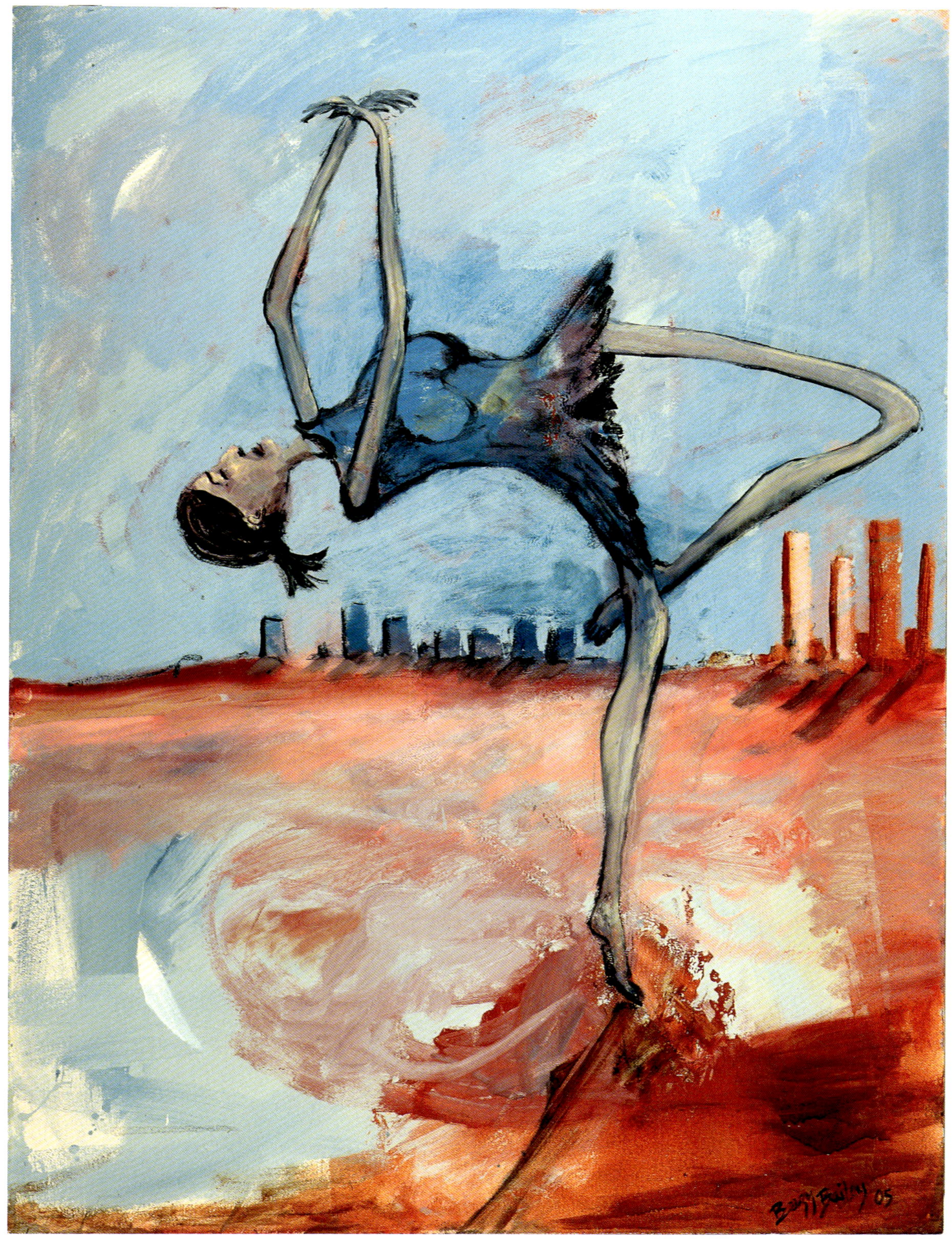

DORIS'S MOTHER WAS A GENIUS 2005 Oil and enamel on canvas 135 × 100cm

FALLING ANGELS IN THE DESERT 2010 Oil and enamel on canvas 170 × 250cm

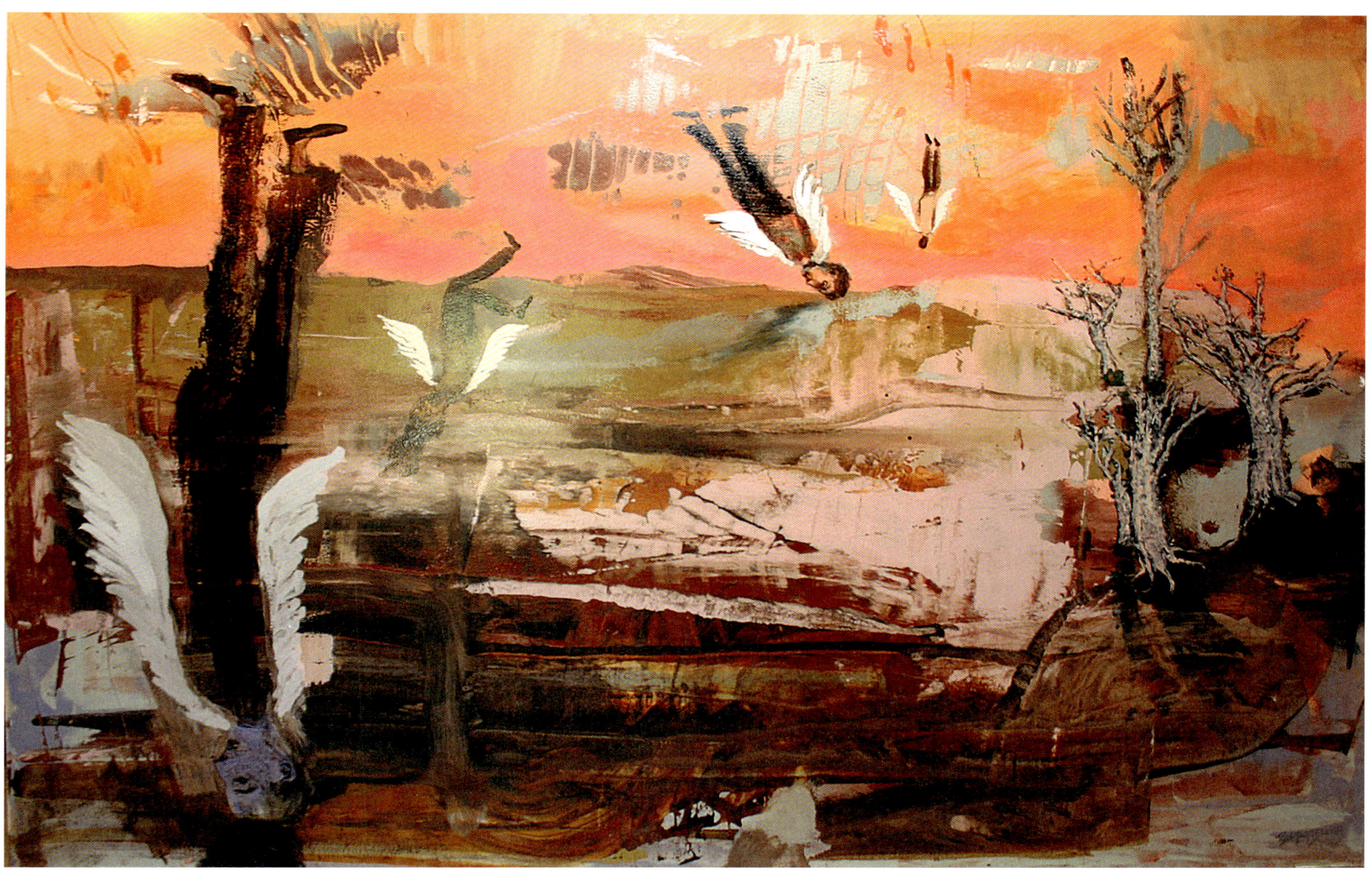

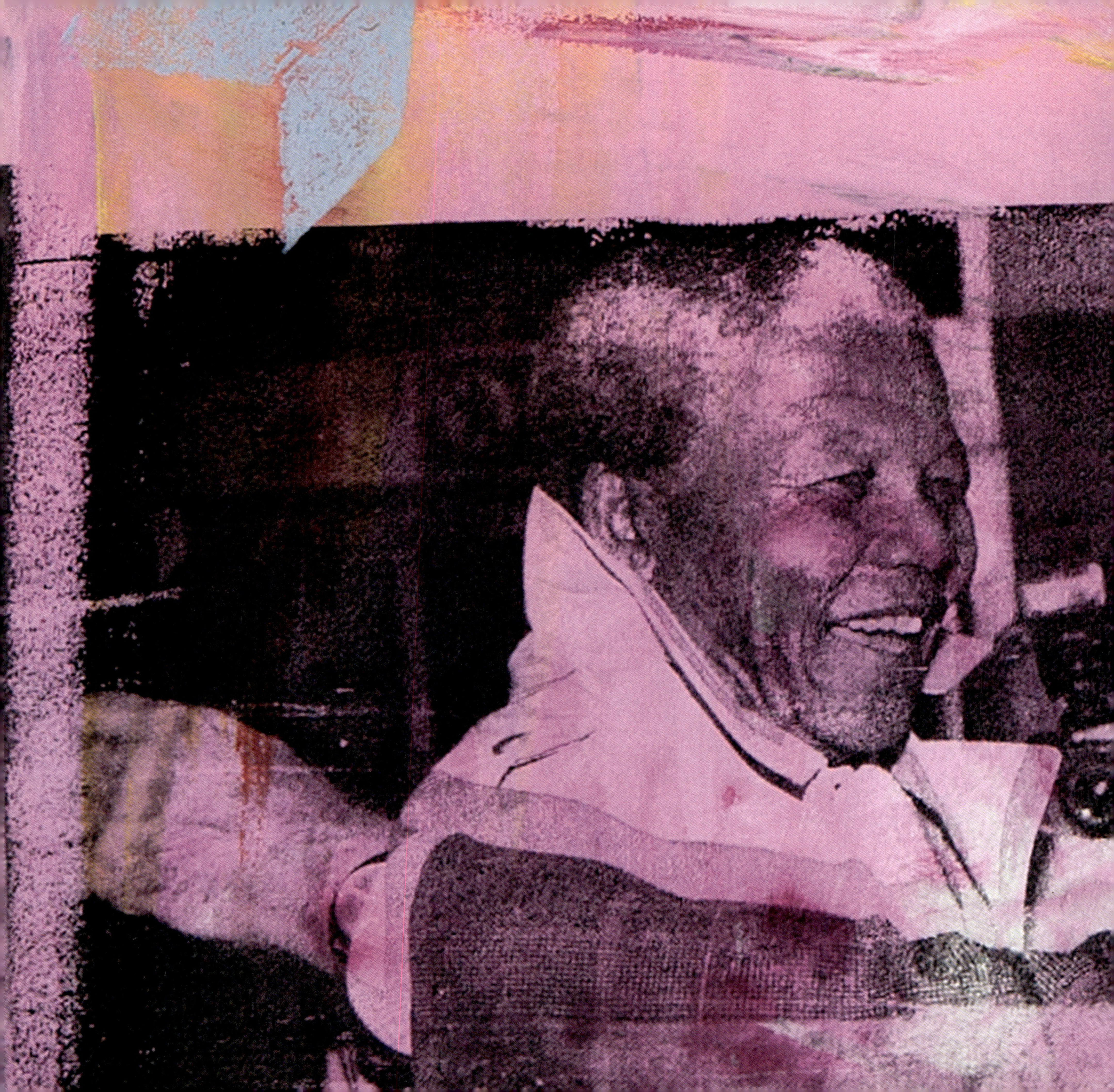

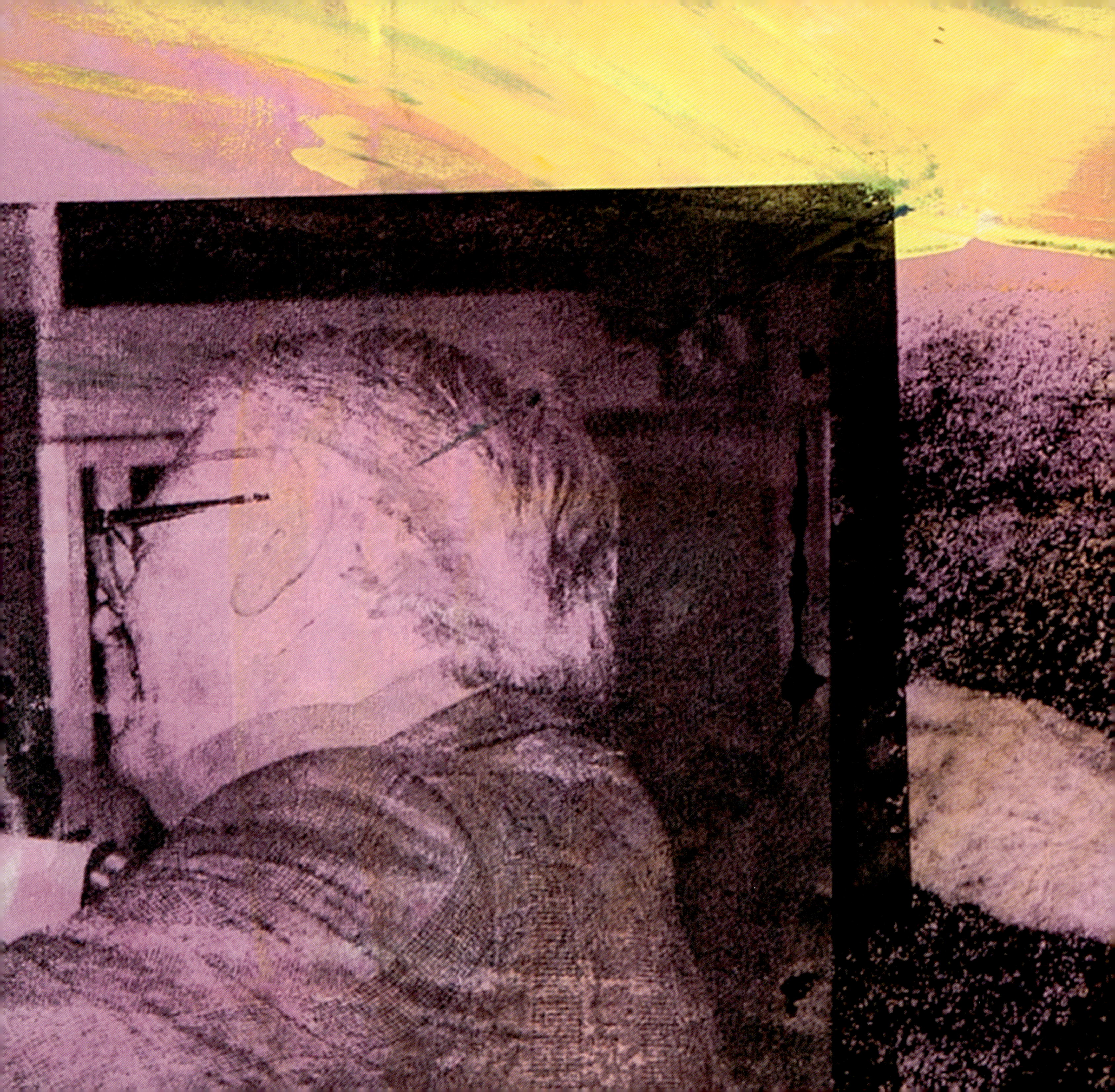

STORMY WEATHER 2010 Oil, silkscreen and enamel on canvas 170 × 250cm

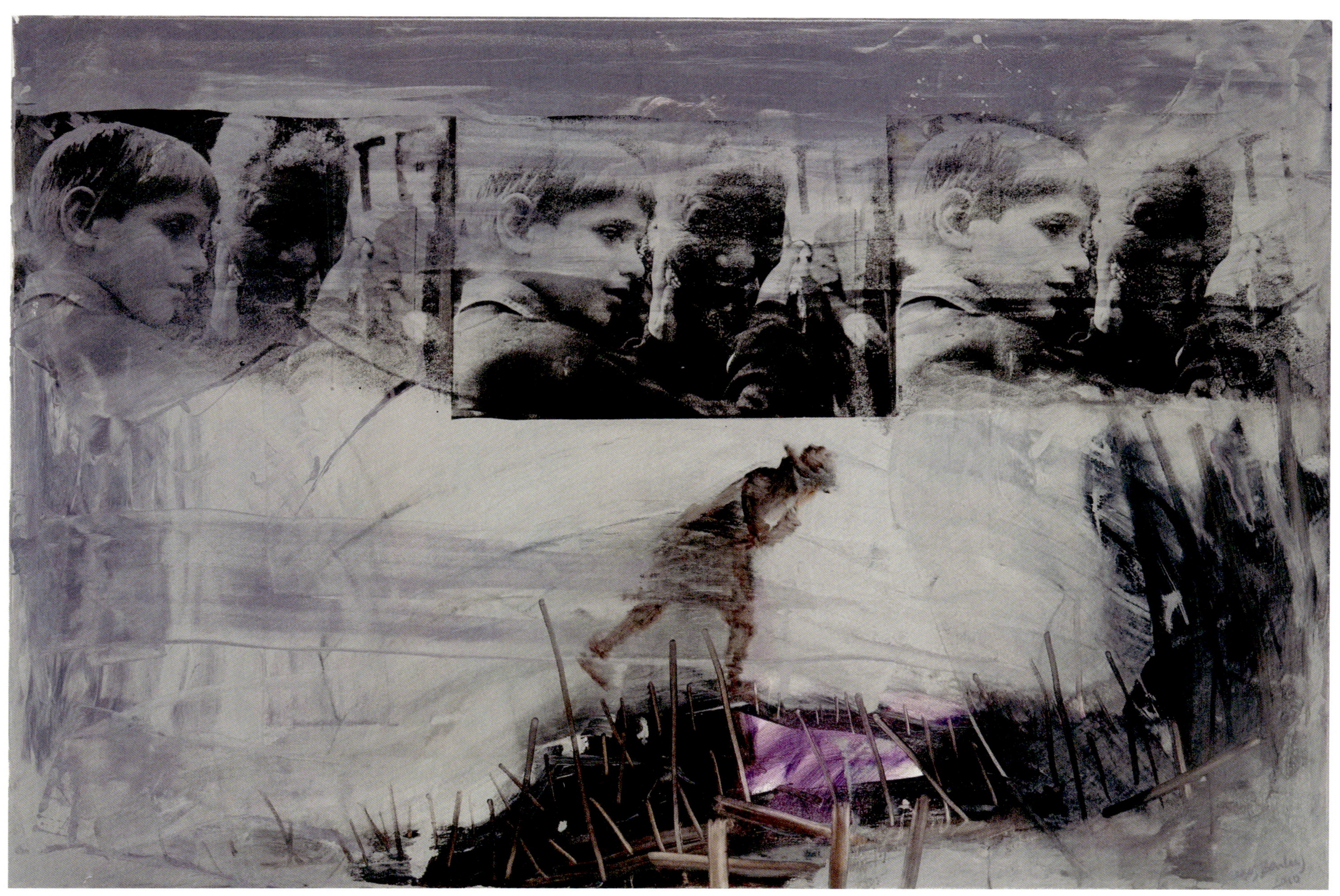

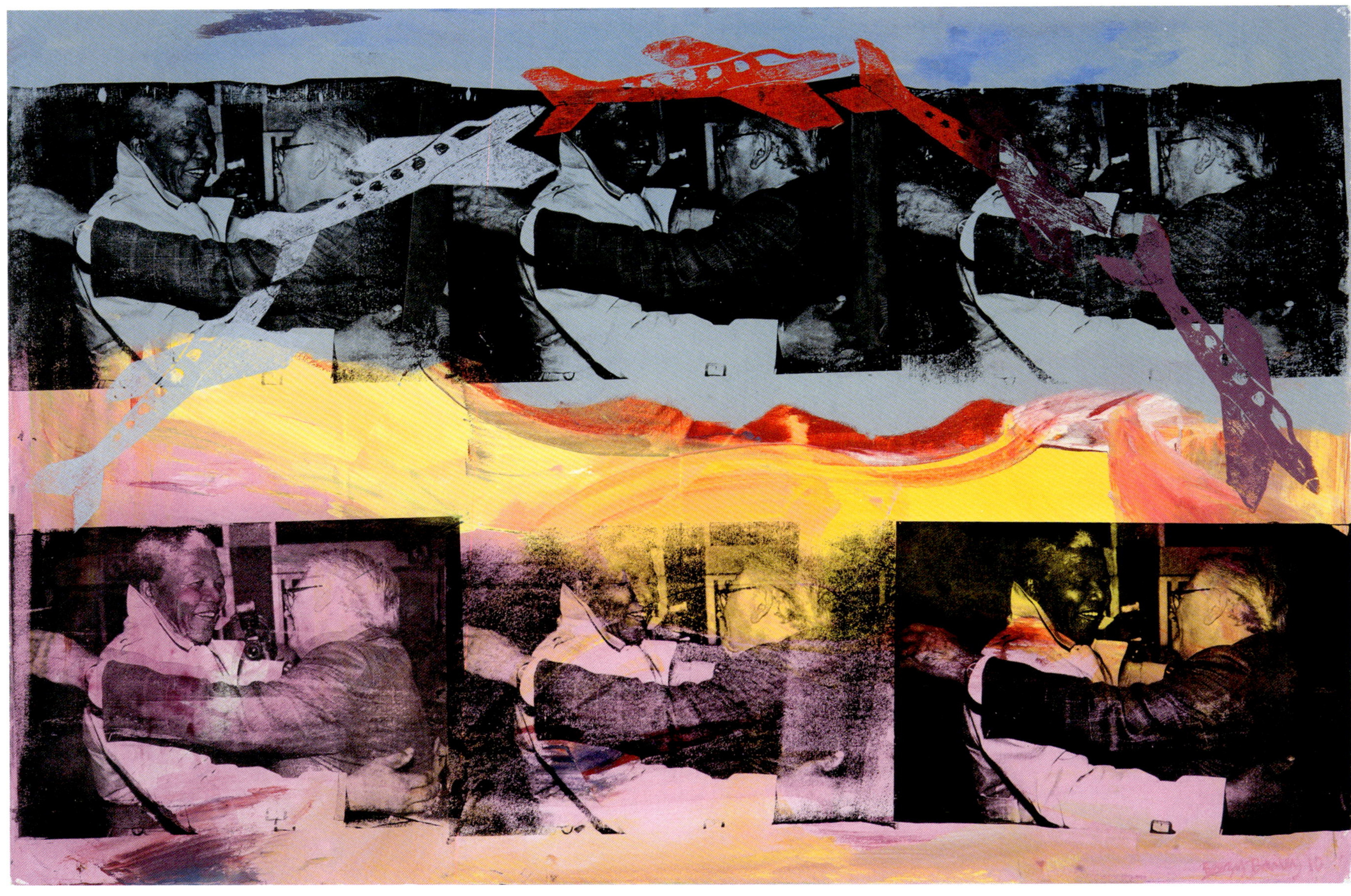

HOMECOMING 2010 Oil, silkscreen and enamel on canvas 170 × 250cm

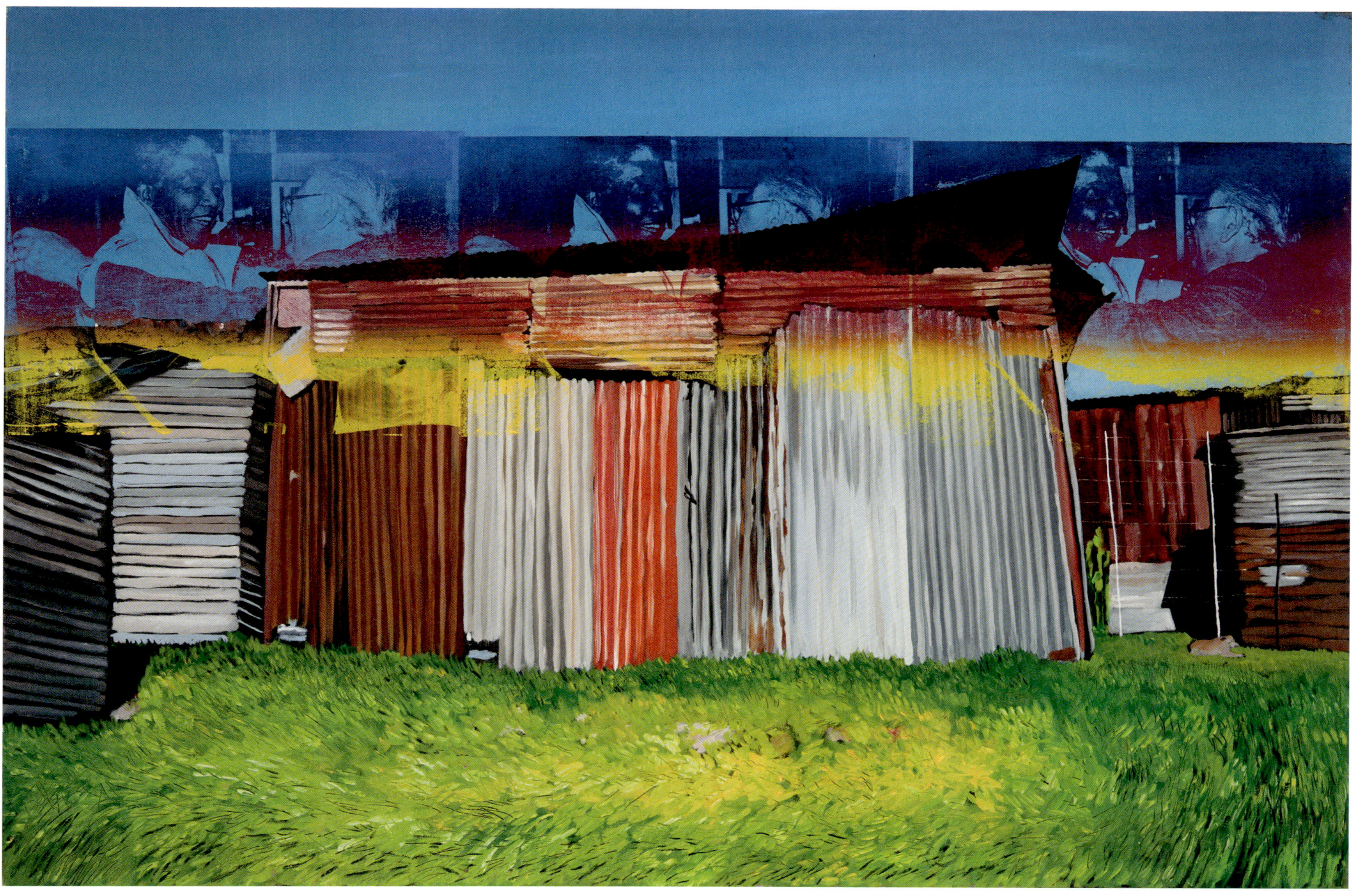

RAINBOW MEN 2010 Oil, silkscreen and enamel on canvas 170 × 250cm

GHOST BOXER 2010 Oil, silkscreen and enamel on canvas 170 × 250cm

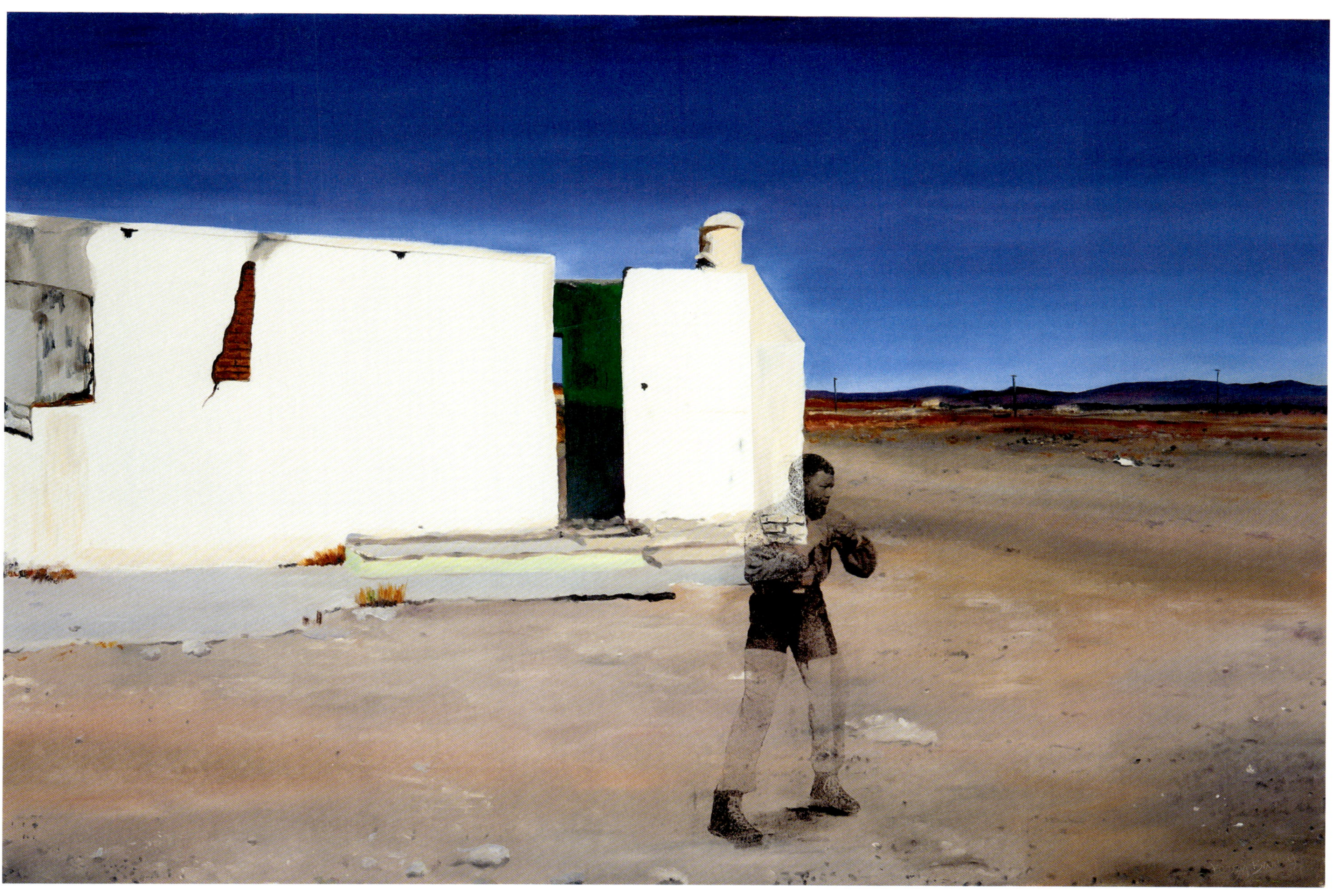

PRISONER OF THE PEOPLE 2010 Oil, silkscreen and enamel on canvas 170 × 250cm

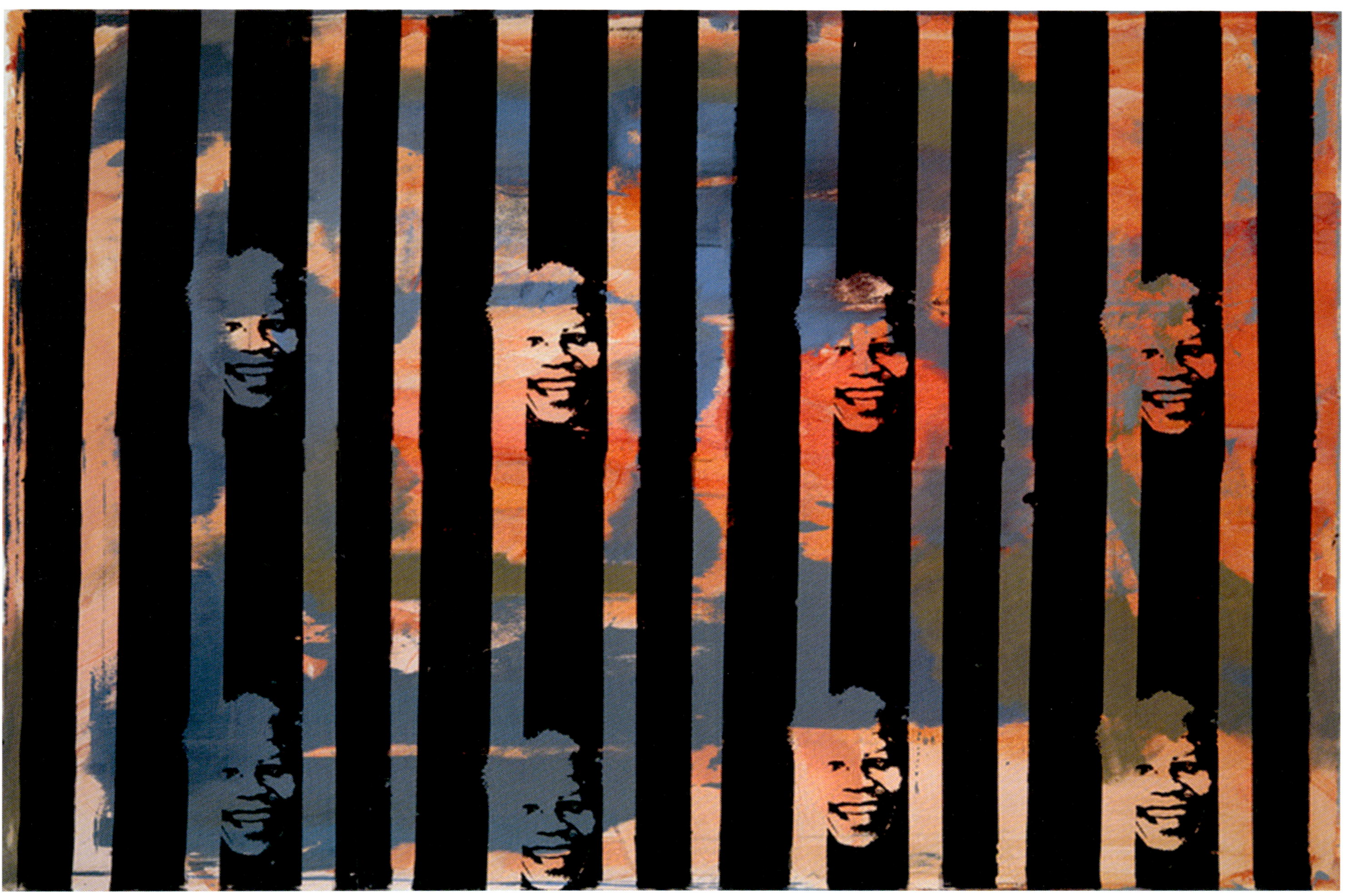

THE END OF WINTER 2010 Oil, silkscreen and enamel on canvas 110 × 125cm

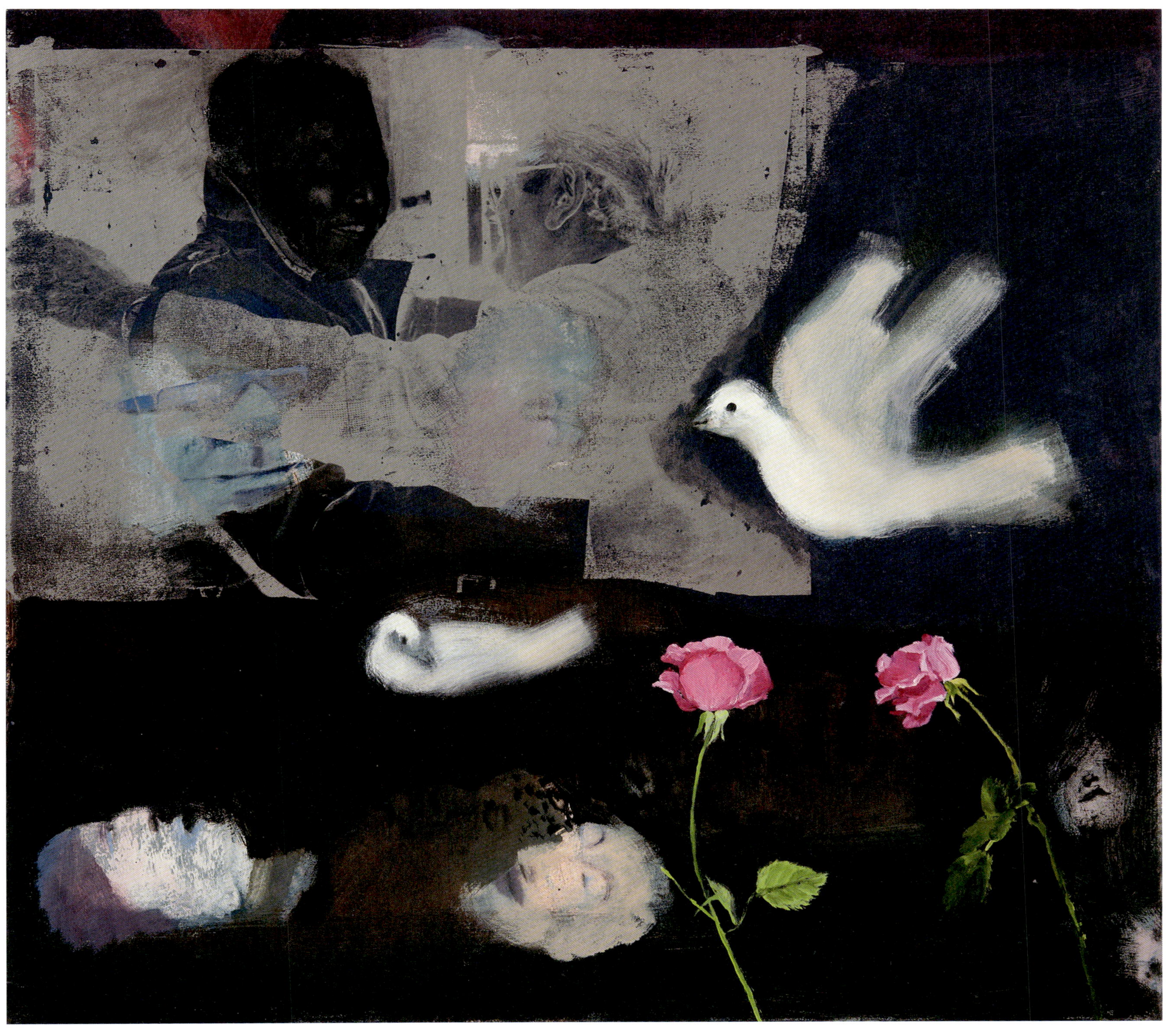

CITATION 2010 Oil, silkscreen and enamel on canvas 250 × 170cm

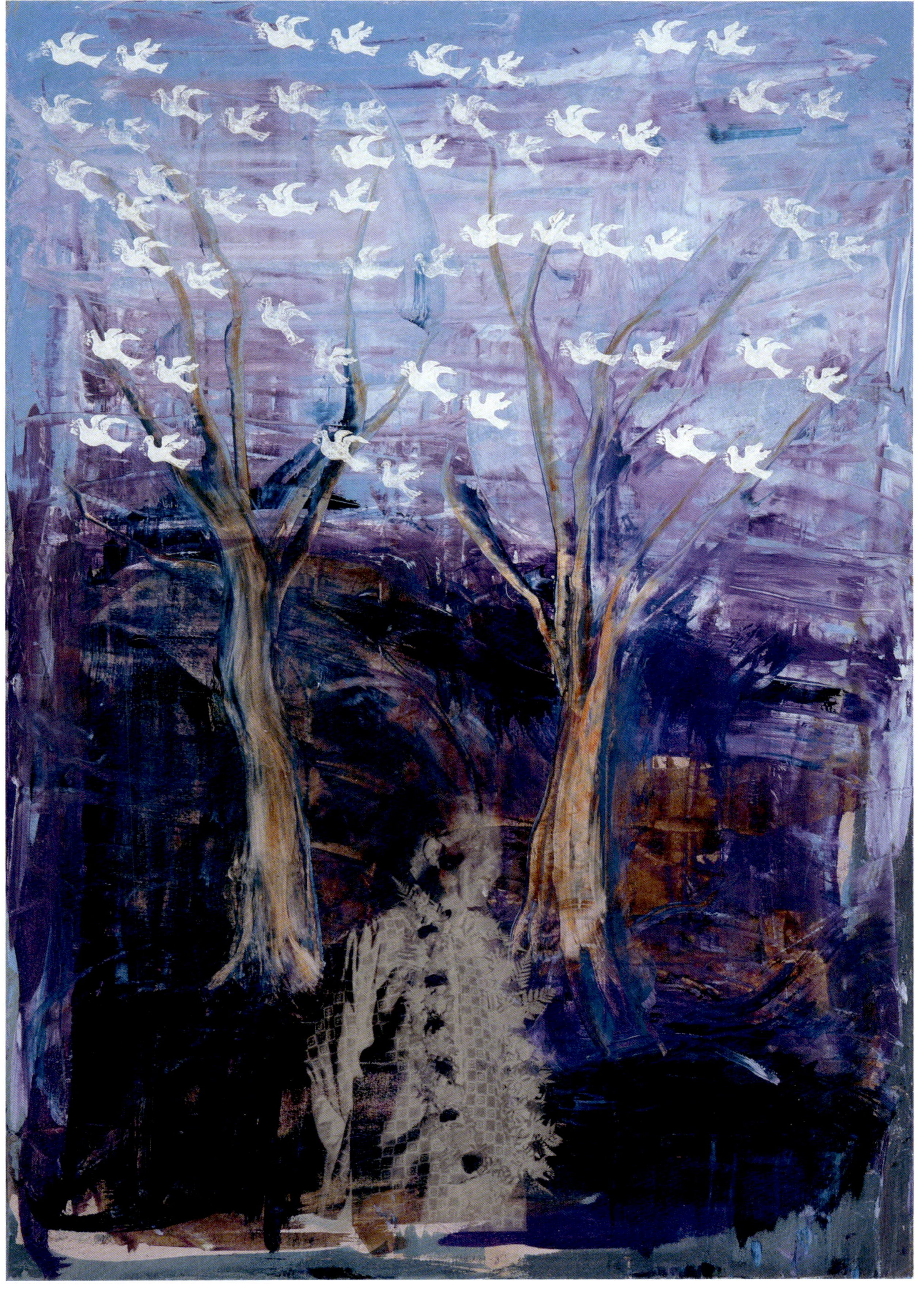

GOODBYE JACOB 2018 Oil on canvas 75 × 60cm

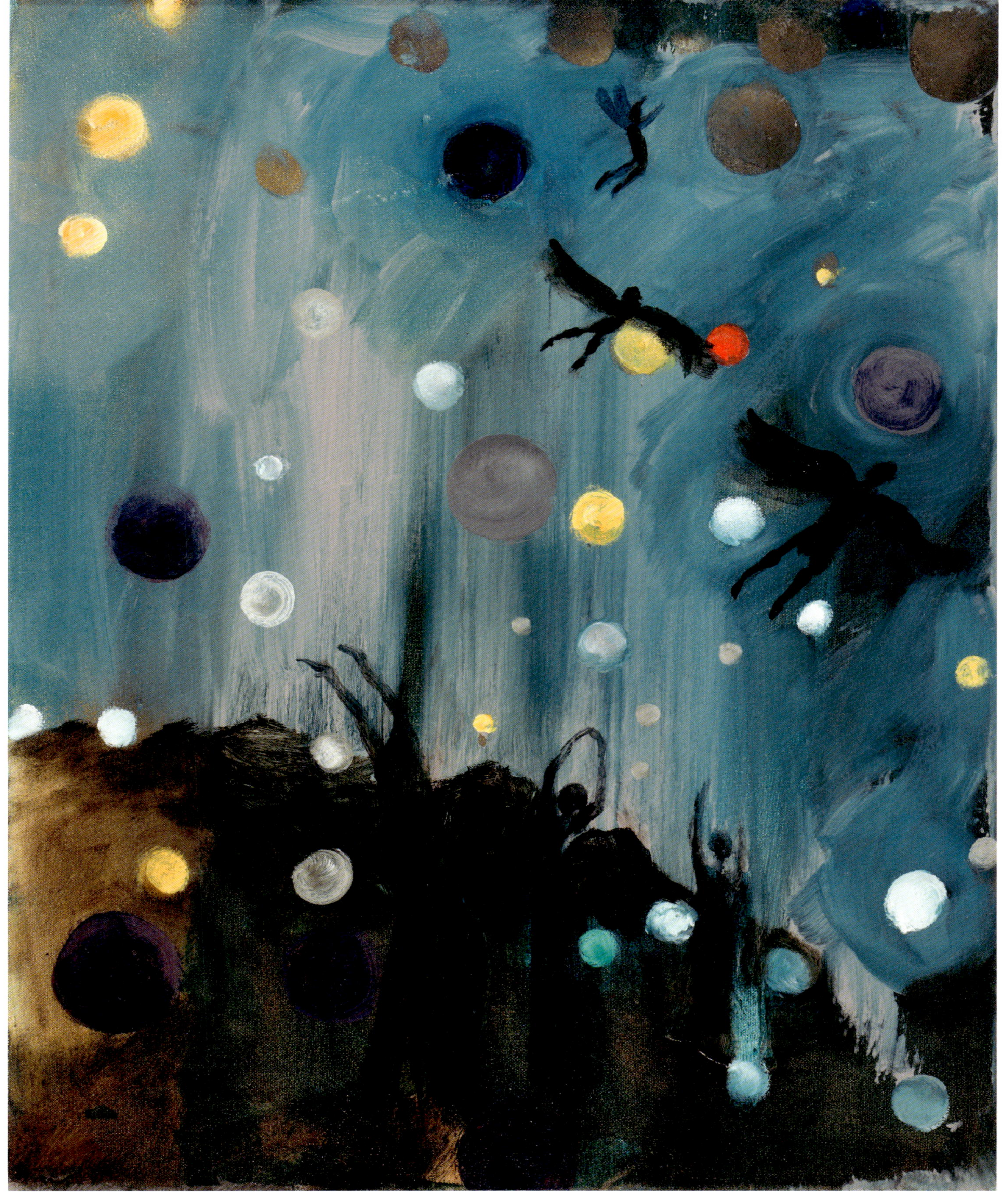

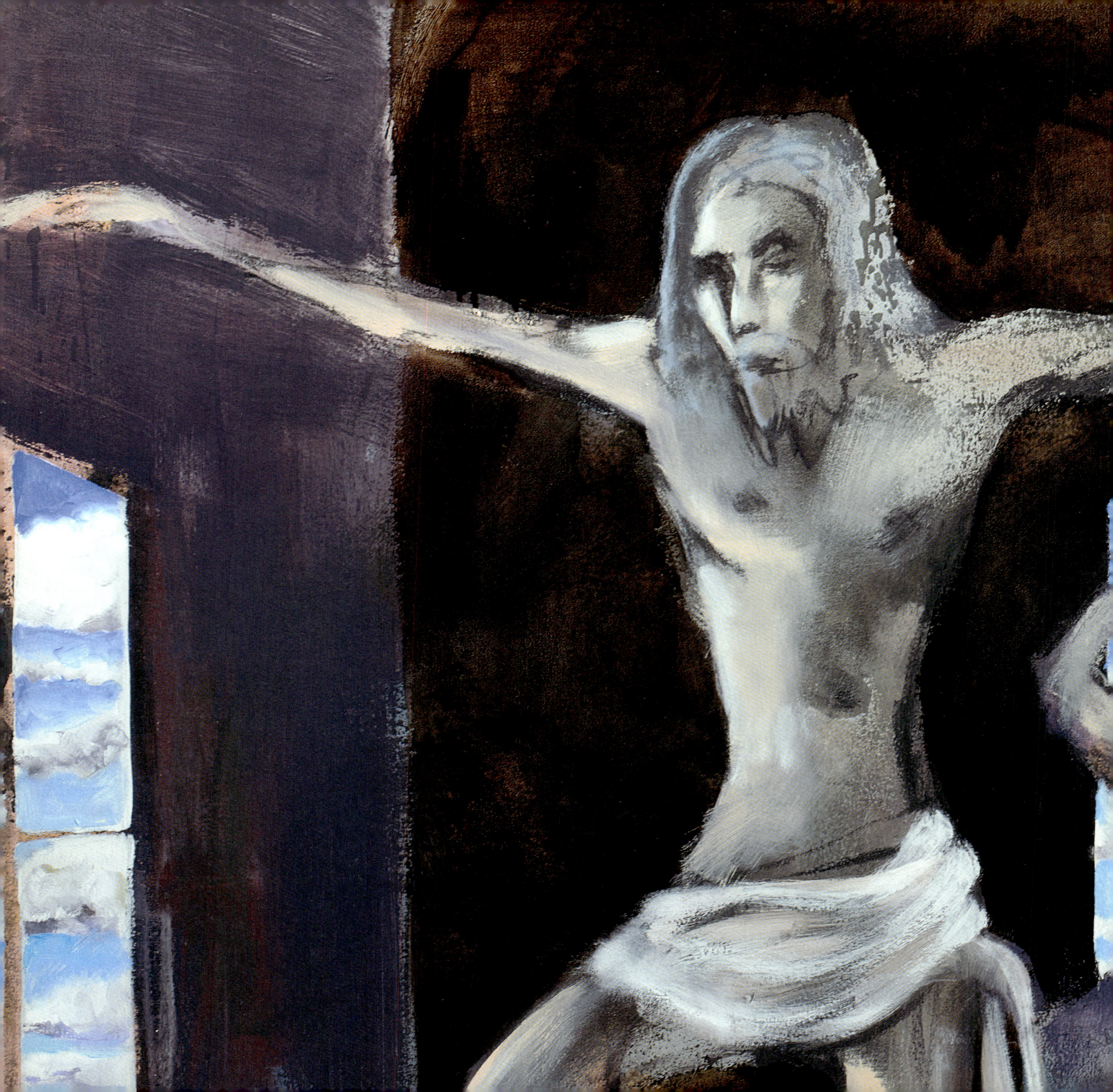

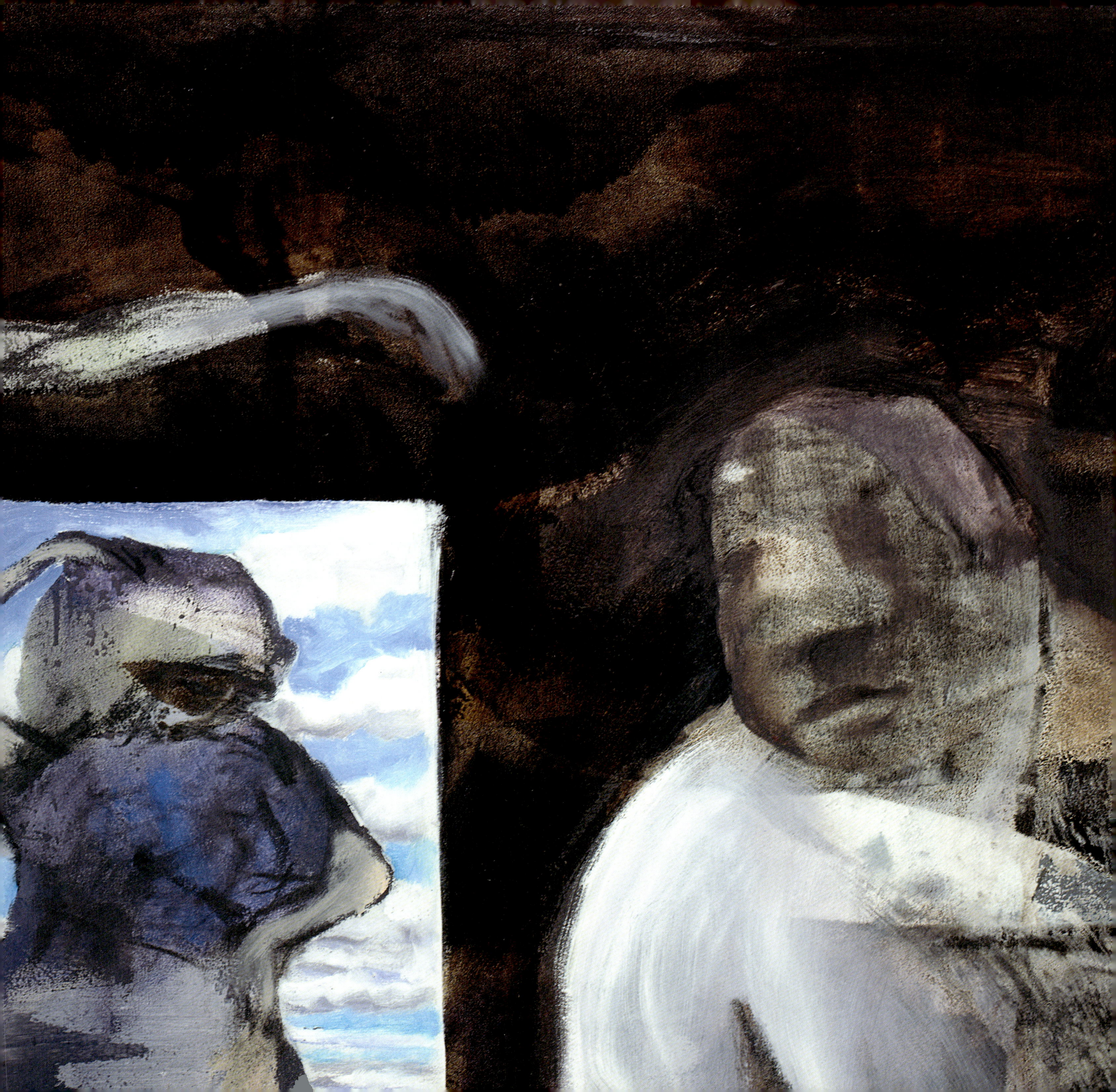

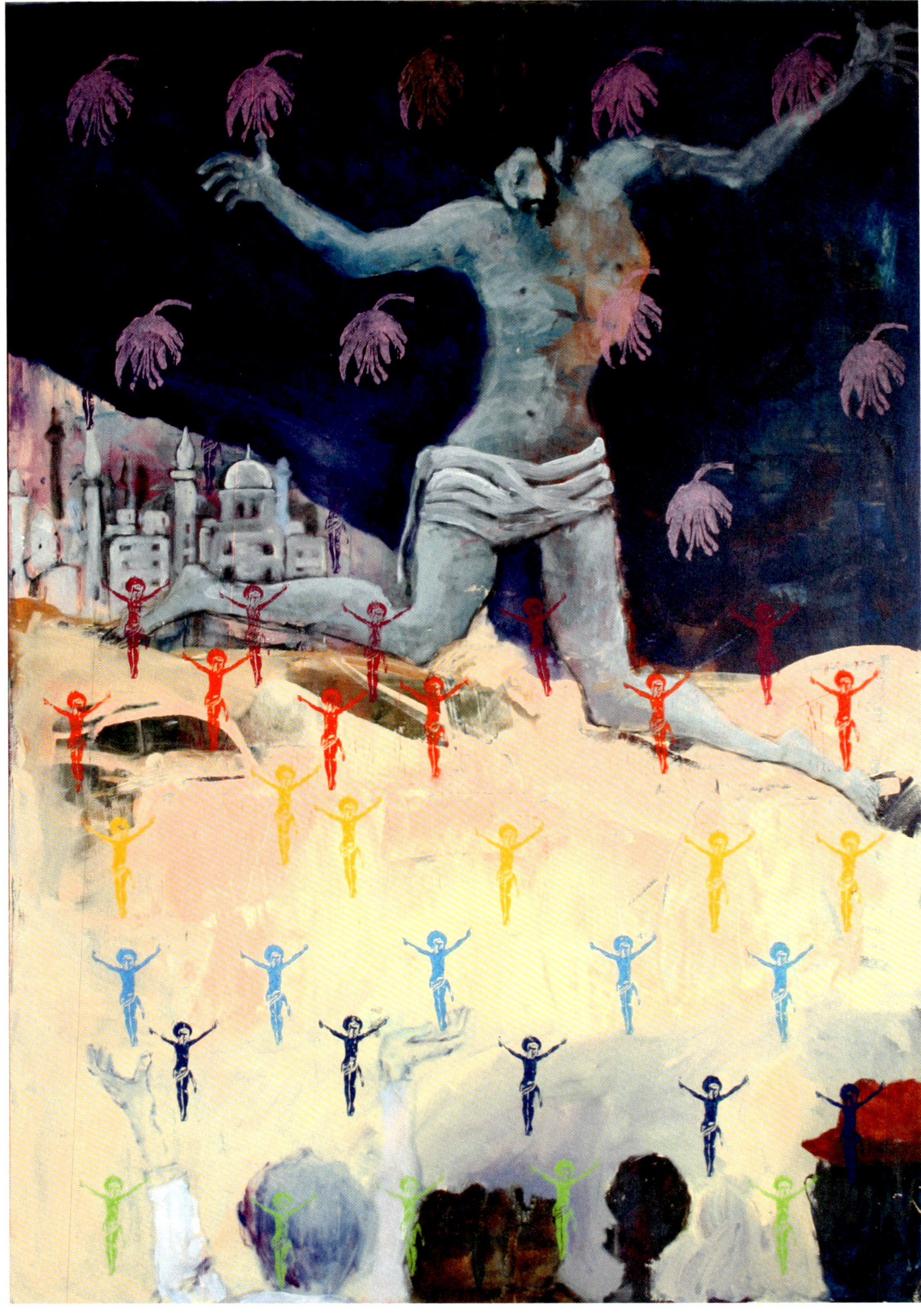

CHRIST JUMPING BETWEEN HEAVEN AND EARTH 2009 Oil and enamel on canvas 250 × 170cm

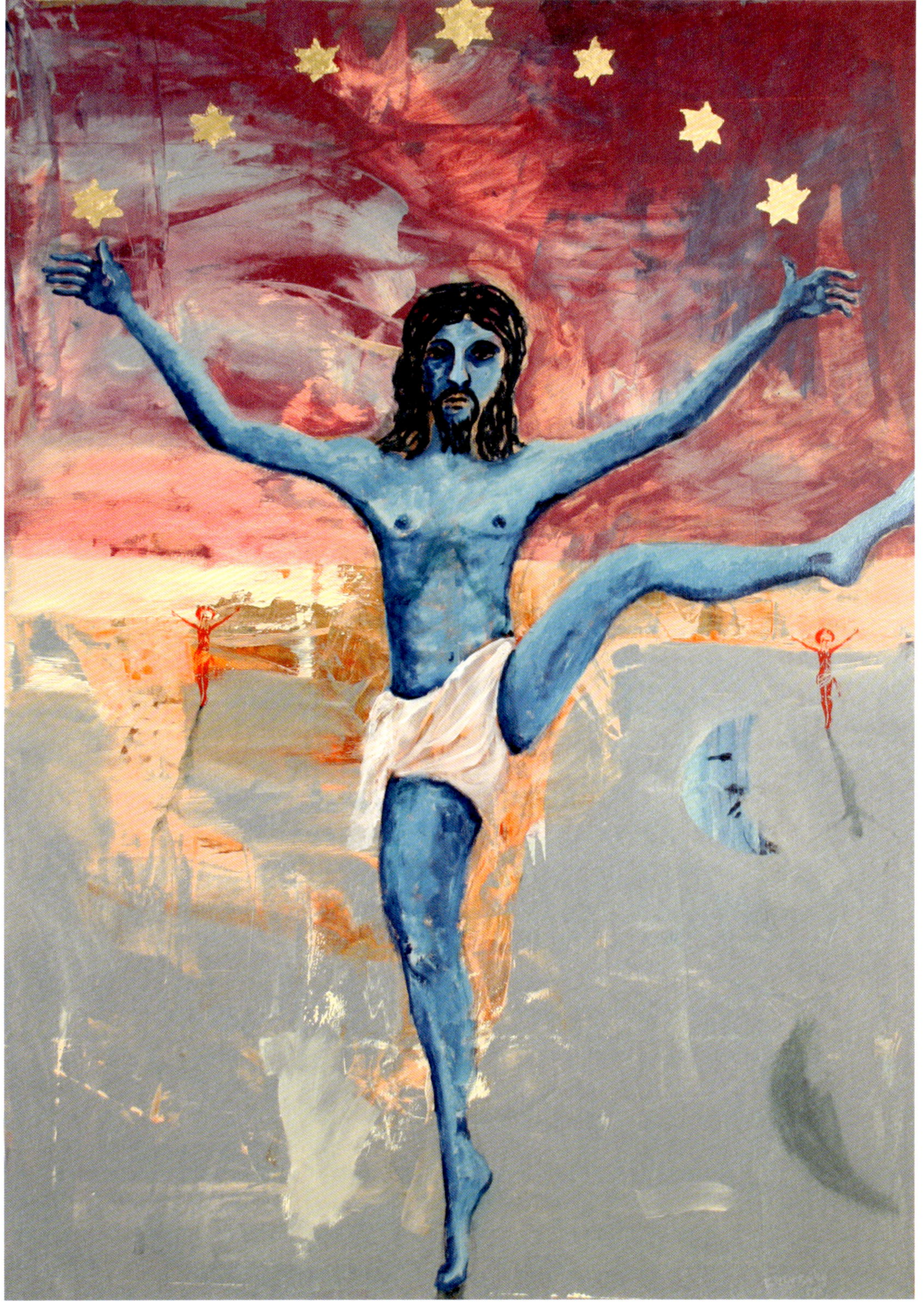

BLUE CHRIST DANCING 2009 Oil and enamel on canvas 250 × 170cm

TWO KINGS MEET 2009 Oil, enamel and gold leaf on canvas 170 × 250cm

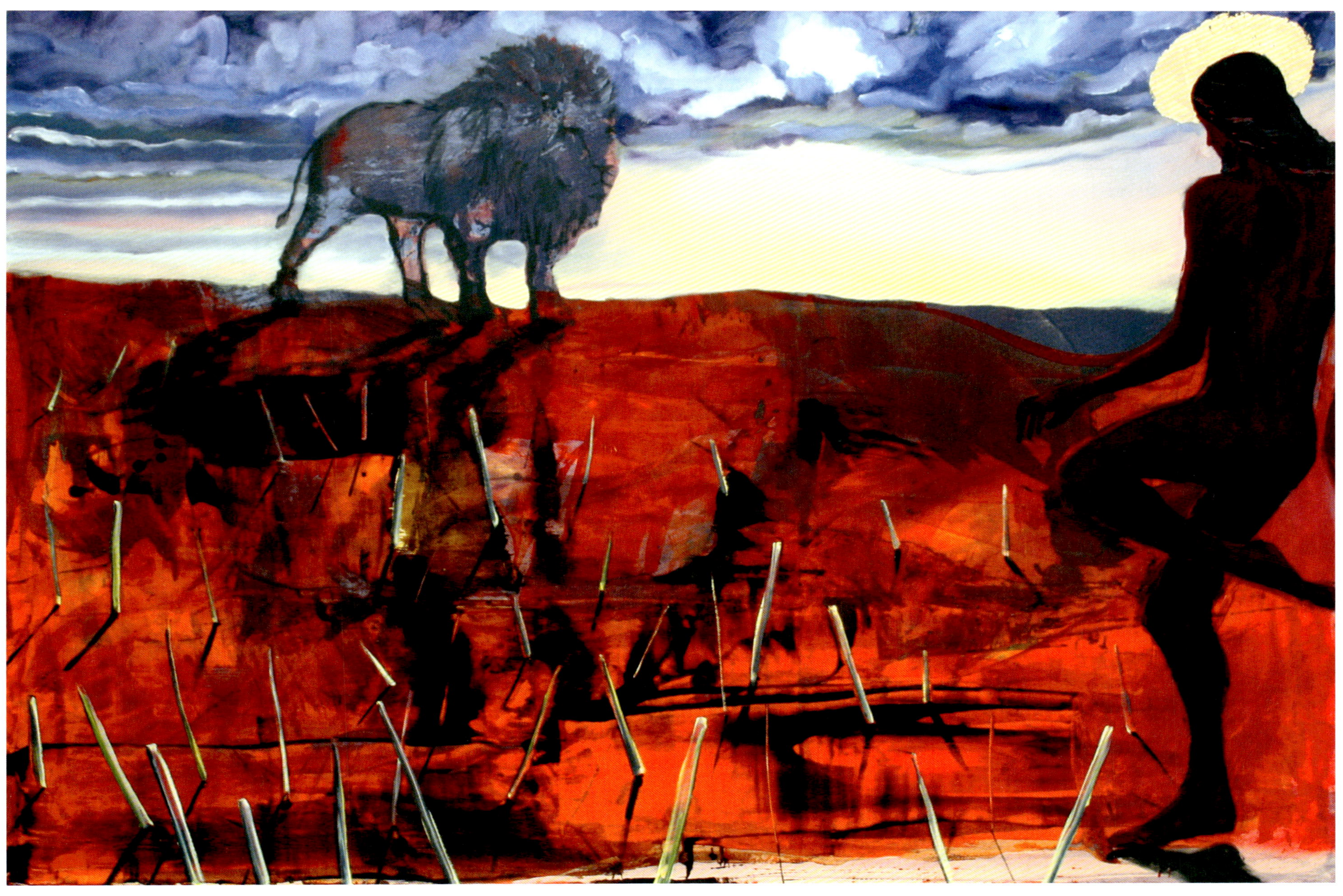

PLAY US A SONG, YOU'RE THE PIANO MAN 2009 Oil and enamel on canvas 170 × 200cm

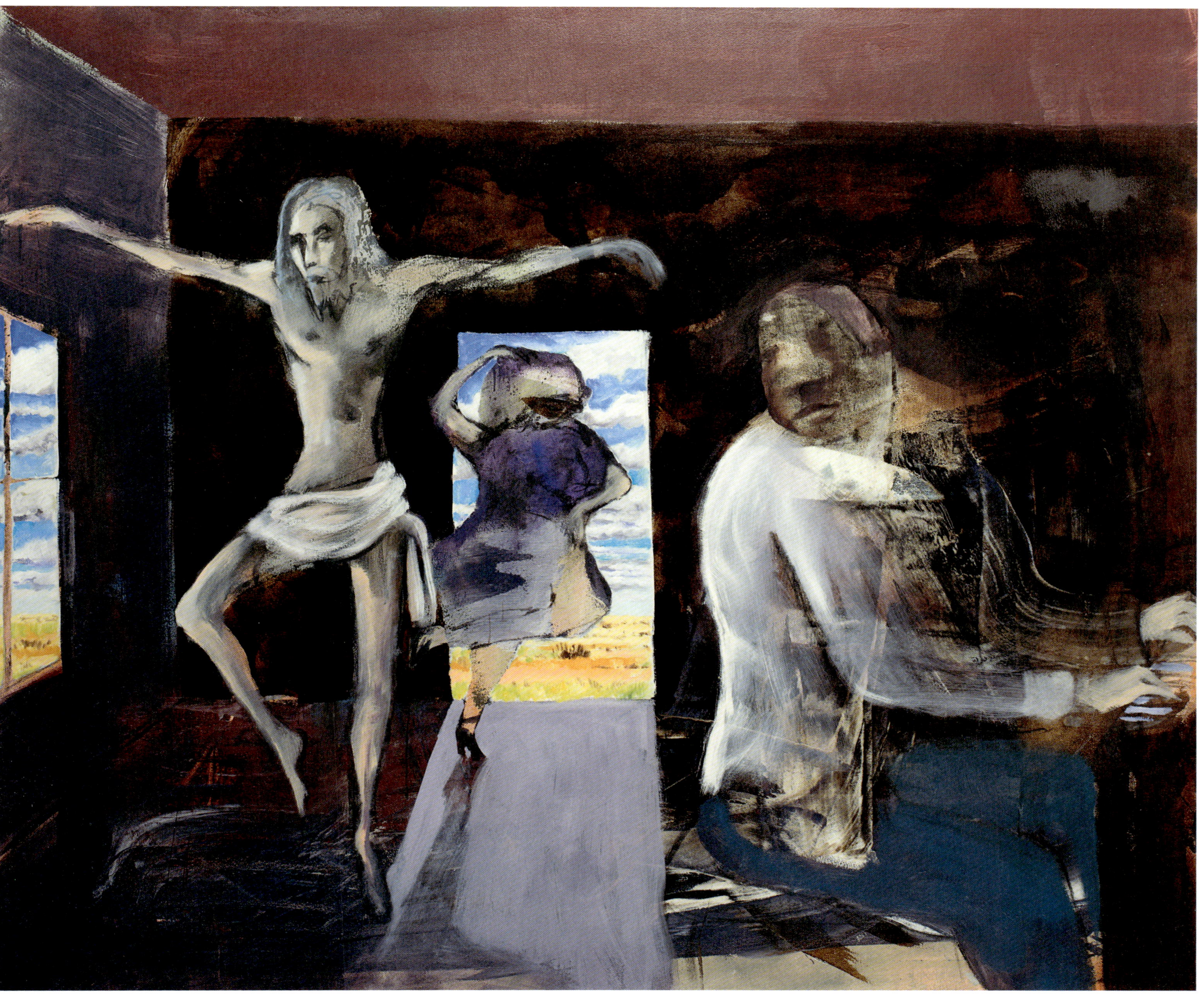

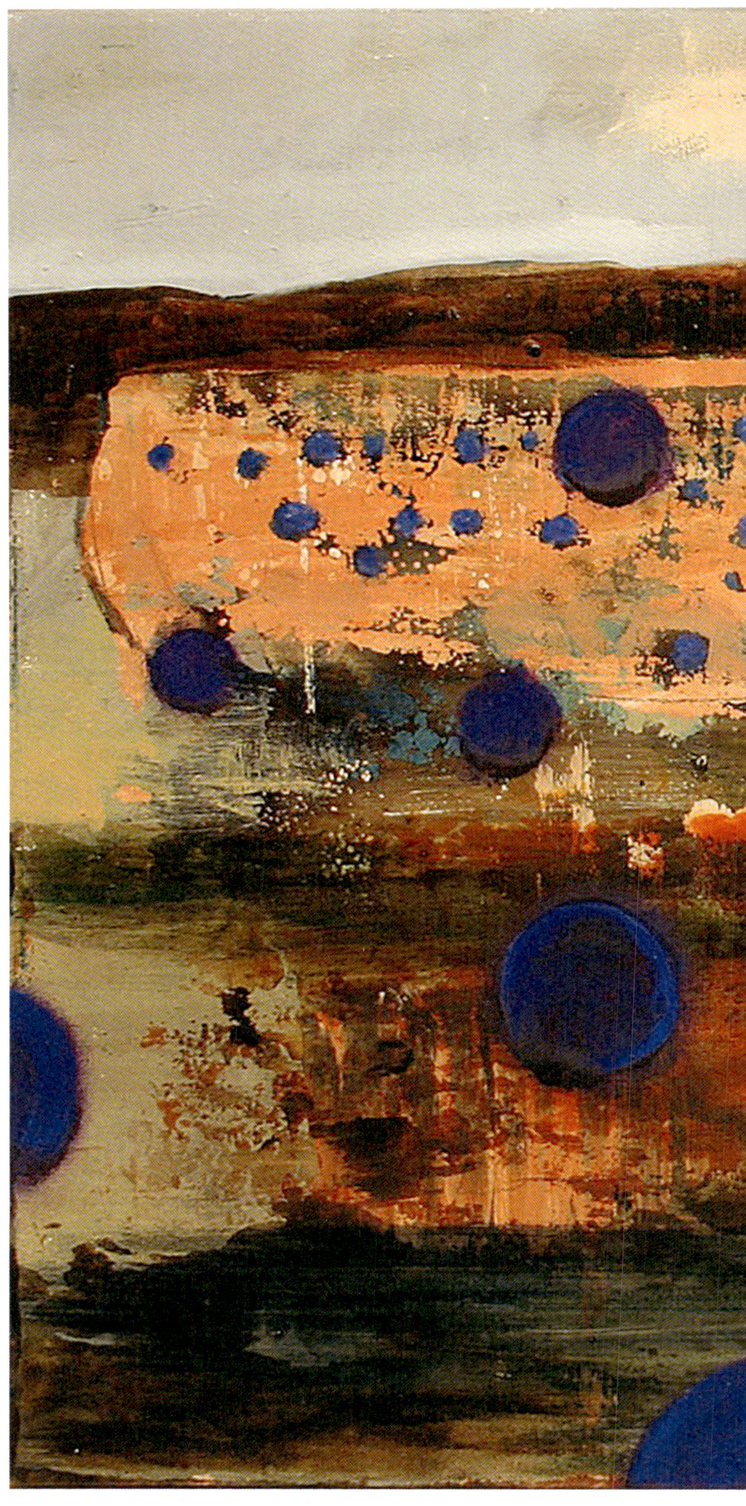

FAILED AVIATOR 2002 Oil on canvas 70 × 190cm

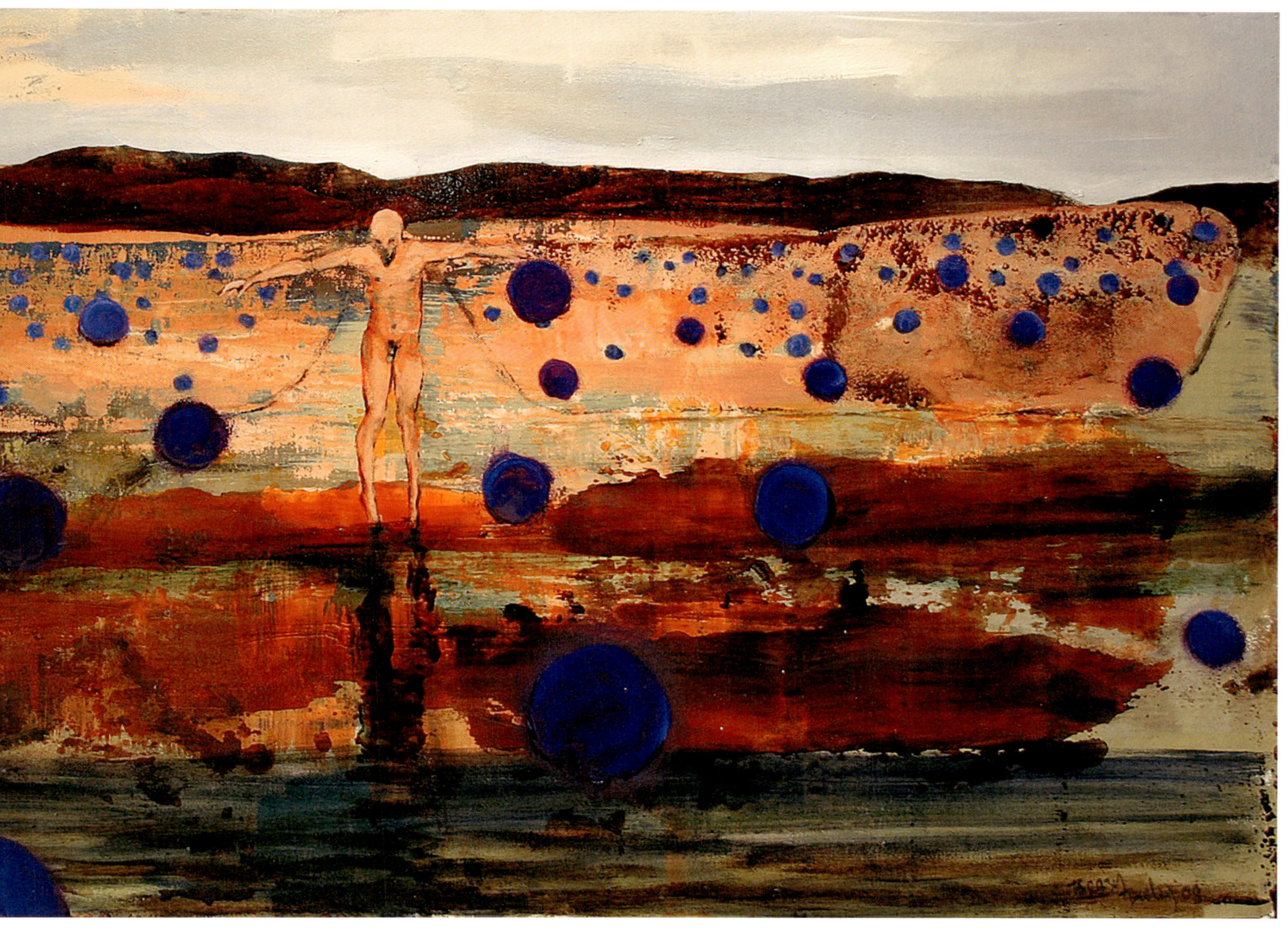

DANCING WITH QUEEN BABA 2015 Oil, enamel and gold dust on canvas 150.5 × 90cm

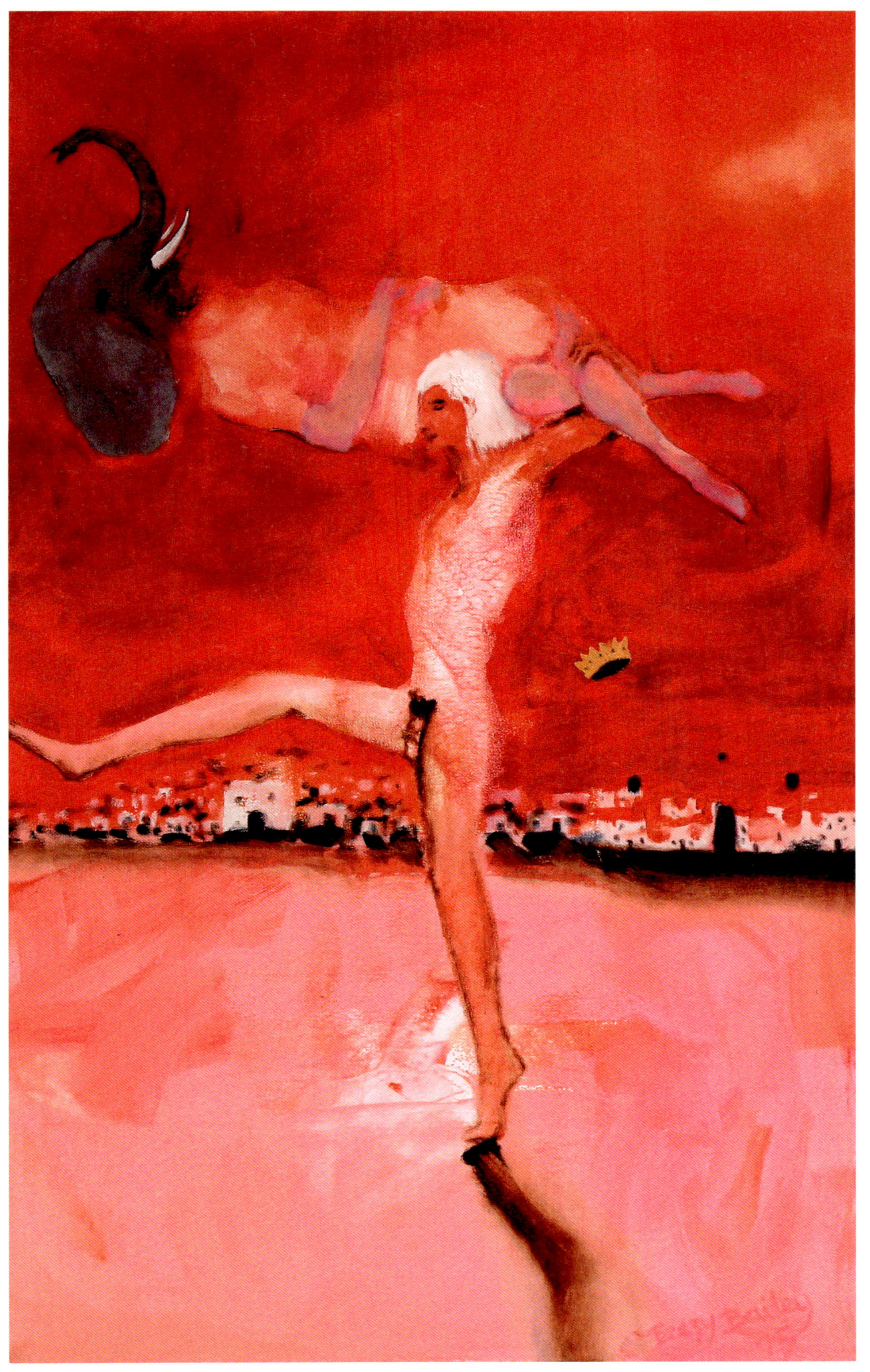

BOWIE DANCER 2016 Bronze 225 × 83 × 55cm

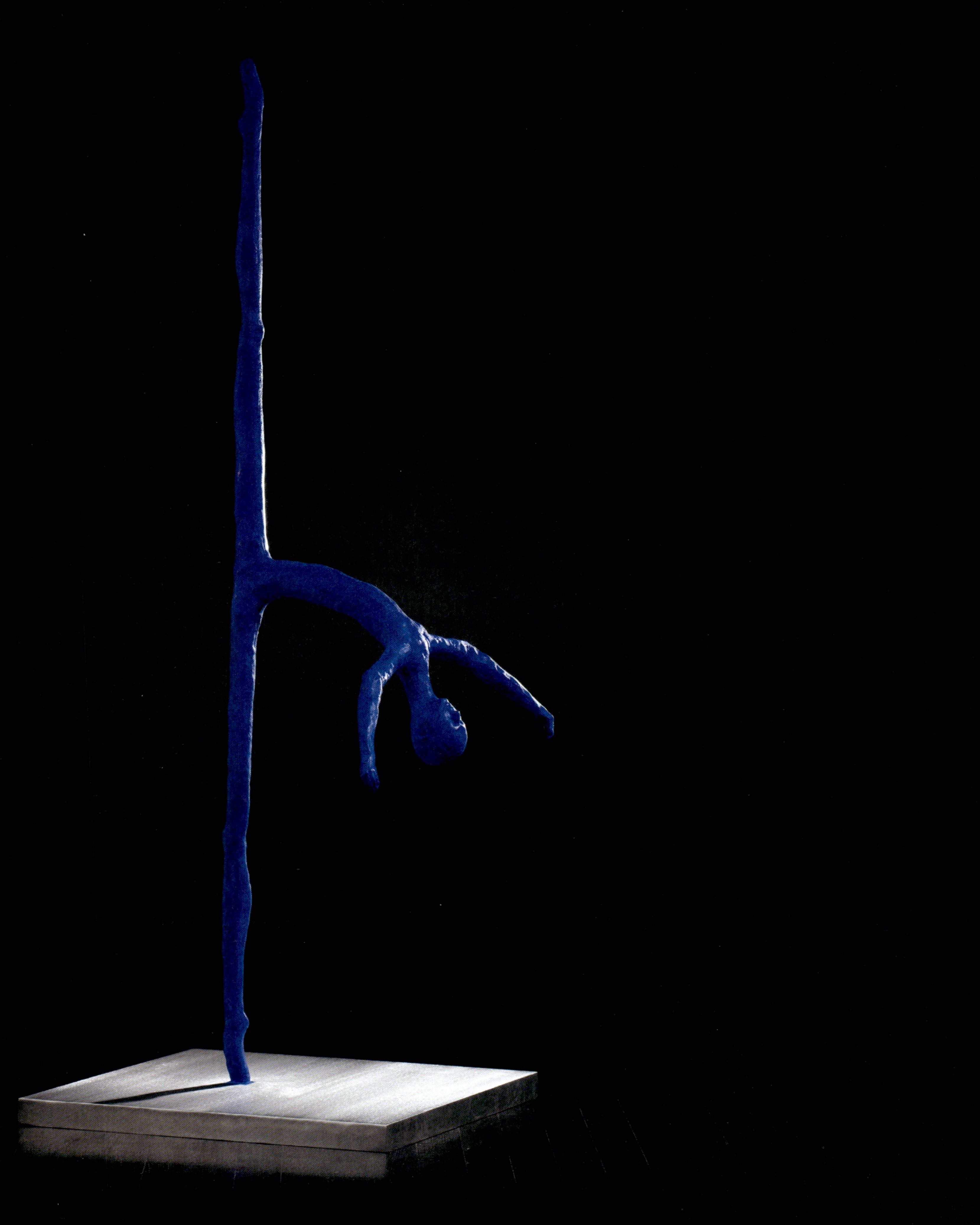

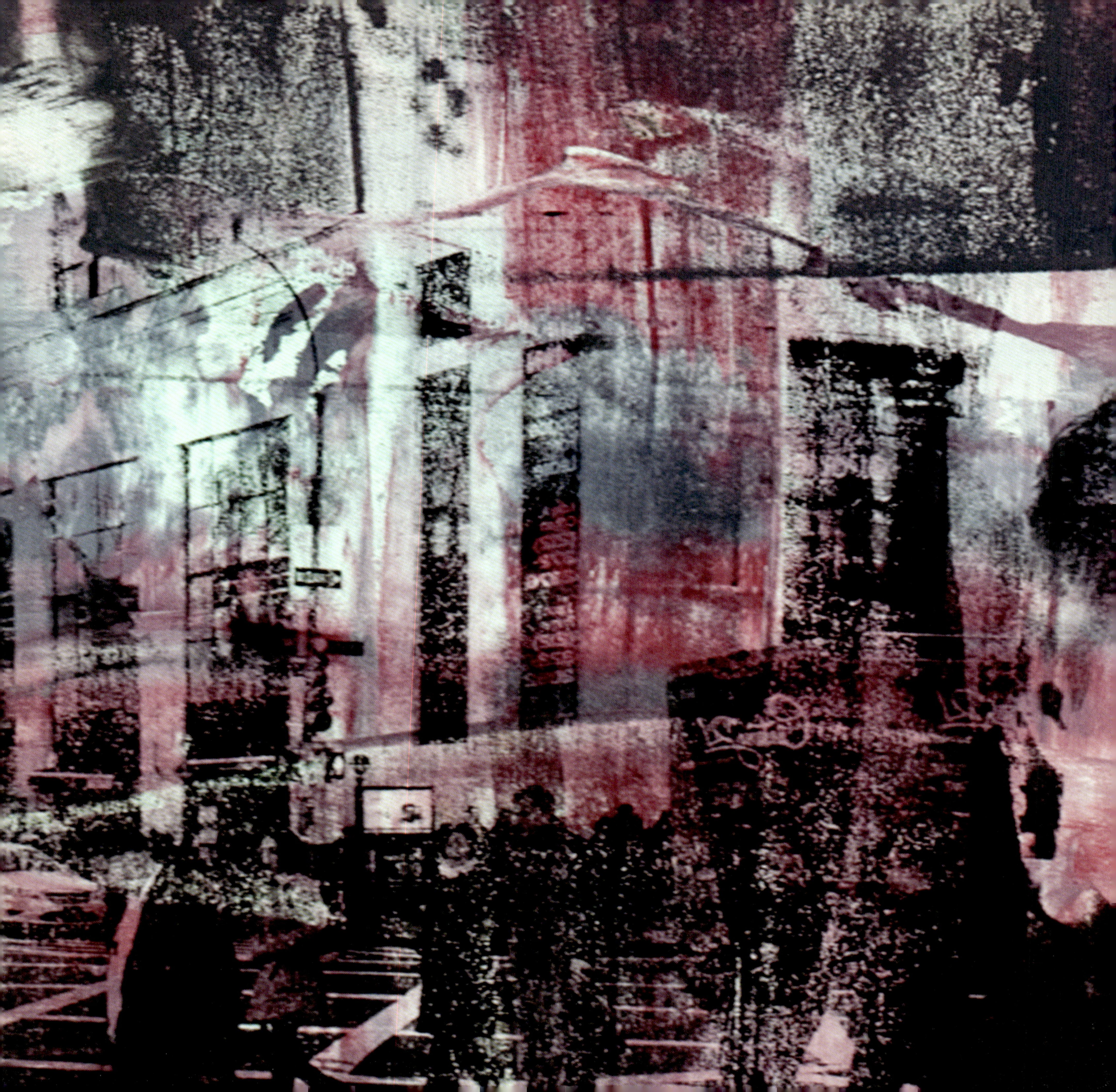

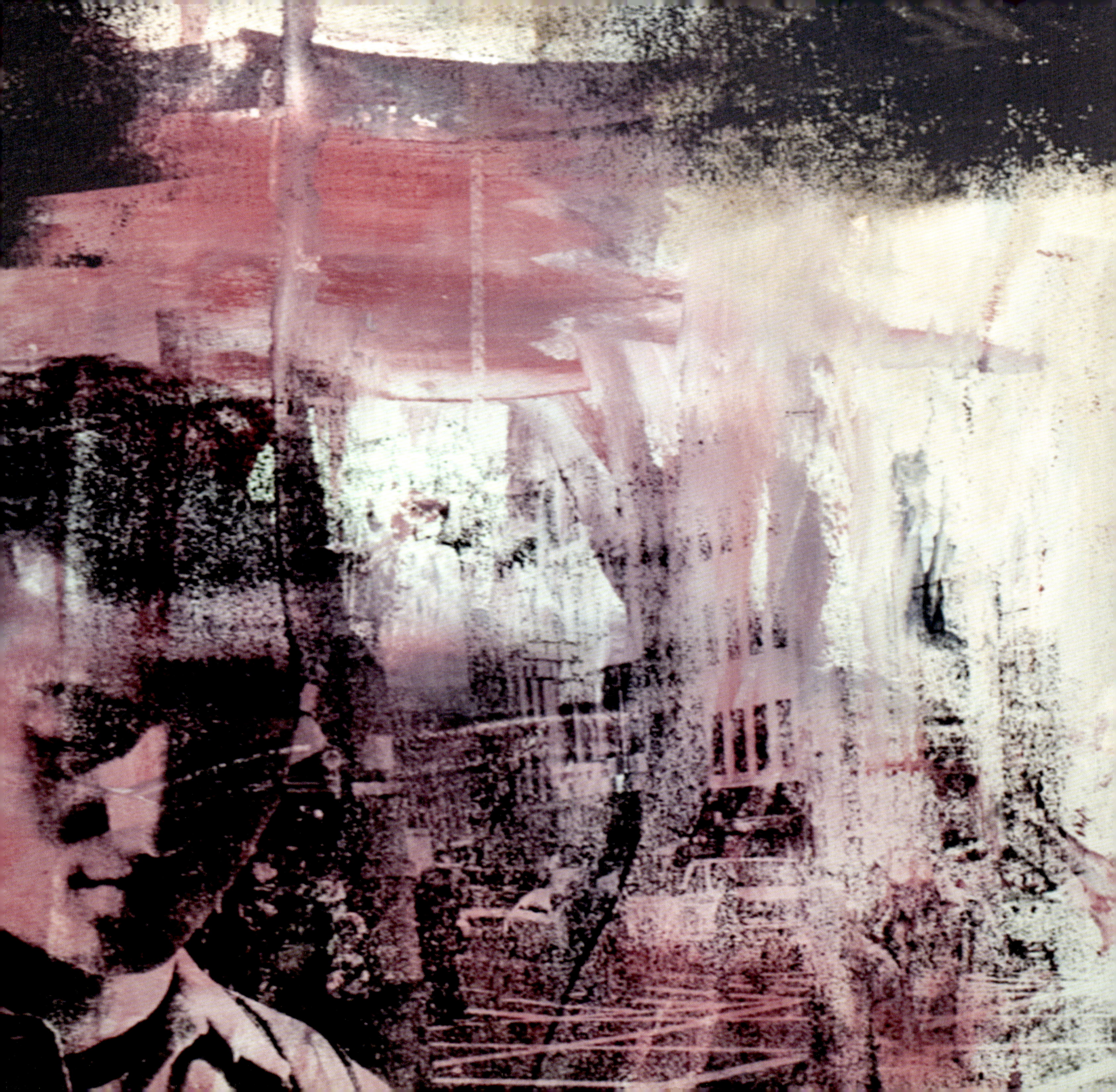

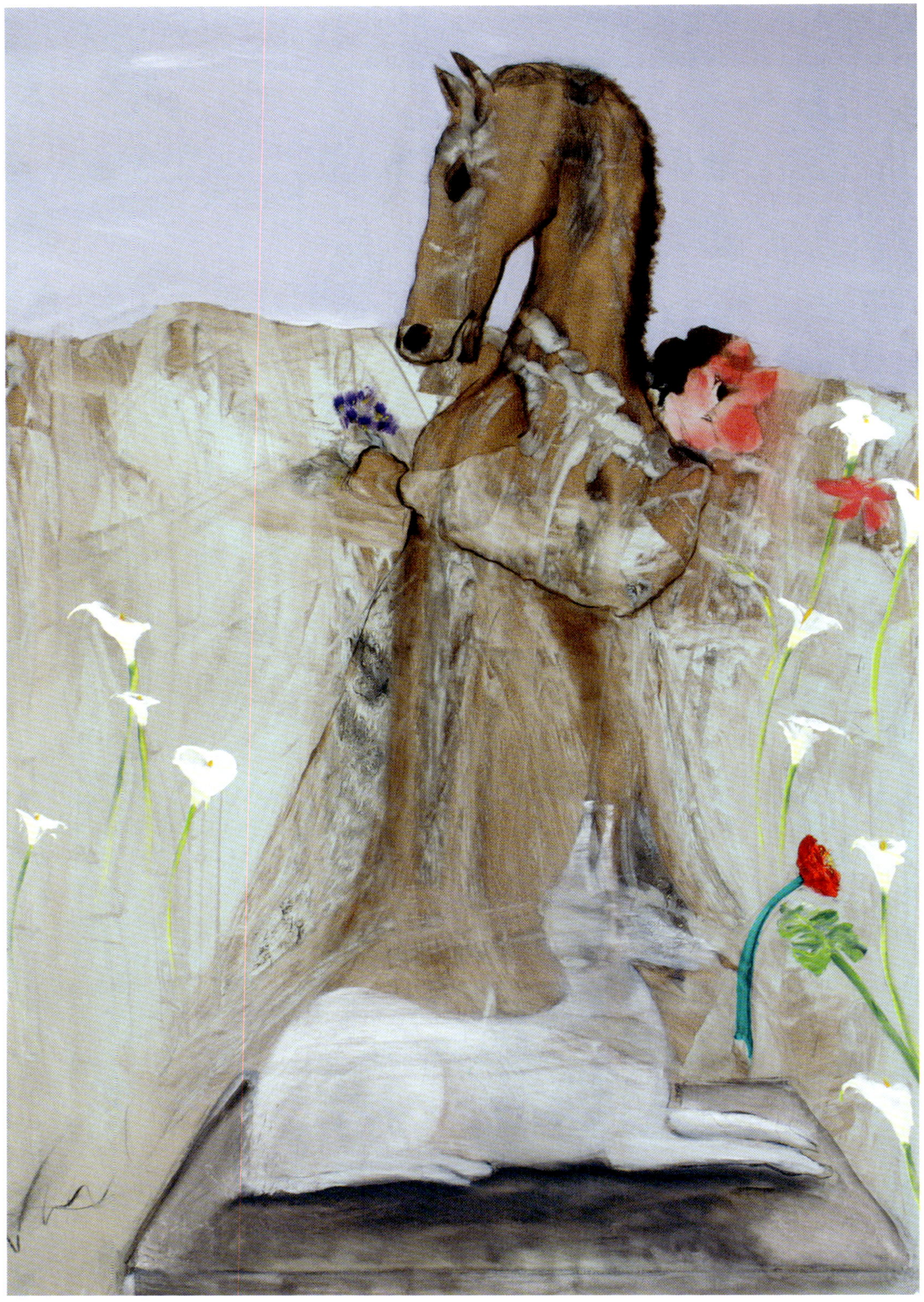

THE HORSE'S GRAVE 2008 Oil and enamel on canvas 250 × 170cm

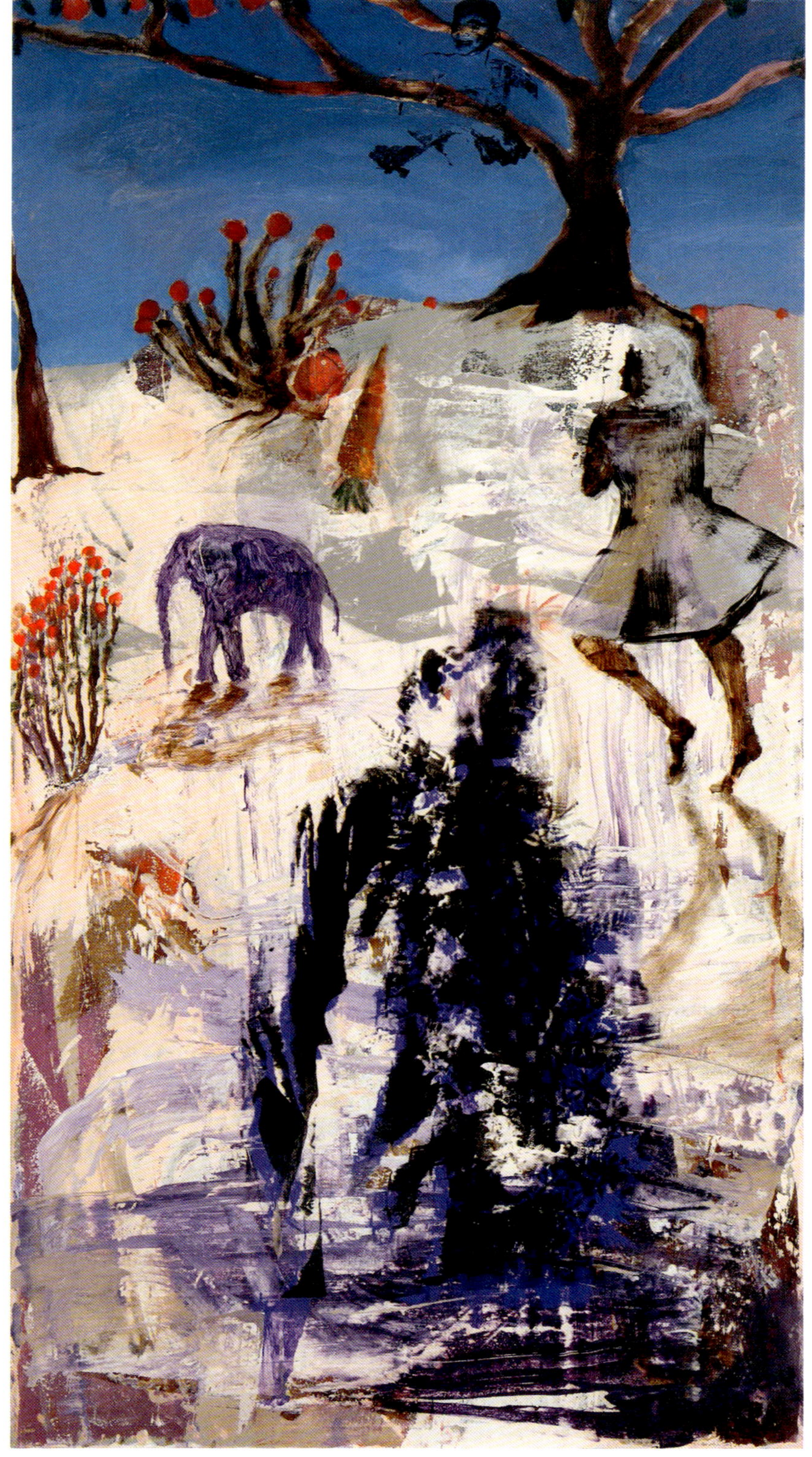

AFRICAN HARVEST 2010 Oil, silkscreen and enamel on canvas 170 × 90cm

BLACK ORCHARD 2012 Oil, enamel and silkscreen on canvas 92 × 120cm

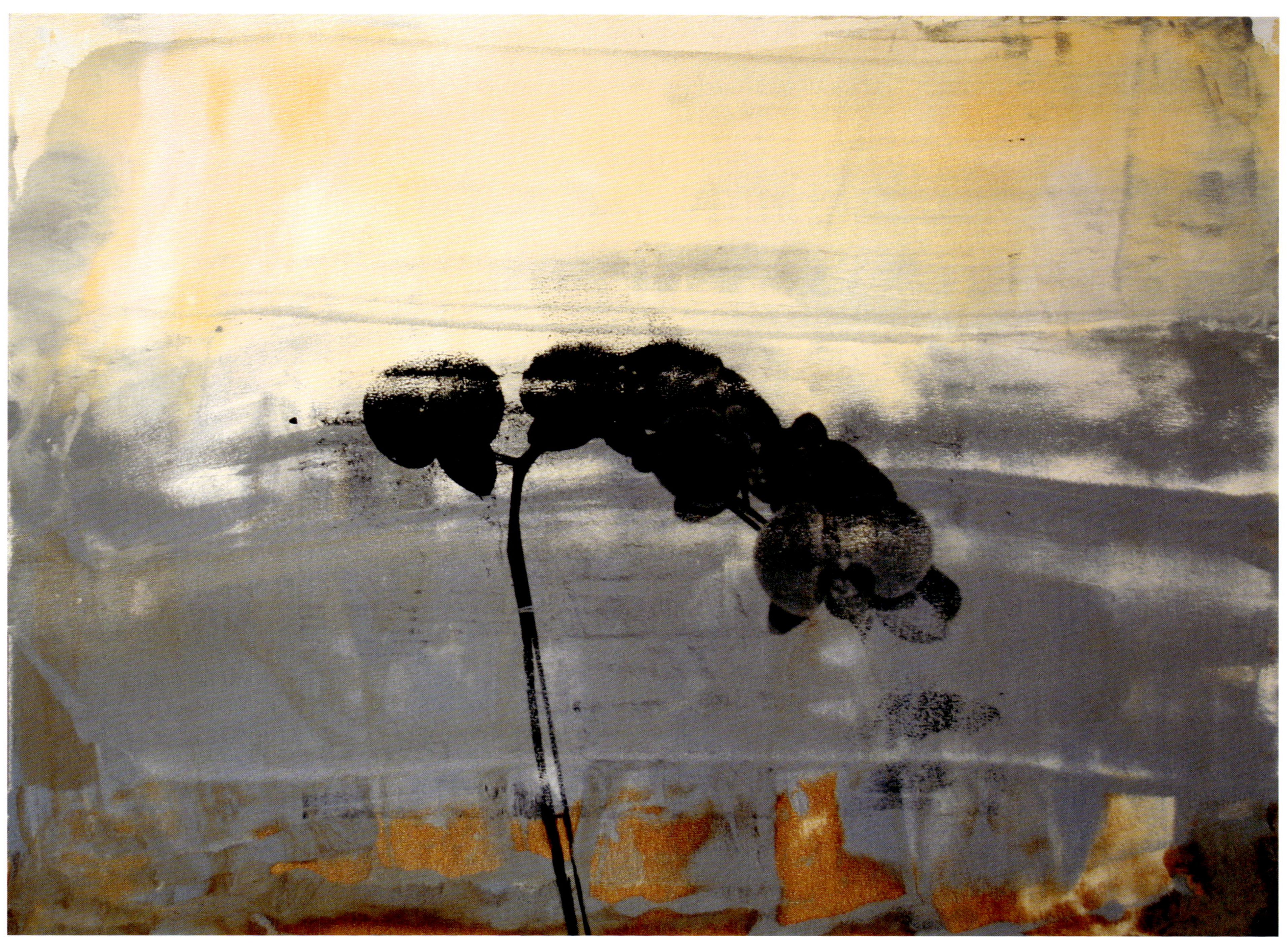

AND THE FOREST ECHOED WITH LAUGHTER 2015 Oil, enamel and silkscreen on canvas 170 × 250cm

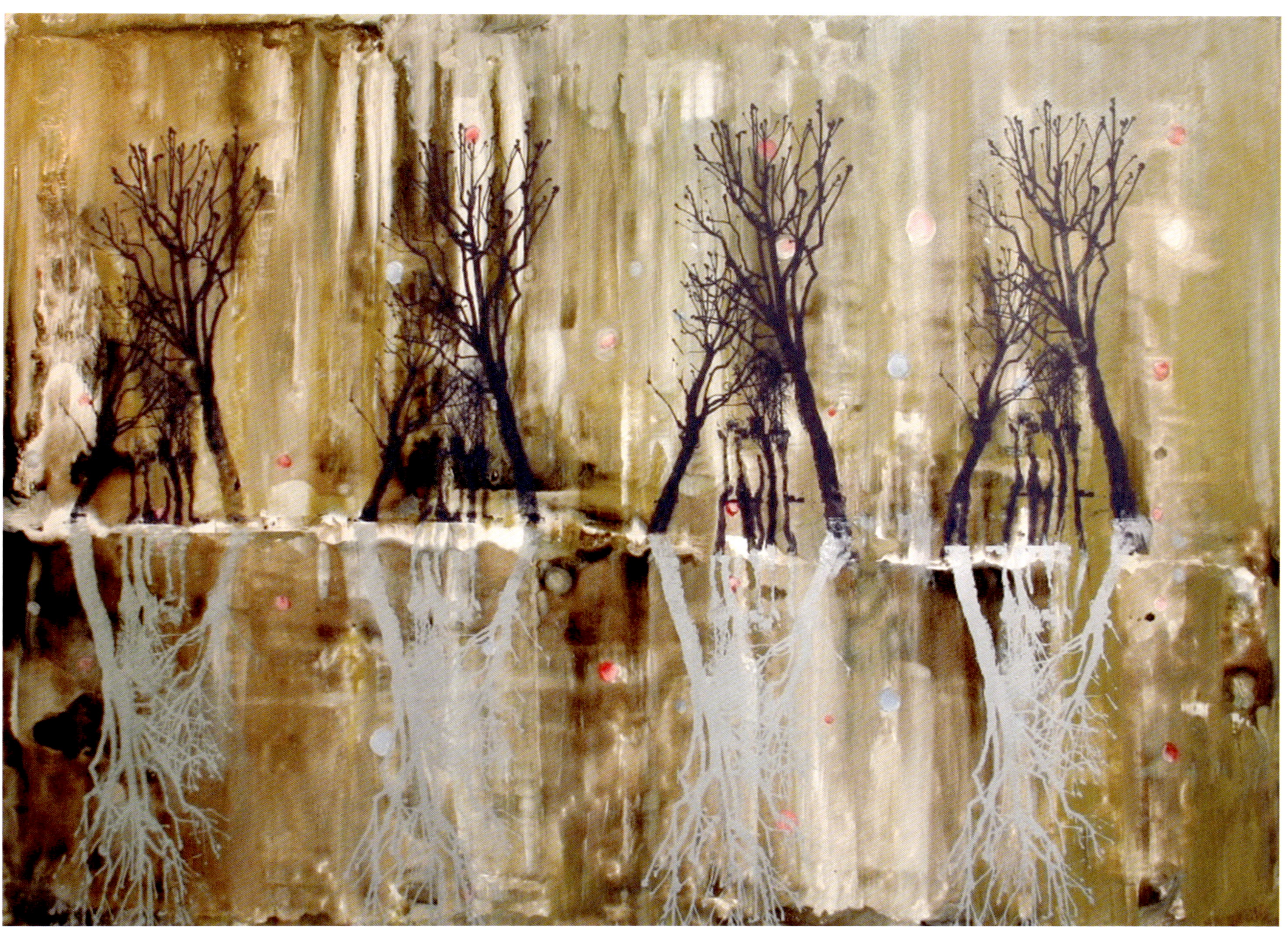

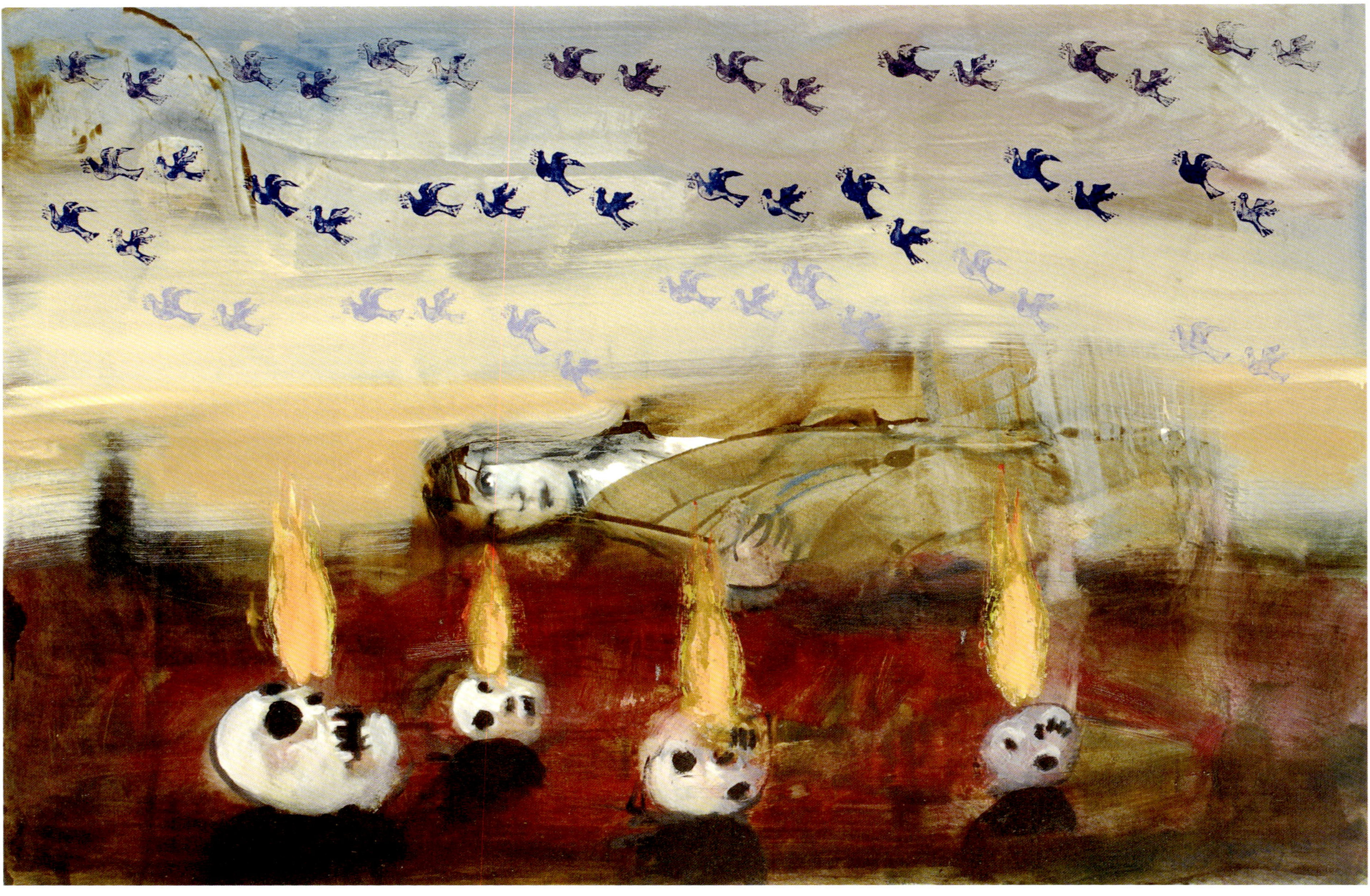

FALLEN ANGELS AND OTHER DREAMS 2007 Oil and woodblock on canvas 170 × 250cm

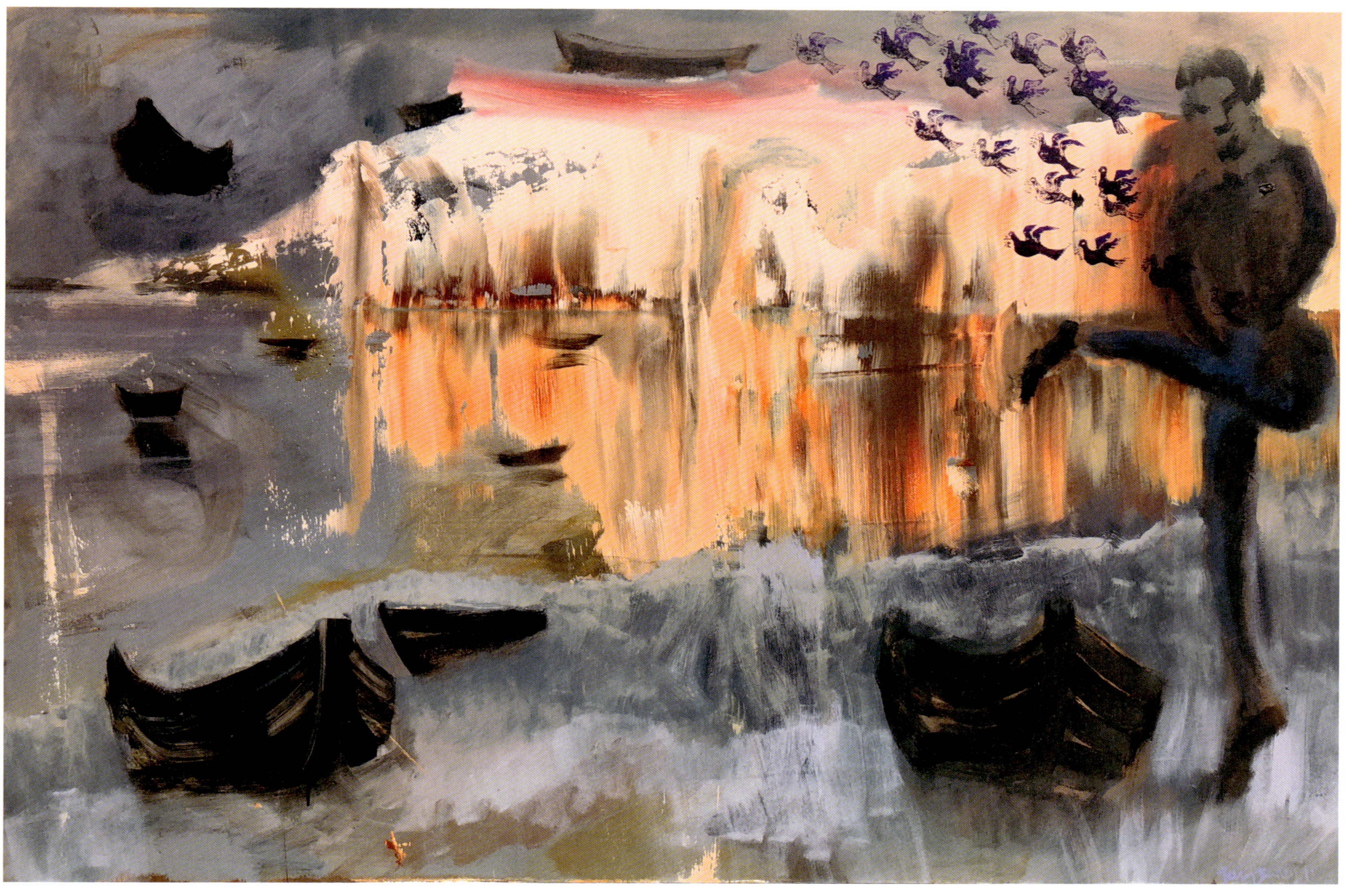

WATER ON FIRE 2011 Oil and enamel on canvas 170 × 250cm

IN THE QUIET NIGHT WOODS, THE DOVE COOS AND THE GIANT DANCERS A RAT-A-TAT 2016 Oil and silkscreen on canvas 150 × 200cm

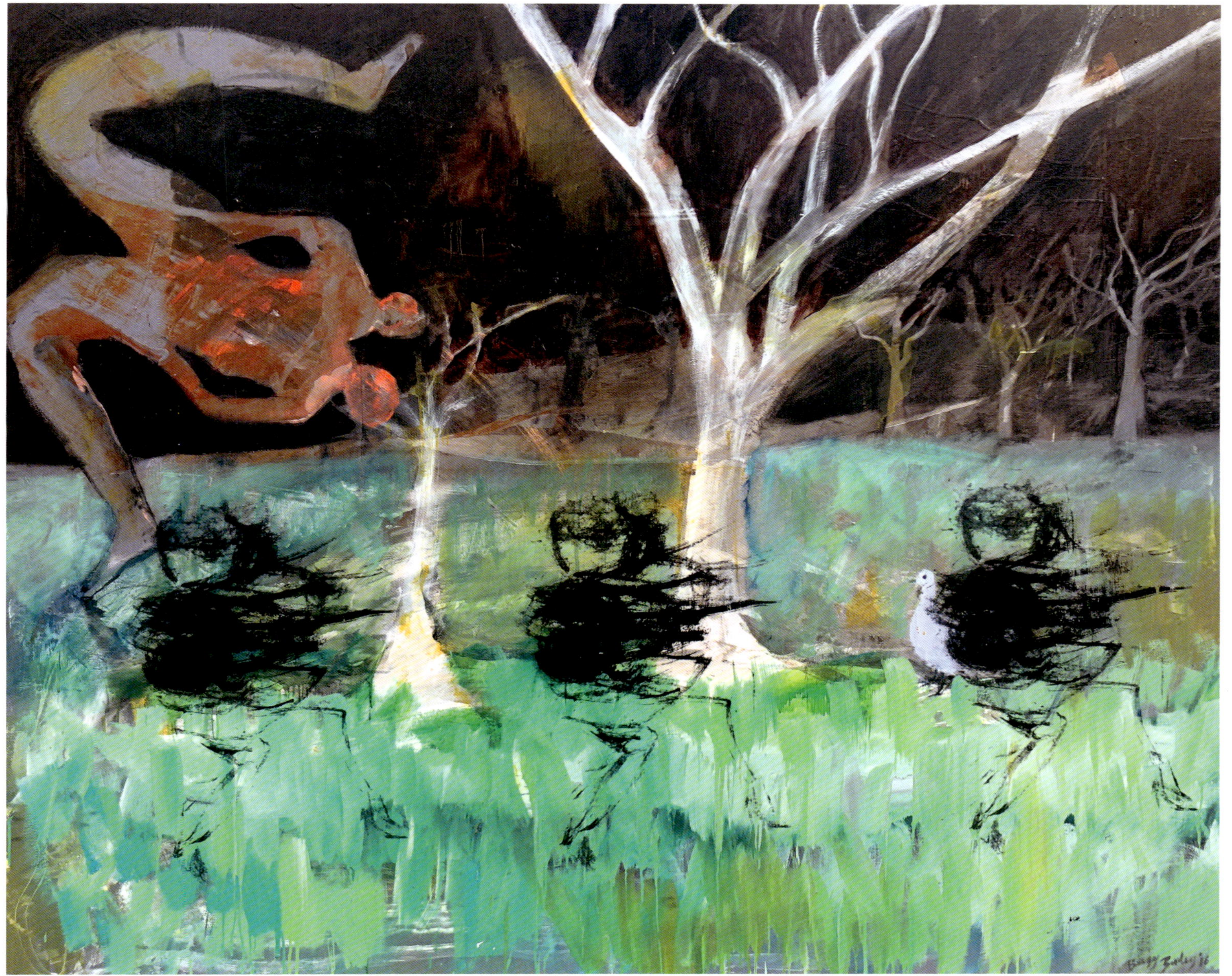

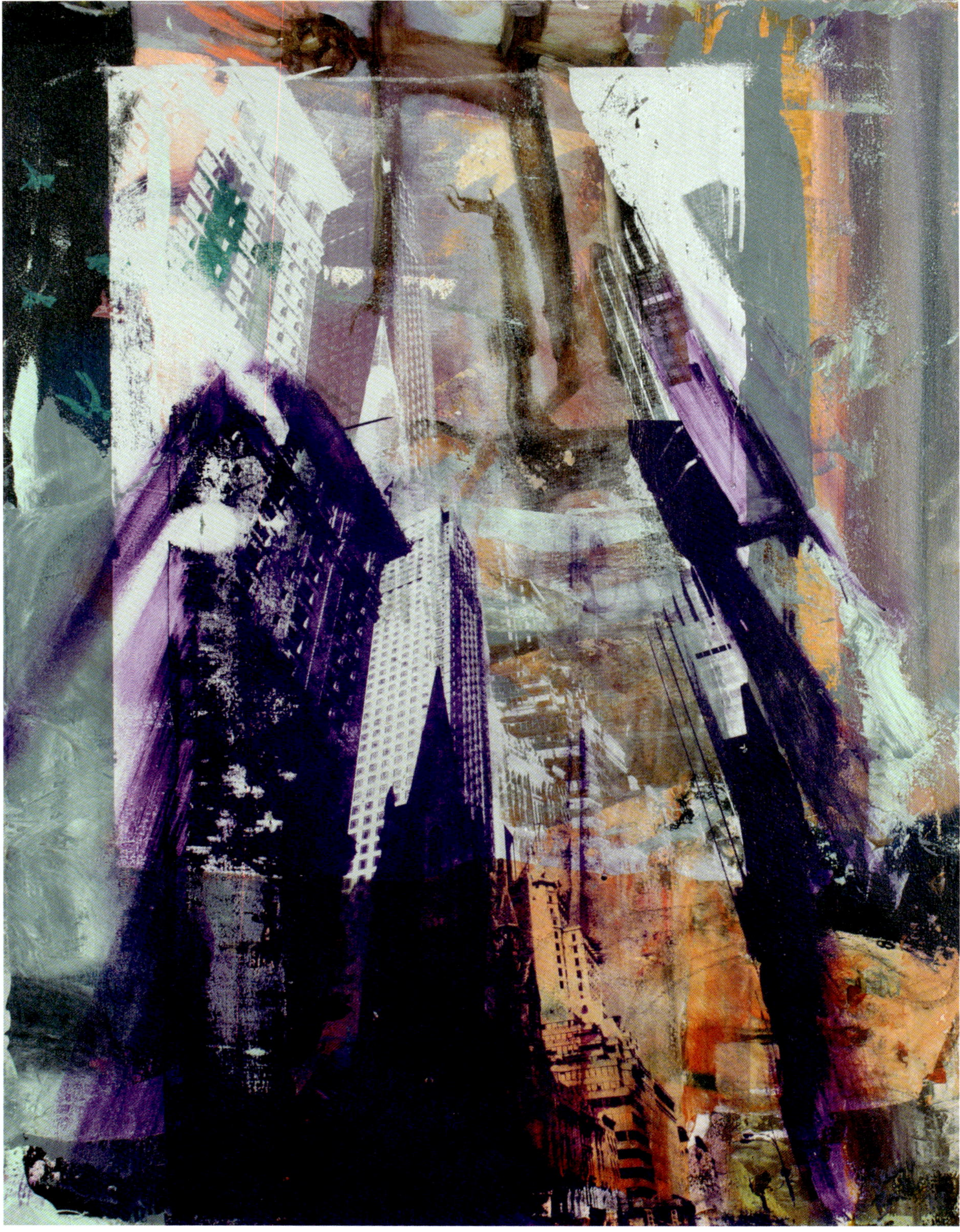

ANGEL JUMPERS 2012 Silkscreen and oil on canvas 120 × 92cm

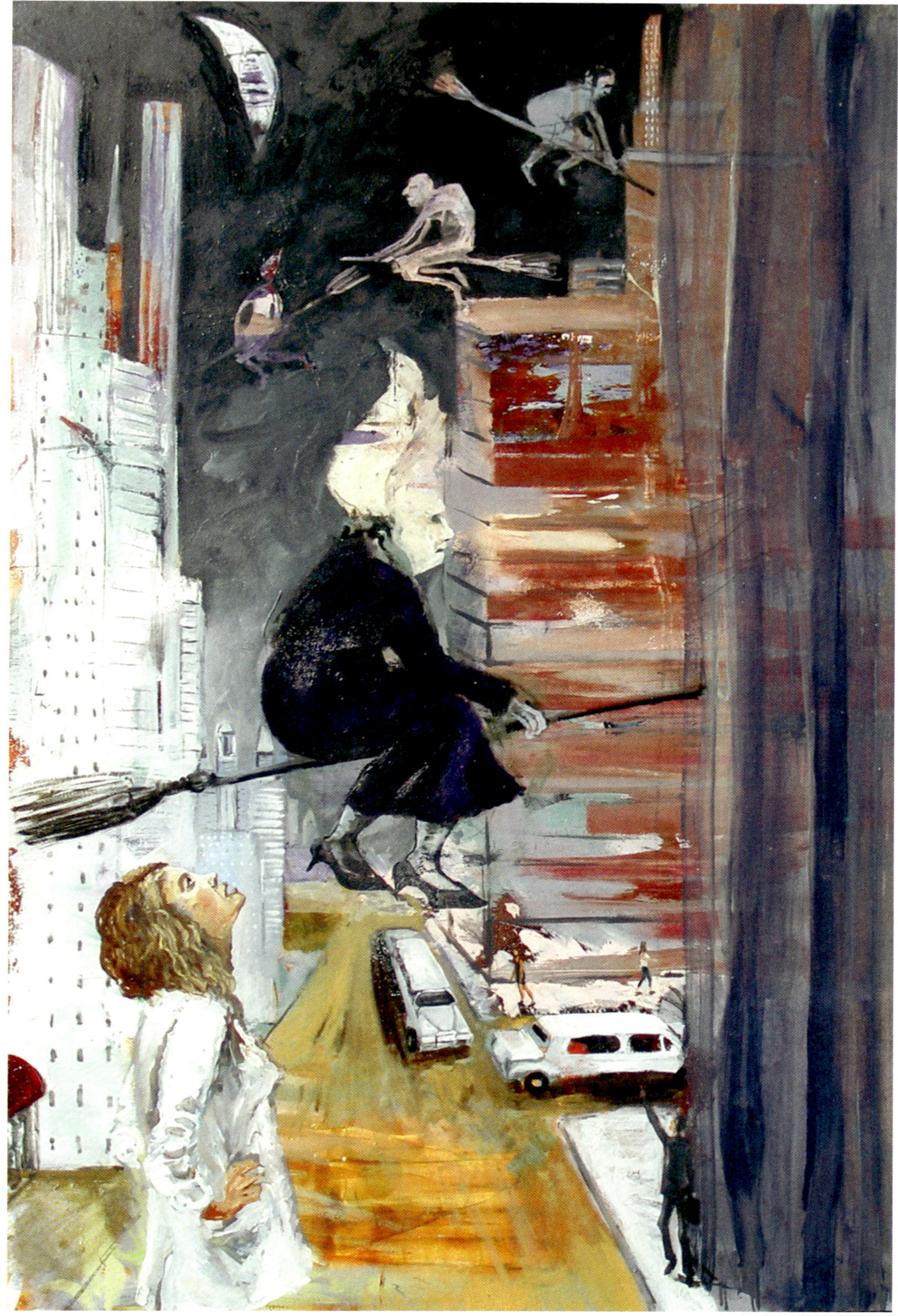

WITCHES ON WALL STREET 2010 Oil and enamel on canvas 120 × 92cm

WOMEN DANCE 2010 Oil and enamel on canvas 92 × 120cm

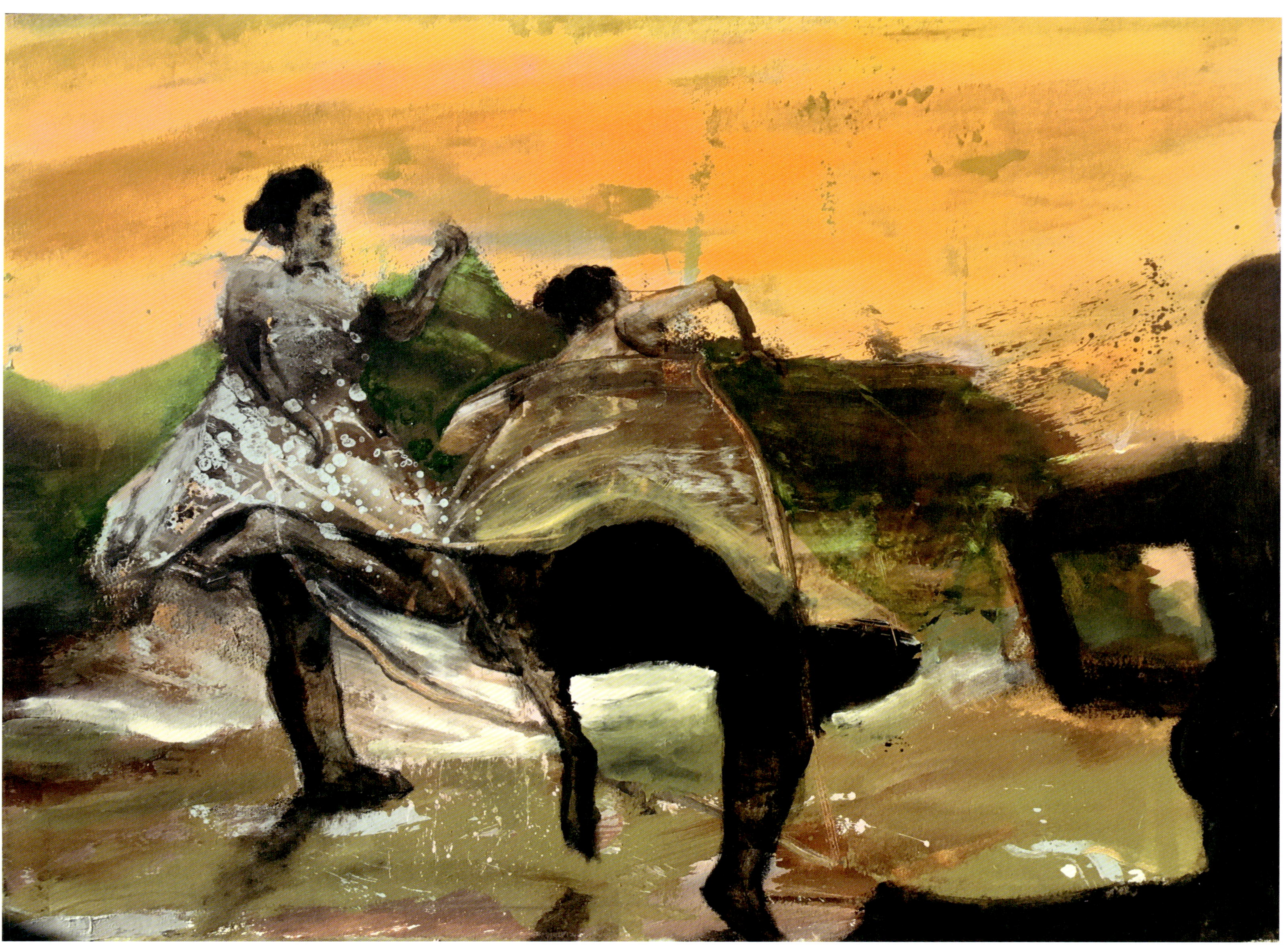

JASPER IN NEW YORK 2011 Oil, enamel and silkscreen on canvas 250 × 170cm

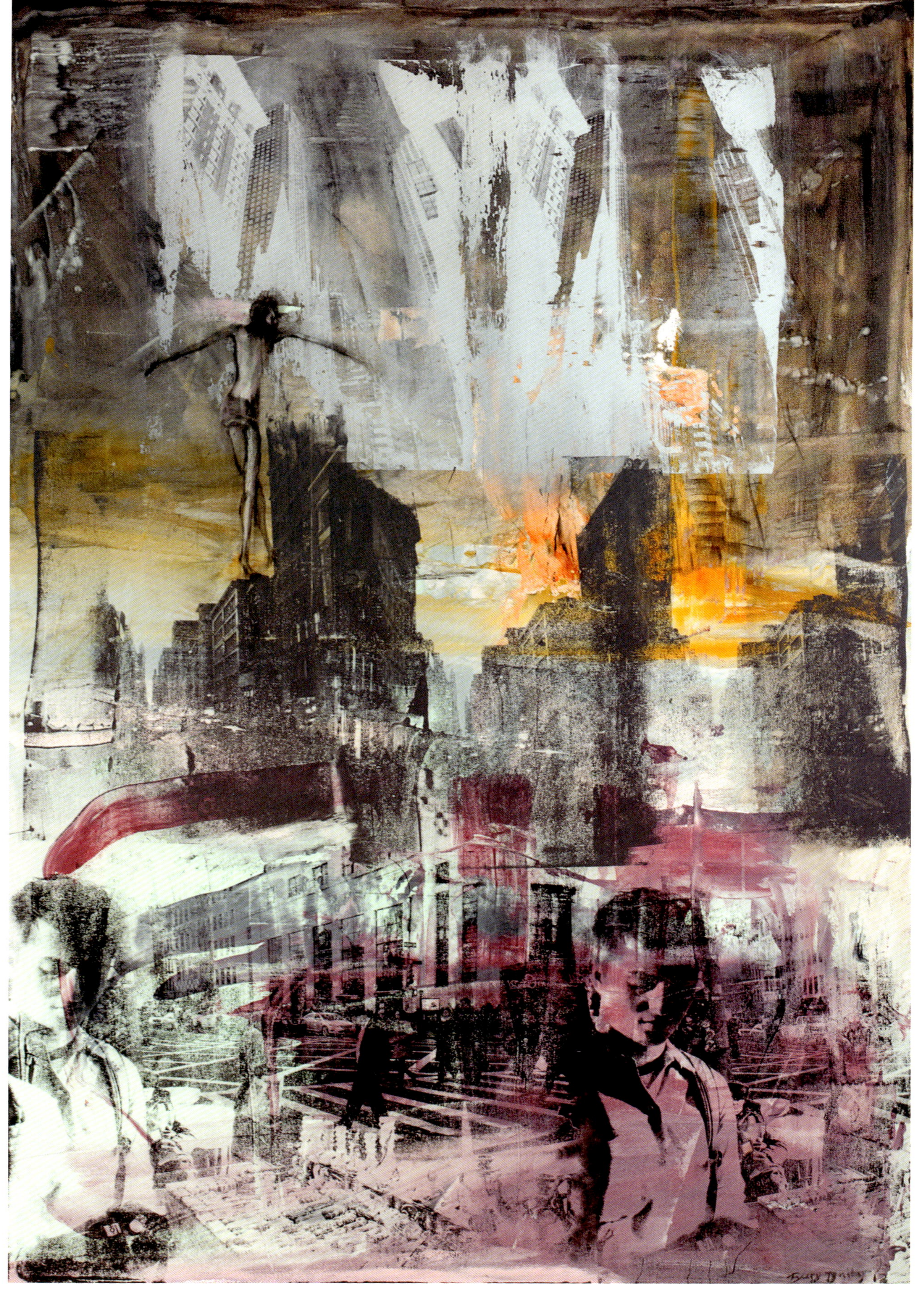

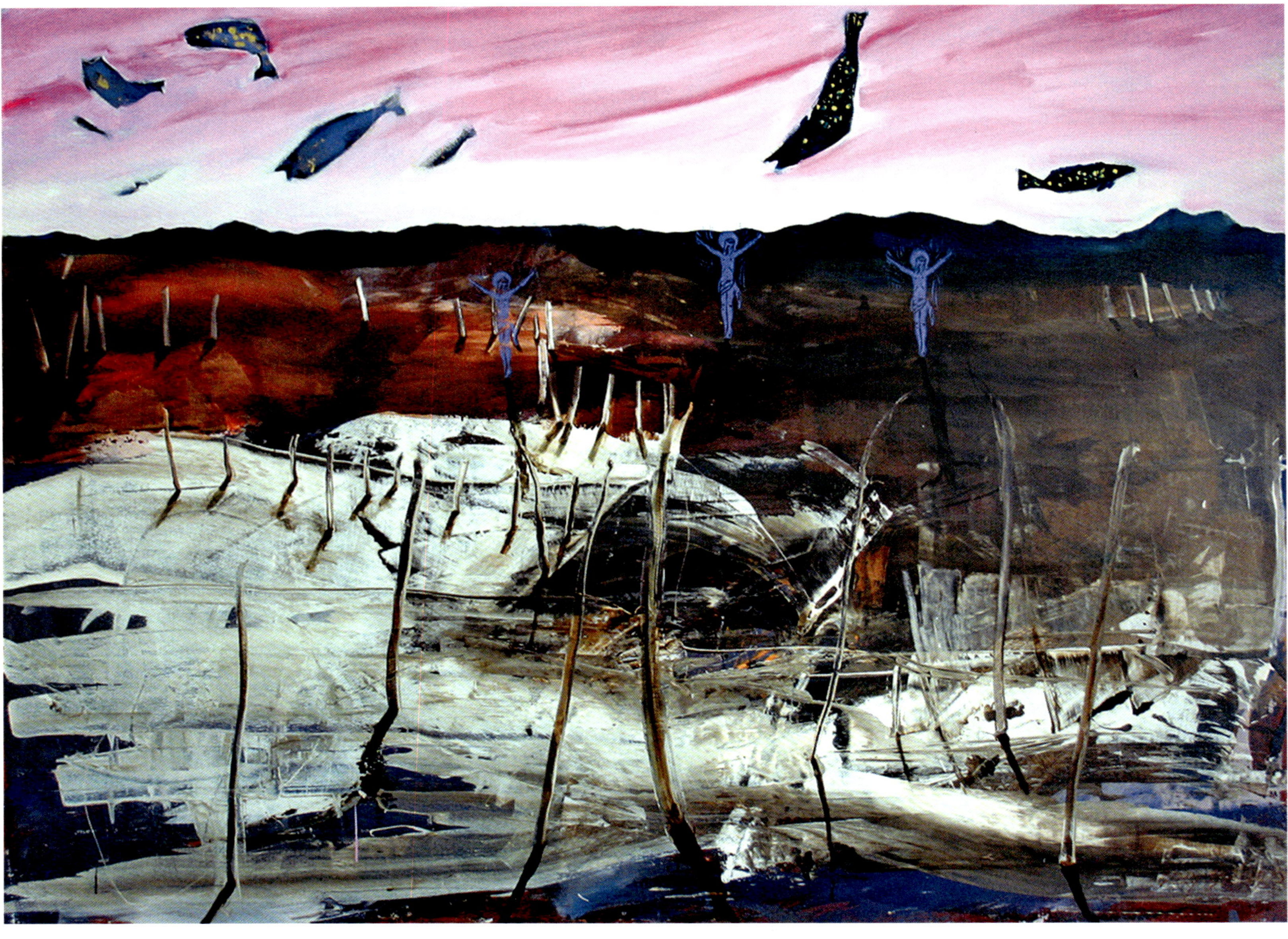

FORGOTTEN SONG: FORGOTTEN SINS 2010 Oil, enamel and silkscreen on canvas 170 × 200cm

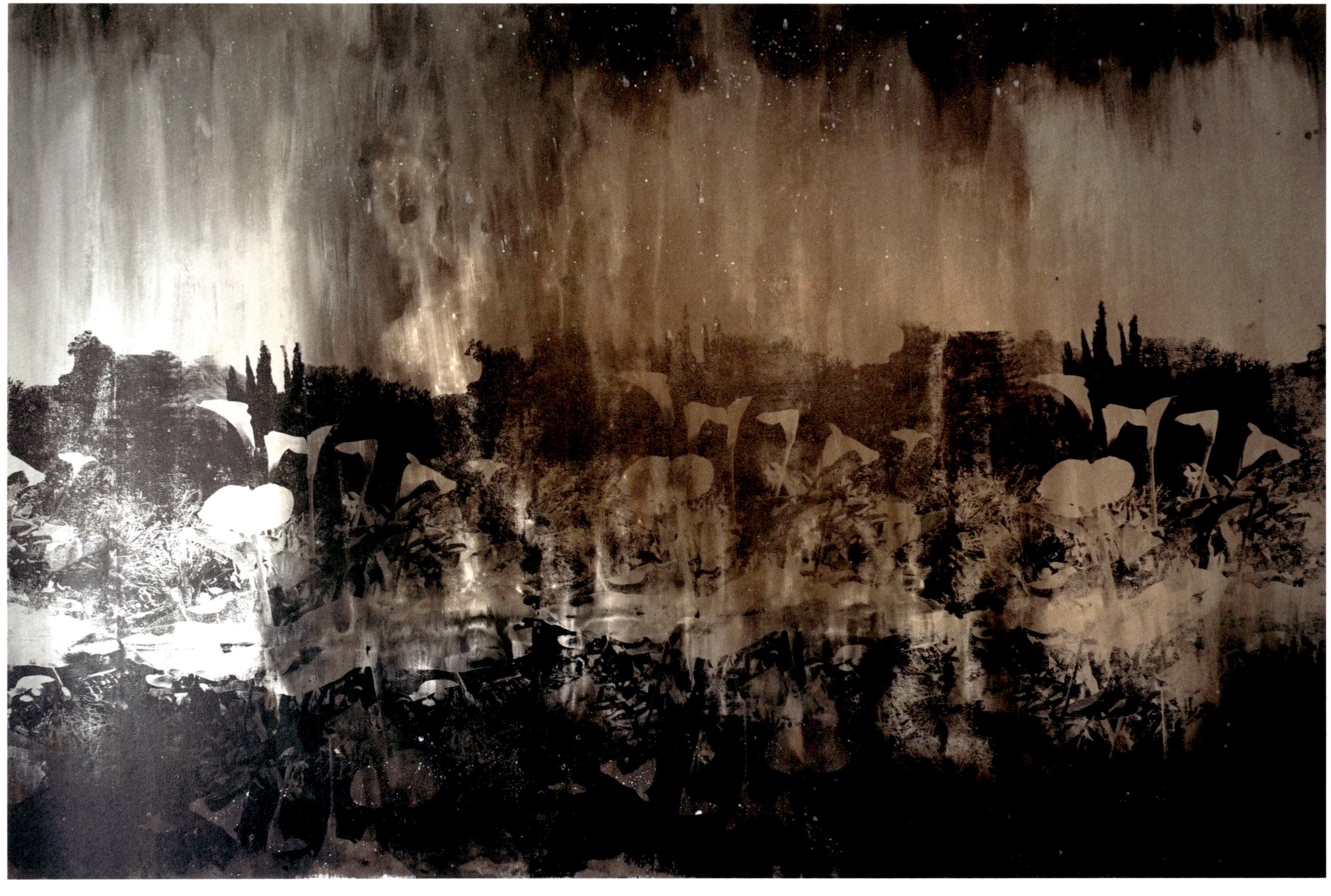

THE LAST EVENING ON EARTH 2013 Oil, enamel and silkscreen on canvas 170 × 250cm

THE APOCALYPSE 2012 Oil, enamel and silkscreen on canvas 92 × 120cm

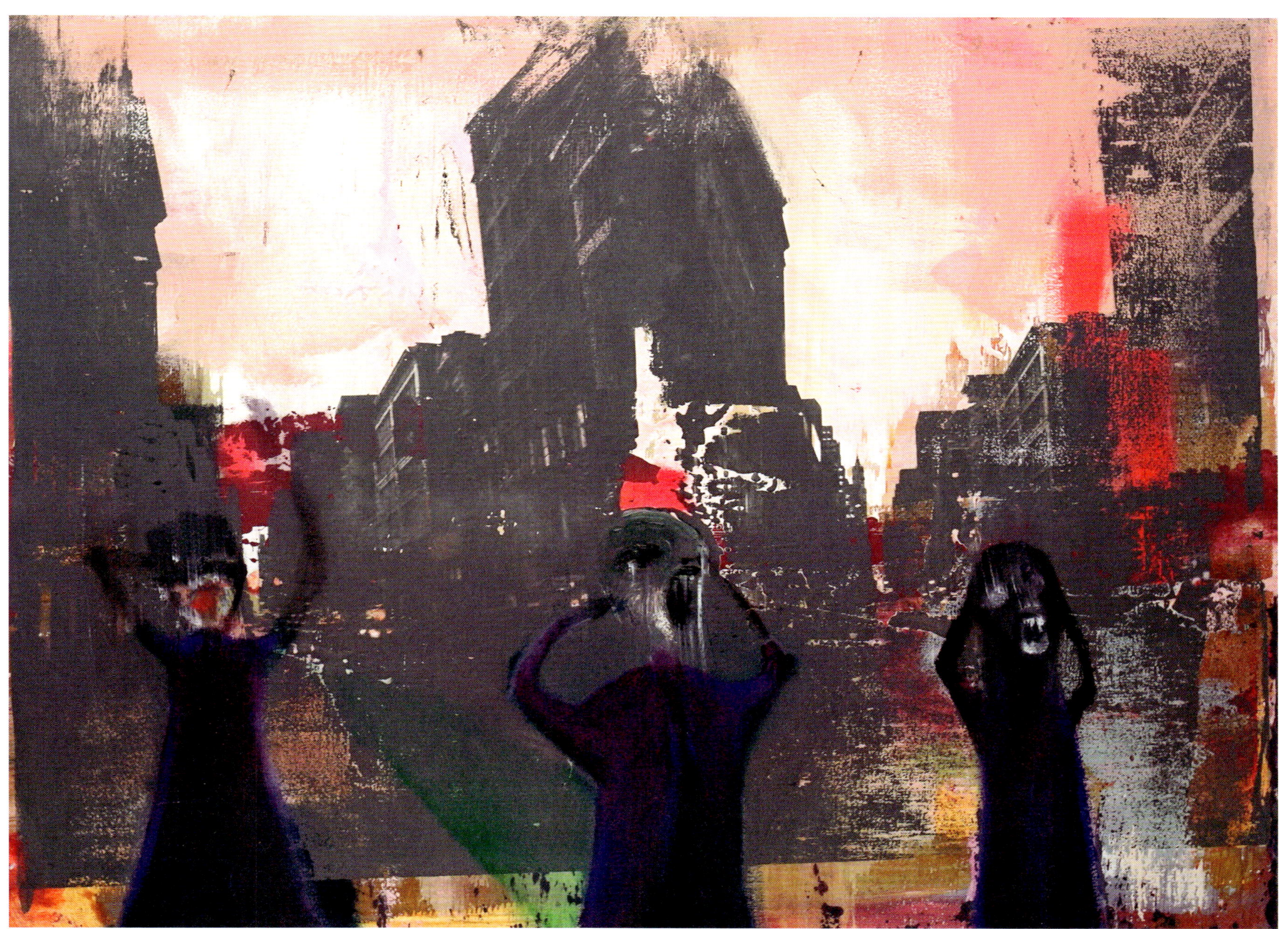

RED BULL 2010 Oil and enamel on canvas 170 × 250cm

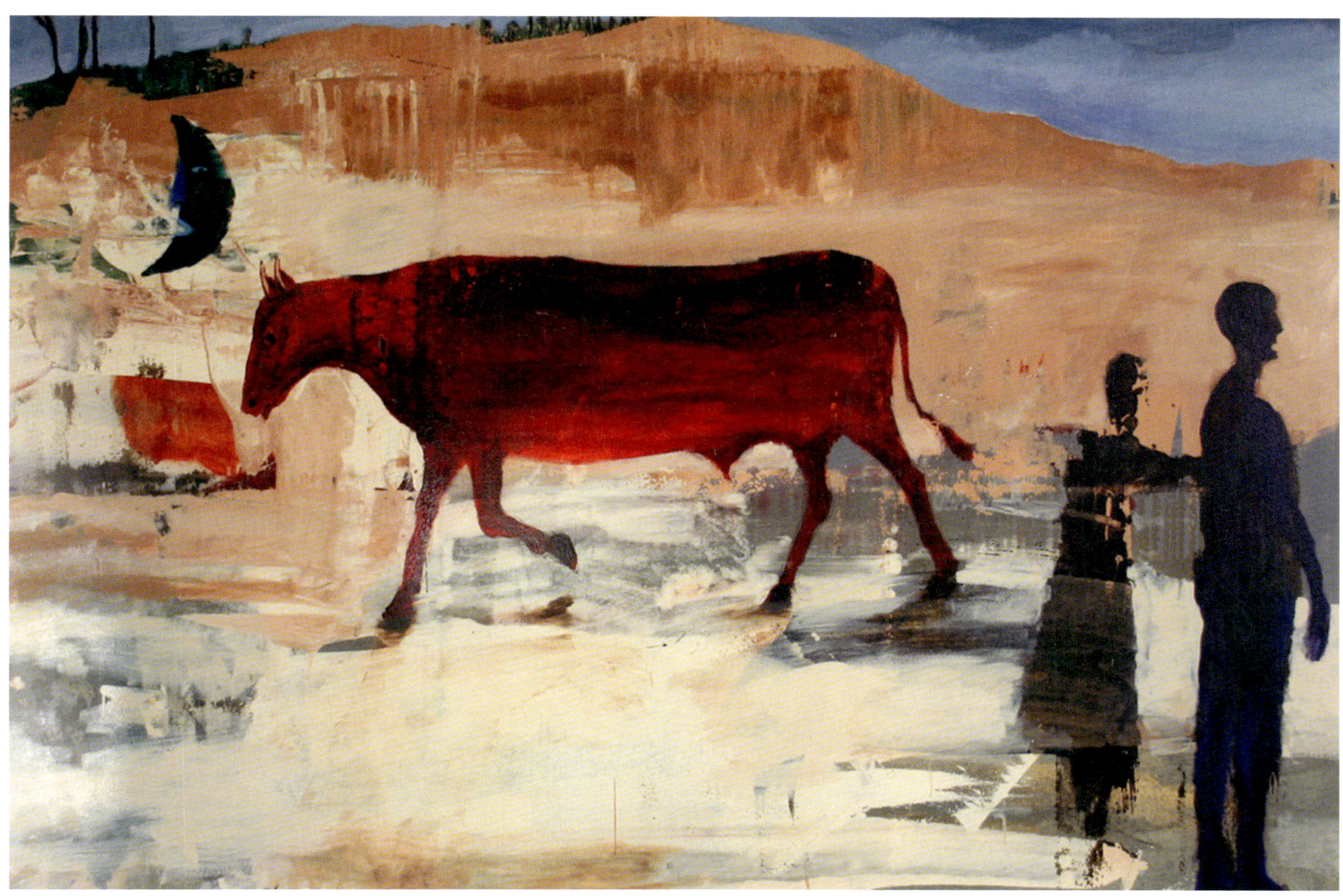

DANCING WITH MR LONDON 2017 Oil, enamel, silkscreen and velvet cut out on canvas 170 × 250cm

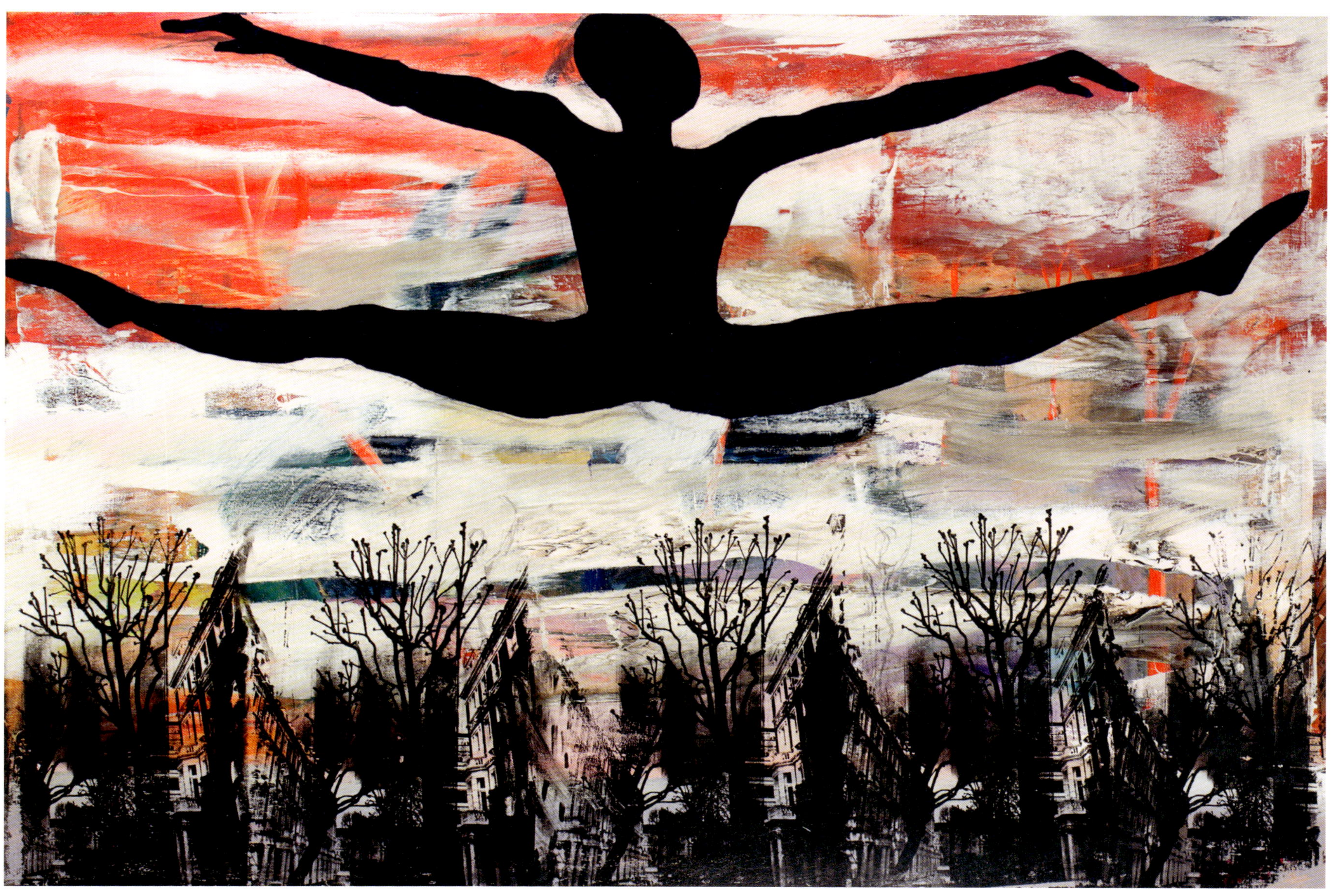

WILD HORSES ON MARS 2017 Oil on canvas 90 × 120cm

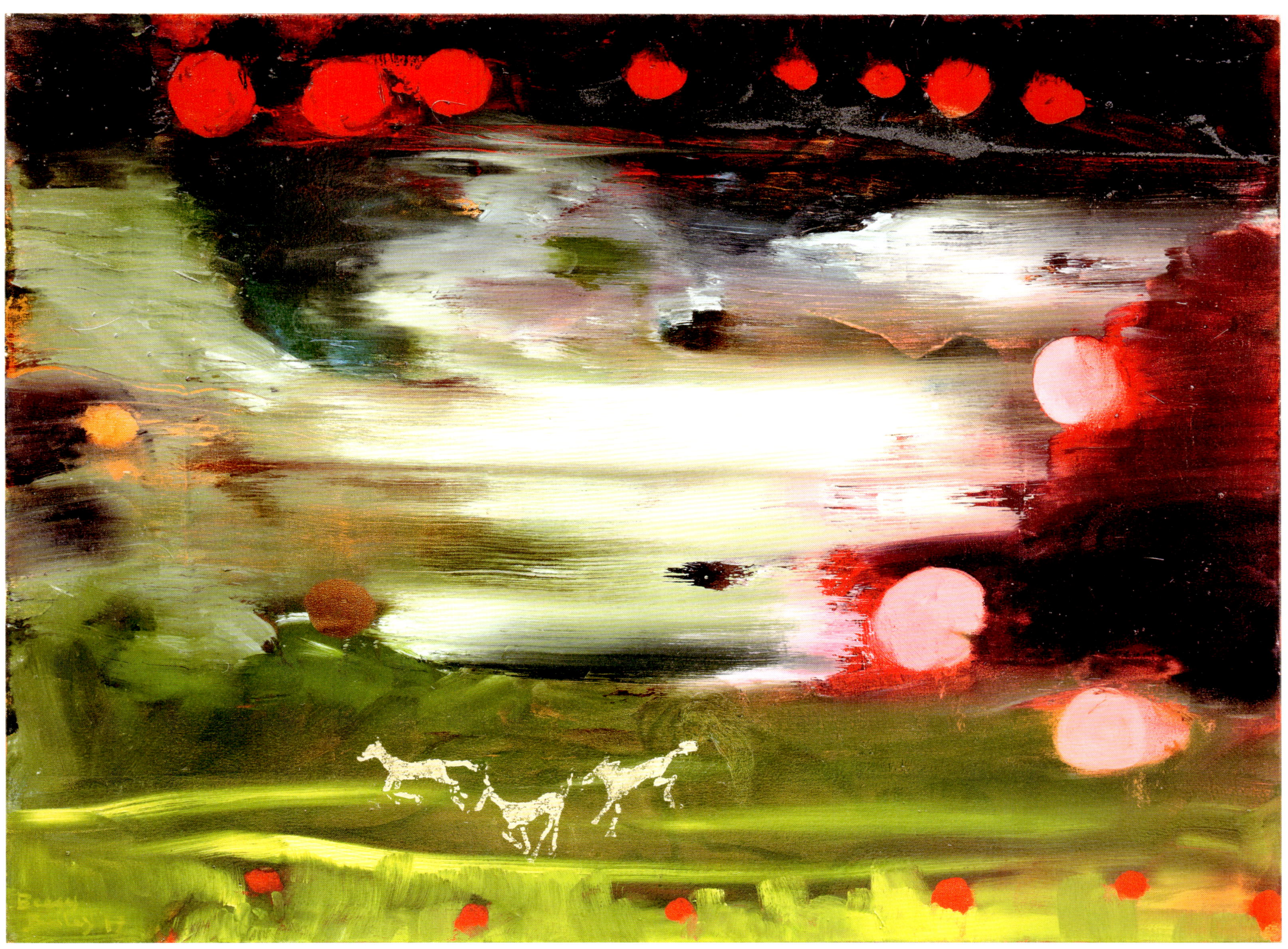

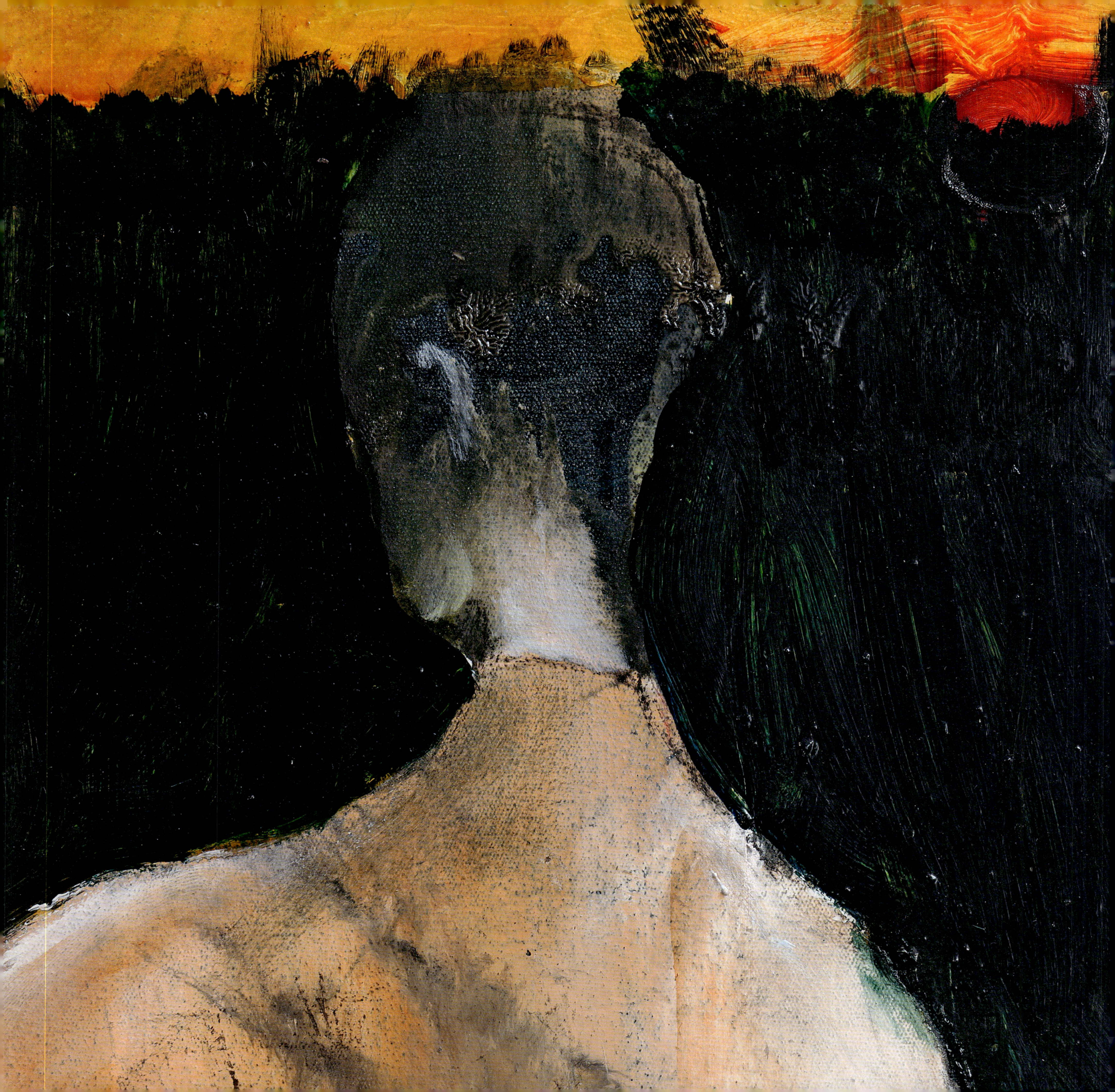

Beezy Bailey in Conversation

Roslyn Sulcas

Painter, sculptor, printmaker, performance artist, exhibitionist, extrovert, Surrealist, collaborator, iconoclast, idealist, opportunist – these are all descriptions that have been given to Beezy Bailey, a white male South African artist who has posed as a black female South African artist; who studied fine art in London and woodcarving back home; who has collaborated with rural artisans and David Bowie; and who is as energised and enthusiastic about sculpture and printmaking as he is about painting and performance.

Bailey lives in Cape Town, in a beautiful old house that once belonged to his aunt, and he works in a studio on the grounds, framed by the mountain, with sweeping views across the city. That environment, he says, is central to his creativity and identity as an artist. I met him there, and he spoke about his upbringing, his beginnings in art, his controversial projects and collaborations, and his South African identity.

Roslyn Sulcas What kind of family did you grow up in?

Beezy Bailey I have a very complicated family. I found out when I was thirty that Jeremy Taylor, my mother's first husband, was not my biological father as I had always been led to believe. It was in fact Dennis Kiley, a family friend, who worked on *Drum* magazine, and then later at the *Financial Times*. My mother had had an affair with him after her first husband left her and before she married Jim Bailey, who legally adopted me shortly after I was born. Jim brought me up, and to this day I consider him my true father. He was extremely eccentric and not very present, but he was an amazing person. He had an incredible strength and wisdom, and read Ancient Greek and Latin, which he used in his research. He ran *Drum*, but his passion was the Bronze Age, and he had an extraordinary collection of artefacts and wrote books about it.

RS Was it an artistic environment?

BB I grew up on a farm, north of Johannesburg, so not artistic exactly. But the house had interesting and original art, including some Augustus John drawings, which Jim bought after the war. My grandmother, Iris Epstein, grew up in London and had been at the Slade with Augustus John. And my mother went to the Michaelis School of Fine Art, in Cape Town, so somehow I feel my art comes through the female side; as, of course, does my Jewishness. But my mother's main passion was and is music – my sister went to the Royal College of Music to study when she was sixteen, and she is still a great cellist. I was musical too, and I played the drums.

It was my father who suggested I become an artist. We knew Norman Catherine and Judith Mason (who had a tremendous influence on Marlene Dumas). Both of them were famous, but because of South Africa's isolation they were far from wealthy. So I said no and considered, as Bowie originally did, a career in advertising as the one avenue that would allow me to be creative and make money. I'm probably the only person whose father tried to persuade him to become an artist!

RS How early did you begin to make art?

BB I was dyslexic and hopeless at school, and the only thing I could do properly was art, so I began quite early. I went to a school called Woodmead, close to where we lived, which was the first school to take black kids in 1975. I grew up with that sense of equality, which I think was unusual in my generation of South Africans. That contributed to my confidence later to invent a black female alter ego without any issues clouding the project.

But it was really during my two years of compulsory military service that my world was opened. I had art lessons on Wednesday evenings, when I was based at the Air Force Museum in Lanseria. (My mother got me in there by sitting on the colonel's lap, dressed in my father's RAF fighter pilot's uniform.) When I came out of the military, I worked selling advertising at *Drum*, which gave me an acute sense of how the industry worked, and taught me how to sell anything. My father always said to me, 'you're a performer, like Dalí', and advertising showed me that too.

After a year I went to stay with a South African friend in New York. As soon as I arrived, I got fired up by the artistic explosion that was happening around me in SoHo, and I began to paint. Kerry Kennedy, my friend's girlfriend at the time, suggested I should meet Andy Warhol, so we went to have lunch at The Factory. She got me to show Andy photographs of the work I was doing and he liked them. When I walked out of The Factory into Union Square, I decided I was never going to do anything else but be an artist. Actually, it was the only thing I was capable of doing anyway.

RS What impression did Warhol make on you?

BB The first thing I was aware of was his extraordinarily unhealthy physical appearance. He was very white and thin, and I wanted to drag him into the sun. His white wig that reflected purple ultraviolet light, plonked on top of his black hair, was very striking. As a person there was a seeming vacancy about him and yet he was clearly as sharp as nails.

But his real impact on me was that he was making art and had become a massive success doing so. He showed me that I could do what I loved most and be successful at it, which I hadn't encountered before.

The second time I met him, I had painted a pair of sneakers for him. He looked at the painting, said, 'OK', called an assistant and said, 'get Tony Shafrazi on the phone'. The next thing I was sitting opposite Tony Shafrazi and thinking, this is the deep end. I instinctively and correctly thought it was too soon. I had been accepted at an art school in London, at Byam Shaw, and I decided I should stick to that. I always say, I started at the top and worked my way down.

RS What were your years at art school like?

BB I loved it, the energy of it, working from nine to seven, then an evening session. I'd paint until two in the morning. I was ridiculously prolific and I wanted to do everything – sculpture, painting and prints. Performance too. One of my teachers, Silvia Ziranek, said: 'no performance is longer than four minutes, because that's how long you have an audience's attention'. I've always obeyed that rule.

But I always felt I could never live in London. I was incredibly lucky that I could go home during the December holidays. I would come home and drive up to Venda, where I learned about carving from the artist Nelson Makuba, who was a big man in his world. It meant learning about the importance of dreams and the spiritual in a way I could never have done in London.

So I had the traditional, formal English training and background, yet I was also deeply rooted in the soil of South Africa, my birthplace, with its ancient rhythms and magic. If I had been ambitious, I would have settled in London, but I wouldn't have made the work I have made here. I think I always needed to be in South Africa, in this incredible house, in this incredible town.

RS When did you begin to exhibit your work?

BB I began pretty early on. My first solo show was in 1986, in London, at a pop-up gallery called Art Show, on Fulham Broadway. It went up on the day my final degree show came down at Byam Shaw, which was close by. Even before then, I was the only student at the school to be selling my work.

Shortly after that show, I had another in South Africa, at Gallery International in Cape Town. I did my own PR. I made slides, sent press releases to radio, television and the newspapers. I ruthlessly promoted myself and was hated for it by the Cape Town art world. That didn't daunt me, but it made me see myself as an outsider. I think when Nicci – my girlfriend and later my wife – and I moved into this house, that further alienated people. I knew a lot of privileged white kids who called each other comrade, and I wasn't part of that whole bullshit thing.

In fact, looking back, I think I was an outsider from the very beginning. When I was at art school, a famous critic came to guest tutor us. I was sticking things on my canvases and having fun making art. She said I couldn't stick things on them and that making art was 'not about having fun'. At first I was in tears, but then I thought fuck that – art *should* be fun!

When I showed Ester Rousseau (the owner of Gallery International) a photo of a painting, and she asked about it, I told her that I'd done it with twenty others in half an hour.

'Whatever happens don't tell anyone that!' she said. I decided to do exactly the opposite, and that's how the 'live painting exhibition' was born.

In the Cape Town warehouse where I had my studio, there was an open area with a balcony surrounding it, where you could fit an audience of about eighty people. So I set up a performance space with lighting and music. Then, to the sounds of the Swiss band Yello, I painted an entire exhibition of more than fifty paintings. The whole thing lasted an hour, and the paintings went up on the wall as I completed them. Some even sold, and I was offered an exhibition by a local gallery, called Art First. I had simply taken my working process, which was at that stage very prolific, into the public realm.

There are no lies in real art.

RS What was the Cape Town art scene like in those days?

BB It was quite tight-knit. Gallery International was the main commercial gallery, and it was located in a shopping centre, so it wasn't at all glamorous. You could very quickly get to know everyone. I became close friends with another artist, the late Barend de Wet, and we literally painted the town red during those mad, wild days.

Johannesburg was very different. You had William Kentridge and Braam Kruger and other young artists working with the Famous International Gallery (FIG) and doing really interesting work. But it was a difficult time politically. It was really the height of apartheid. The South African army was fighting the Soviet-backed ANC armed wing on our borders. And anyone sympathetic to the cause was viewed with suspicion. I'd been to Moscow with my art school, and at my first Cape Town exhibition I'd worn a Communist lapel badge (next to the South African flag). I had the security police eyeing me.

As an artist, I felt it was hugely important to use art to try to break down the wall of fear that existed then between black and white; and so I curated an exhibition I named *Zebra Crossing*. I gathered works on paper by Kentridge, Robert Hodgins, Norman Catherine, Wayne Barker, Tommy Motswai, Billy Mandindi and others, to show how our non-racial art transcended the narrow confines of apartheid. I intended to take the show to Moscow, but only got as far as London before the funds ran out. Sadly it never travelled any further.

Later, when Kentridge and South African art really got discovered, money and competition among us somehow broke down the sense of community we'd once had. I would never have imagined that the Cape Town art scene would usurp the Johannesburg one, as it seems to have done recently. A lot of the big money has moved down to Cape Town along with a massive and growing tourist industry, which Johannesburg, despite being a financial centre, does not enjoy.

RS You opened a hybrid ceramics and printmaking studio, gallery and shop in the 1990s. How did that fit in with your artistic trajectory?

BB In 1990, I bought a 1930s building at the top of Long Street in Cape Town, and collaborated with a craftsman called Koos Malgas, who worked on Helen Martins' famous Owl House. He created statues from drawings I made, and we hoisted them onto the roof. I made a fabric range, and showed my other work, and did performances.

I called it the Art Factory. It was inspired by Keith Haring's shop in SoHo, in New York, as well as Warhol's Factory – right down to the tinfoil ceiling in my loft office. It was clearly ahead of its time; no one else was doing homeware. You could watch people making ceramics and prints, and then you could buy them downstairs in the gallery.

I had a kind of Warholian idea about art for the masses, and I wanted to take it to a bigger scale. But of course the same elite group who bought my paintings were the people who bought my fabrics. Not that people bought much. We kept it going for four years, but I didn't even know how to open the till! I realised I had no idea how to run a business and returned full-time to making art in my studio.

RS Is it fair to say that what really made your name in the early 1990s, was creating work in the name of a black woman?

BB Yes, that propelled me into a spotlight around 1992, although I really didn't do it for that reason. Wayne Barker pioneered the idea, doing work as a black person for the Standard Bank award. He suggested we all do it, but I was the only one who took him up on it. I made linocuts as a black domestic worker called Joyce Ntobe. I entered them in what was to be the last Triennial art competition, and they weren't chosen, but the National Gallery spotted and bought them. In fact, linocuts aren't really a black tradition, which is much more about woodcarving, but it was something that was being taught to black artists by NGOs, which I felt was ironic. At the time, the chief curator was working on a paper on three black female artists (which was never completed) and one of them was Joyce, which was pretty amazing considering she had only ever made three rather mediocre illustrative linocuts! It exposed the desperate need, now worldwide, to right the wrongs of the past.

I went on to have three group shows with Joyce, further illustrating aspects of her life –going shopping, attending church, travelling back to the Transkei, and going on holiday. She went on to become a feminist and conceptual artist. The feminist piece was an installation of eight Mother Earth figures, made in resin, containing objects relating to her life as a black woman, such as tubes of hair straightener. She also created a Mother Earth figure from 300 tampons.

Joyce freed me in a way. It was like being an actor, having a portal into another world. Unfortunately, I am now inhibited by the climate of aggressive political correctness, but perhaps I'll just lie low until it's all over. Joyce definitely isn't dead.

RS In the mid-1990s you met David Bowie and worked with him for a while. How did that happen?

BB I had always wanted to meet David Bowie. In fact, he was the only person in the world I really wanted to meet. He came to South Africa in 1994, with his wife Iman, who was here for a *Vogue* shoot with Bruce Weber. I received a phone call, asking if he could meet and interview me for *Modern Painters* magazine, which he was involved with. We immediately clicked. I felt we were kindred spirits.

When he arrived at my house, he told me that like most rock stars, he had started at art school. I suggested to him that we do the interview while painting together. We painted and chatted. Afterwards, he said, 'Why don't you come to New York and paint with me there?'

Of course I went, and it was amazing to be around him. He had a kind of demonic energy. He was a sort of magic fairyman, with a childlike openness and freedom about trying new things. He also had a great sense of humour. At the time he was playing Warhol in Julian Schnabel's movie *Basquiat* and making his brilliant *Outside* album. He called me Spaceboy. There's a song on that album called 'Hallo Spaceboy'. I'm so vain I bet you think it's about me.

We made about fifty paintings, collecting scraps from the street and shiny bits of plastic and fabrics, bought from a hardware store on Canal Street, which like Pearl Paint is sadly no longer there. It was all about the act of creation. The painting fed the music and vice versa: it was a creative energy machine, and we exhibited the work in 1995 at The Gallery in Cork Street, London. It was called *New Afro/Pagan and Work: 1975–1995*. After that it went to Thorens Fine Art Gallery, in Basel.

RS What came next?

BB The next phase of my work also came out of that time in New York. One day I went into Pearl River, a huge shop full of Chinese goods. I bought a wad of banknotes that they burn at funerals, and painted them. There was a Chinese mandarin on them, who I called Lee Ping Zing. I created a story around him by illustrating my pictures with words, as opposed to the other way round. It was very influenced by Bowie, by the imminent birth of my son Jasper, and the discovery of the identity of my biological father – Lee Ping Zing looked a lot like Dennis. I created a kind of mythology around him, a character, like Mickey Mouse or Tintin.

I ended up making a huge body of work, including silkscreens, paintings and bronzes, some of which I later exhibited in Wuhan in central China in a private museum that acquired more than 200 of my pieces going back to my art school days. Largely as a result of the South African National Gallery turning down a request for a mid-career retrospective, that work has now left South Africa.

I even did a performance where I dressed up like Lee Ping Zing and painted his self-portrait with a long brush. I published a limited-edition book about Lee Ping Zing, with the title *We Are All Gods* (in Chinese characters), for which I painted his life story on a series of banknotes. I dedicated the book to Jasper. *Learning to Fly* was my next project, largely based on Da Vinci's drawings of flying machines. They were impossible to get off the ground, but pioneering. I did a performance in collaboration with theatre director Brett Bailey, where I was painted blue, with a propeller on my head, and wore wings and flying goggles. I composed and sang soundtracks for both this and the Lee Ping Zing performances.

I've never stayed for a long time with any one theme. Something that Brian Eno and Bowie both exemplified was not repeating, always reinventing oneself. I had very successful moments with paintings I made called *Falling Flowers*, and also with a series of Mandela pictures. But I soon moved on. I've always admired Gerhard Richter, who has such different languages, from abstraction to Photorealism, and I aspire to that.

RS Nonetheless, landscape has been a continuous thread in your work.

BB That's true. When I arrived at art school, I was incredibly full of myself because I'd met Andy Warhol. I was doing all these Surrealist paintings, and they called me in, and said, 'if you don't do any serious work, you're out'. They suggested landscapes, and I painted my first one in the Alps.

Initially my landscapes were slightly more abstract than the works I make now. Later I worked in a more realistic way. I painted with Walter Meyer, who encouraged me to work from photographs, which I had always avoided before then. But he was right. You can't do an oil painting of a sunset from life; you would only have ten minutes! And of course I realised that Marlene Dumas and Francis Bacon only painted from photographs.

RS Were you represented by a gallery from early on?

BB I had been with a number of galleries, Linda Goodman in Johannesburg, Vanessa Devereux and Jibby Bean in London. But I always also represented myself and was very busy marketing my own work. After I did my first Art for AIDS Orphans (later Art for Africa) auction in 2000, Mark Read called to ask if he could represent me, which I was very pleased about, because I think it's essential that a gallery approaches you. And I feel I've grown with the gallery; plus the international art world has opened up in a way that I could never have imagined when I was younger. My first thematic show with the Everard Read Gallery was the Mandela exhibition. I collaborated with Benny Gool, the photographer, and also used iconic images of Mandela boxing on a Johannesburg rooftop, before his imprisonment, taken by *Drum* photographer Bob Gosani. I repeat silkscreened them onto canvases, which I painted in homage to Warhol and Rauschenberg. It was very successful, but I didn't want to repeat it or to exploit the figure of Mandela.

I also did a collaboration with Zwelethu Mthethwa, who took photographs of me as Joyce, done up as a black woman. We would go to the township with him to take the photographs, and everybody would fall about laughing when they eventually realised I was a white man. There was never any issue in terms of political correctness. I called the body of work, *Ticket to the Other Side*. It felt like going to a party that I hadn't been invited to. In Joyce's world, there is a sense of community that is completely lacking in the white community that I live in. There is something poignant and tragic about that. We exhibited around the world, and then last year Zwelethu was sent to jail for murdering a sex worker, which was a huge shock.

RS Have there been other thematic bodies of work?

BB About seven years ago, I made a series of paintings, drawings, sculptures and prints around the theme *Dancing Jesus*, based on the Resurrection. I included a classic Christ figure, with one lifted leg, and cast editions of this in silver, bronze and gold. I called it *Hava Nagila – The Dancing Jew*. The origin of that went back much further, to doing a full-length portrait of David Bowie in New York. I got him to pose as if he were Christ on the cross, but without a cross. Many years later, I began to explore that idea again. I think the coming of the Messiah will be the emergence of a higher consciousness inside each one of us.

I also did a performance version as part of a festival in Cape Town. I hired a dancer called Karabo, who would come out of an old hall on Greenmarket Square in the centre of town, and dance, as Christ removed from the cross, to a jazzed-up version of Sydney Carter's 'Lord of the Dance'. Karabo was flanked by two life-size bronzes I'd made of dancing Christ figures in high heels, one doing the Charleston. I later performed the same dance myself at an art festival in Copenhagen.

Another theme, which has been strong in my most recent exhibition, is *Falling Angels*. I've gone from figurative images, of an actual angel falling down, to more abstract versions of bubbles falling. I believe that when you die, you shatter into energy fields, like spheres, the same as planets and stars.

Looking ahead, I'm going to be working with a new theme around the Anthropocene, which I touched on in my London exhibition. Struggling with insomnia one night in London, thirty years ago I decided to lull myself to sleep by associating a different colour in my mind with each of the multiple bird sounds coming out of the dark dawn. Nowadays you hear far fewer varieties of birds, as the bird population is slowly being destroyed. So I want to create an exhibition inspired by the decimation of the bird population and make something that is endangered beautiful again.

RS Have you always worked across different media, or do you sometimes concentrate on painting, sometimes on other forms?

BB Painting always remains my main addiction, but when I'm working at my best, I'm working across media. There is a richness that emanates as a result of combining these forms. That's largely forgotten about today, when you get an artist who just does one thing – the guy who works on photocopies, the guy who does stuff with boxes. I find it impossible to do one thing. Even if I'm focusing on painting, I work on about ten pieces at one time. It's not multi-tasking because it's all one task; they are directly related. I call it 'cloud-painting', because it's like liberating the images that we all see in clouds.

RS Are there mediums you no longer work in, or have begun to work in?

BB Yes, I didn't do prints for about ten years, and have only just started that again. And I'm also starting to work in clay, which is new to me, because my heart is in woodcarving. Usually I need objects and things to create with. I have just made a steel sculpture from found materials, for example. So just having a lump of clay is a challenge. I've also been thinking about a new fabric range. Printing techniques have changed so much since I last worked with fabrics, and you can do so much more now.

RS Can you describe your process when you begin to paint?

BB My starting point is making abstract marks or 'colour clouds'. They are a way in, and when a painting is really working, it's like dream reality. I think that my painting process is very similar to the dreaming process in that abstract ideas or forms end up creating a figurative narrative. The quicker I can get that down, the happier I am, and the more successful I feel the work is.
Those instantaneous brushstrokes capture energy and give a specific, luminous quality to the paintings. I have always felt light has to emanate from a good painting. I am inspired by those qualities in the work of Rembrandt, Velázquez, Goya and

more recently Bacon, De Kooning and Picasso. To some extent, my process is the same in other media, but not always; for example, I recently did a very traditional drawing of lovers, and then made a large sculpture based on the drawing. That wasn't based on the materials, although more often my sculptures do emerge that way. Sometimes, ideas just come to me. For example, when I made the Bowie dancer, I based it on the flight of a flamingo, the shape of which dictated the dancing figure.

RS At other times, your work has emerged out of collaborations, which have been a strong feature of your career.

BB Yes, there has been a pattern of collaborations. The first serious ones were with Koos Malgas, from the Owl House, and with Adam Letch, a photographer. When I worked with Adam, it was the year Windsor Castle caught fire. I made a crown out of a ploughshare and was photographed naked and screaming. Then in the printing, we turned the body parts around and painted or printed on them. I called that theme, *Love and the Fall of the House of Windsor*. It was inspired by the inhumanity of Princess Diana being raped on a daily basis by the media. We made enough for a show called *Two Collaborations*, which we did at the Association for Visual Arts in Cape Town.

A year later I met Bowie and worked with him, and later Brian Eno and Dave Matthews. I think somehow music is in my art and I respond well to musicians. I always wanted to be a rock star and they always wanted to be painters in a way. The relationship with Eno has probably been the most intense because it has been ongoing, and he is also a visual artist in his own right. We met again about ten years ago and he said, come back to my studio and see some stuff. We started to paint on some pieces of wooden offcuts from the hardware store, which evolved into sound paintings. We put together a body of work where he would make sounds to go with particular paintings; you would put on headphones as you looked at the painting, and see the sound. We exhibited that work at the 2015 Venice Biennale and thereafter in Lisbon.

RS Who are the artists who have most influenced you?

BB I was lucky to grow up surrounded by art. My father had his incredible collection of bronzes, and there were a lot of paintings. My first big influence was Matisse. At fifteen, I would go to the school library and copy his drawings. Picasso too was monumentally influential. I remember picking up a book by the photographer

David Douglas Duncan, who had incredible access to Picasso, and just drinking it in. It was a seminal influence on how I live and how I make my art. Painting, sculpture, prints, everything related. Andy Warhol was a pivotal influence in making the decision to become an artist, and in the way he embraced the commercial side of art. Then there's Giotto, Bacon, De Kooning, Richter. I think Rembrandt is the greatest painter of all.

My real mentor though, was Nelson Makuba, who when I was a student showed me how to find the African within me. That was my moment of discovery, realising that I have a European ancestry and education, but that I have African culture coursing through my veins. I feel very strongly about that, particularly in the present climate of racial disharmony, stoked by extreme right- and left-wing political parties in South Africa. It's completely contrary to our constitution, and to the Mandela dream of racial harmony.

RS Do you think of yourself as a political artist?

BB No, I have always been opposed to that. My father once said to me that if you are a political artist, you are creating propaganda, and then it ceases to be art. Having said that, Joyce Ntobe was an entirely political exploration, and that was political art. But I could only do that as an alter ego. There are a lot of political messages in my art, but it's not what art history would define as political art.

RS How important is your South African identity to your art?

BB It's everything. The tension, the stress of life in South Africa, is central to my creativity. I could never live somewhere calm like Denmark. We live in heaven with this undercurrent of hell – the poverty, the crime of a brutalised society – that feeds my work. There is a feverish edge that I need, and we're not short of it here. From the driest thorn tree in the desert, the reddest blood of all flows.

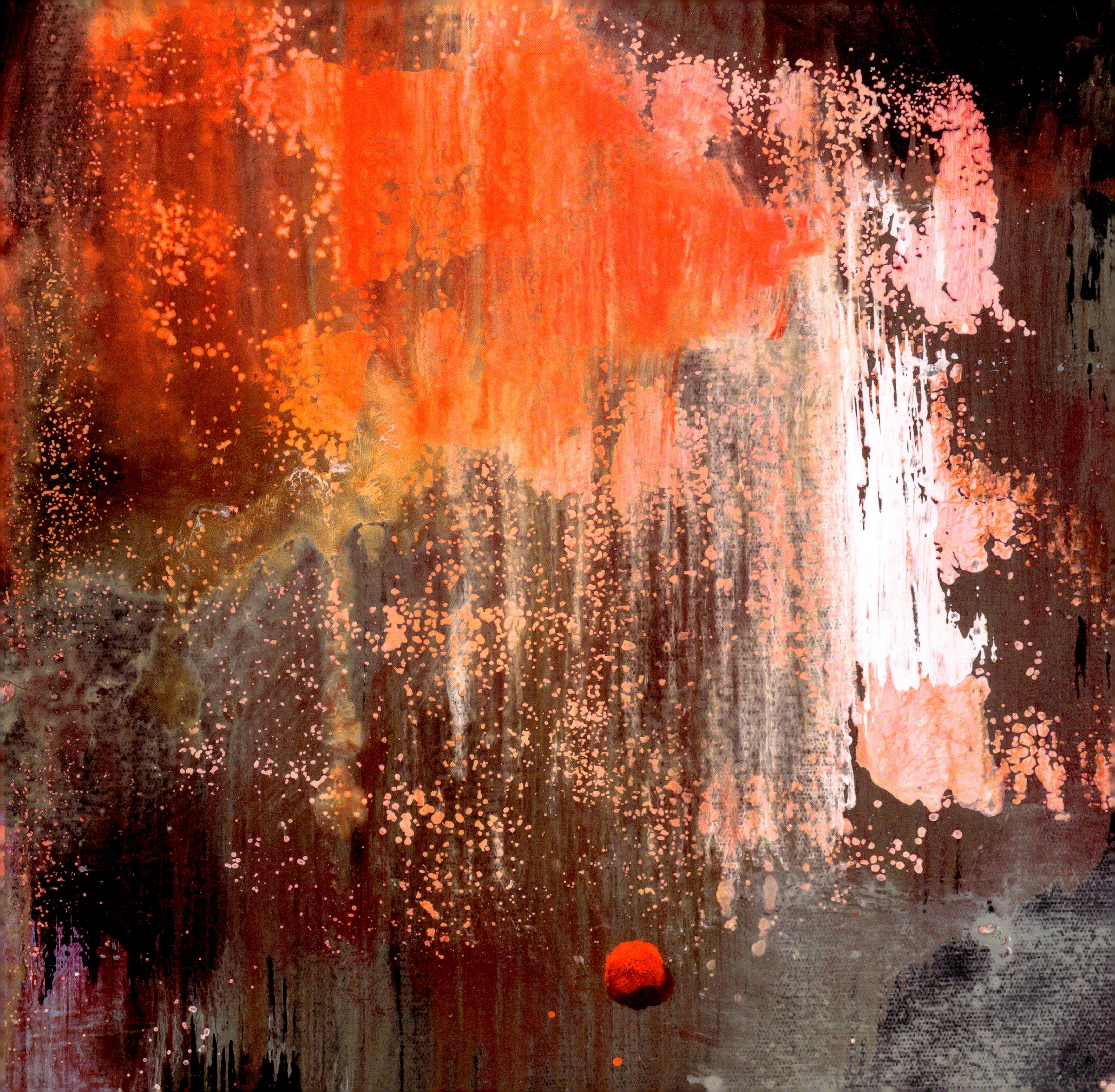

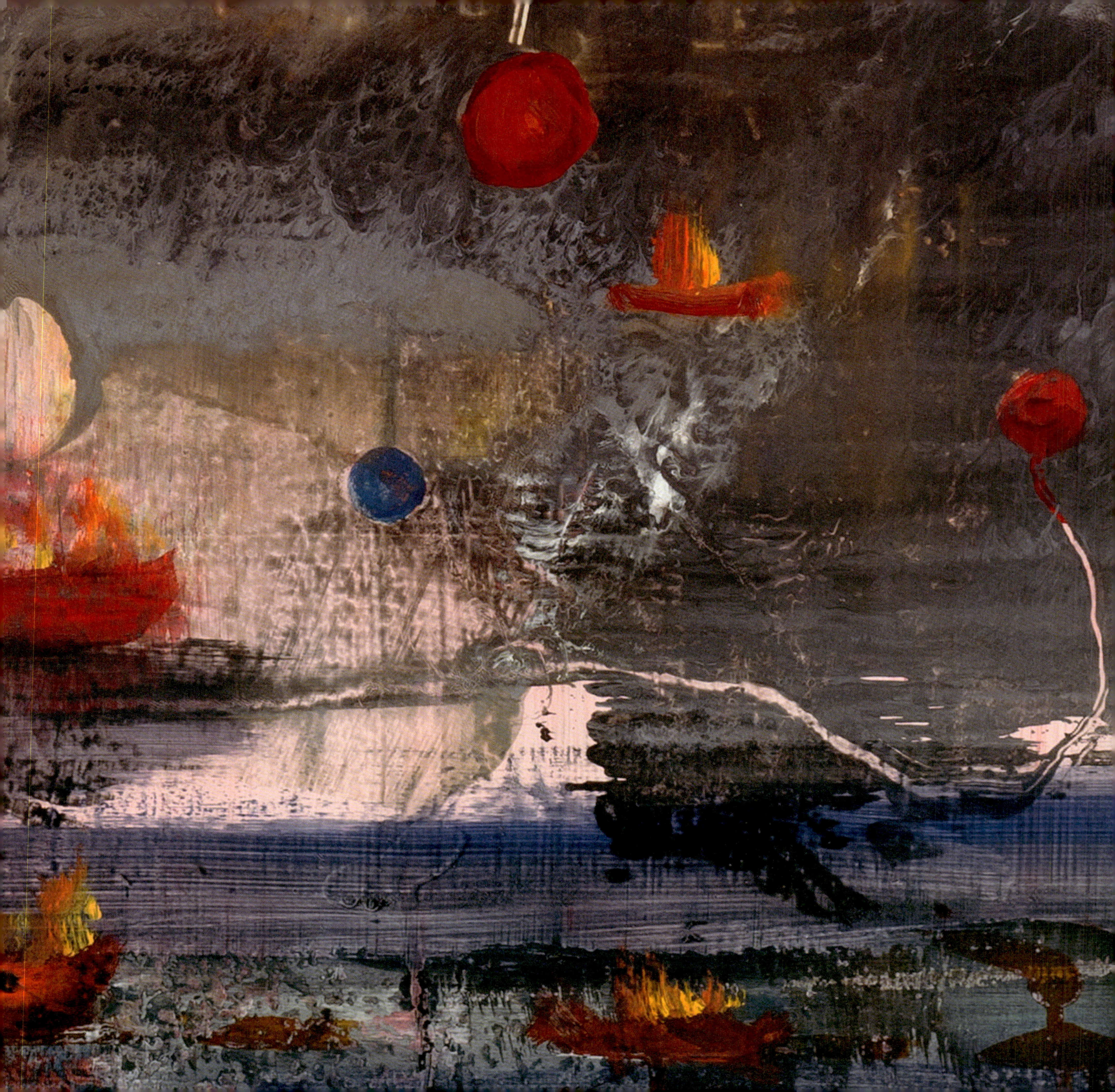

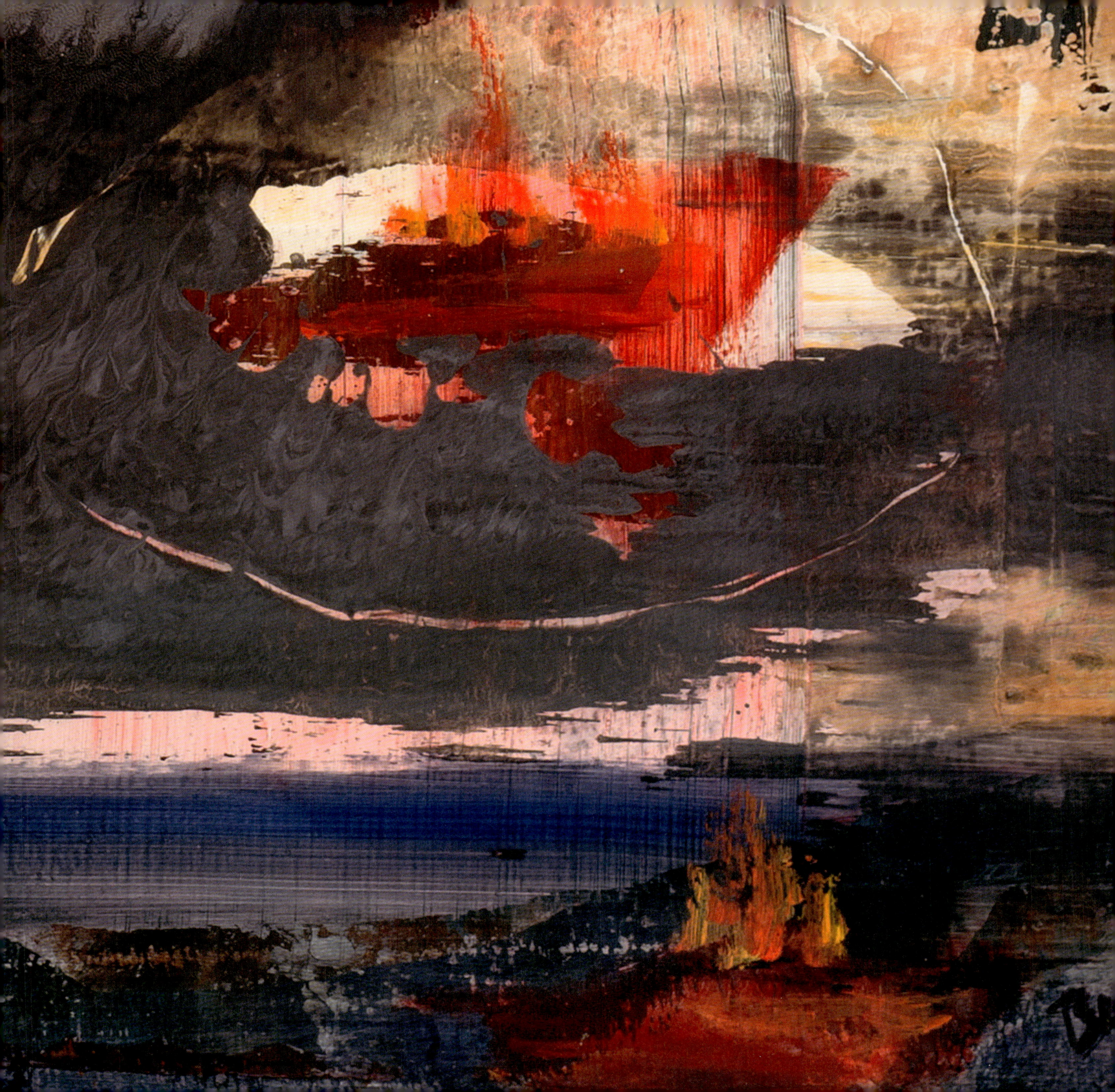

ANGEL BALLS FALLING 2017 Oil on canvas 60 × 75cm

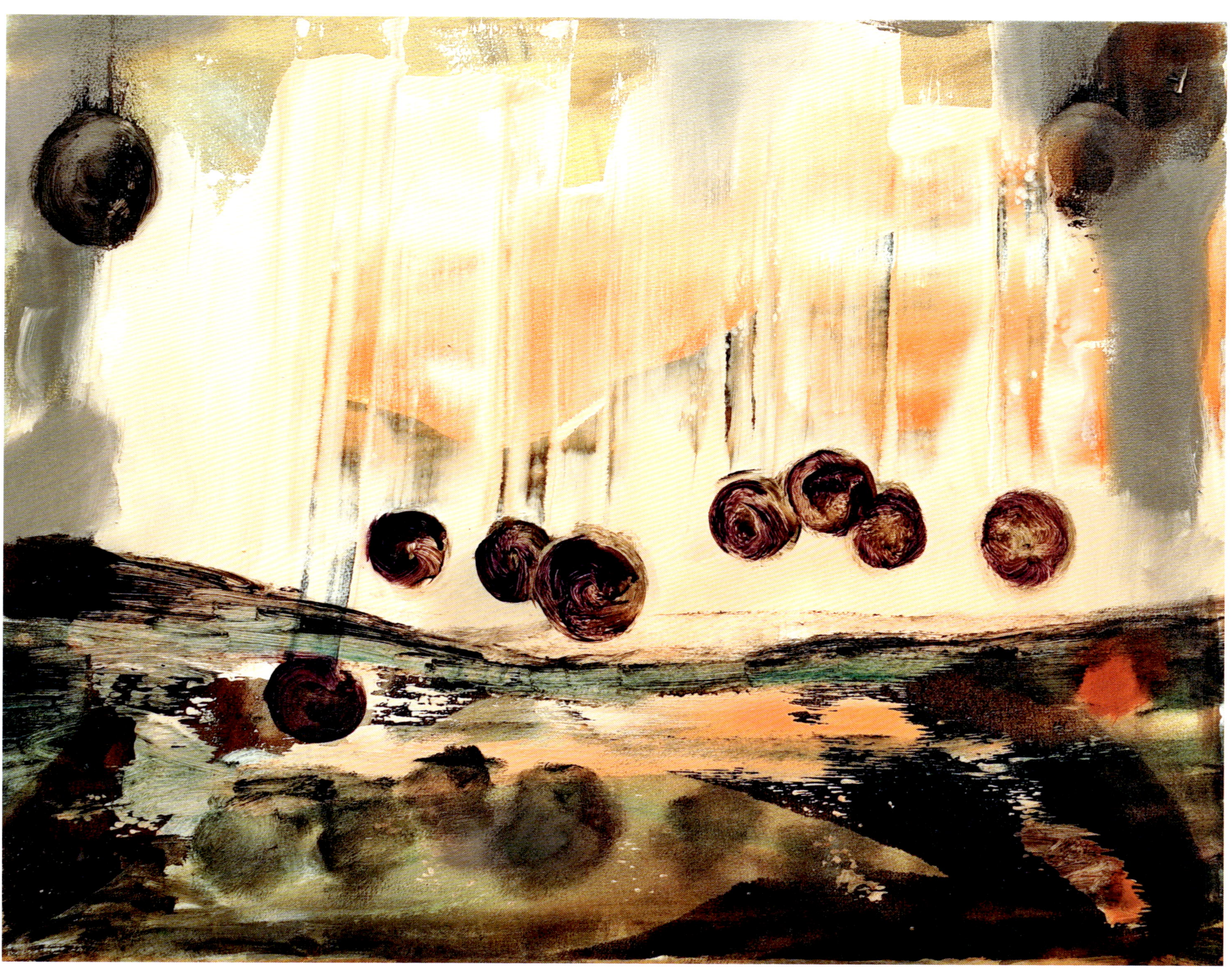

MY HANDS ARE TIED 2017 Oil on canvas 122 × 92cm

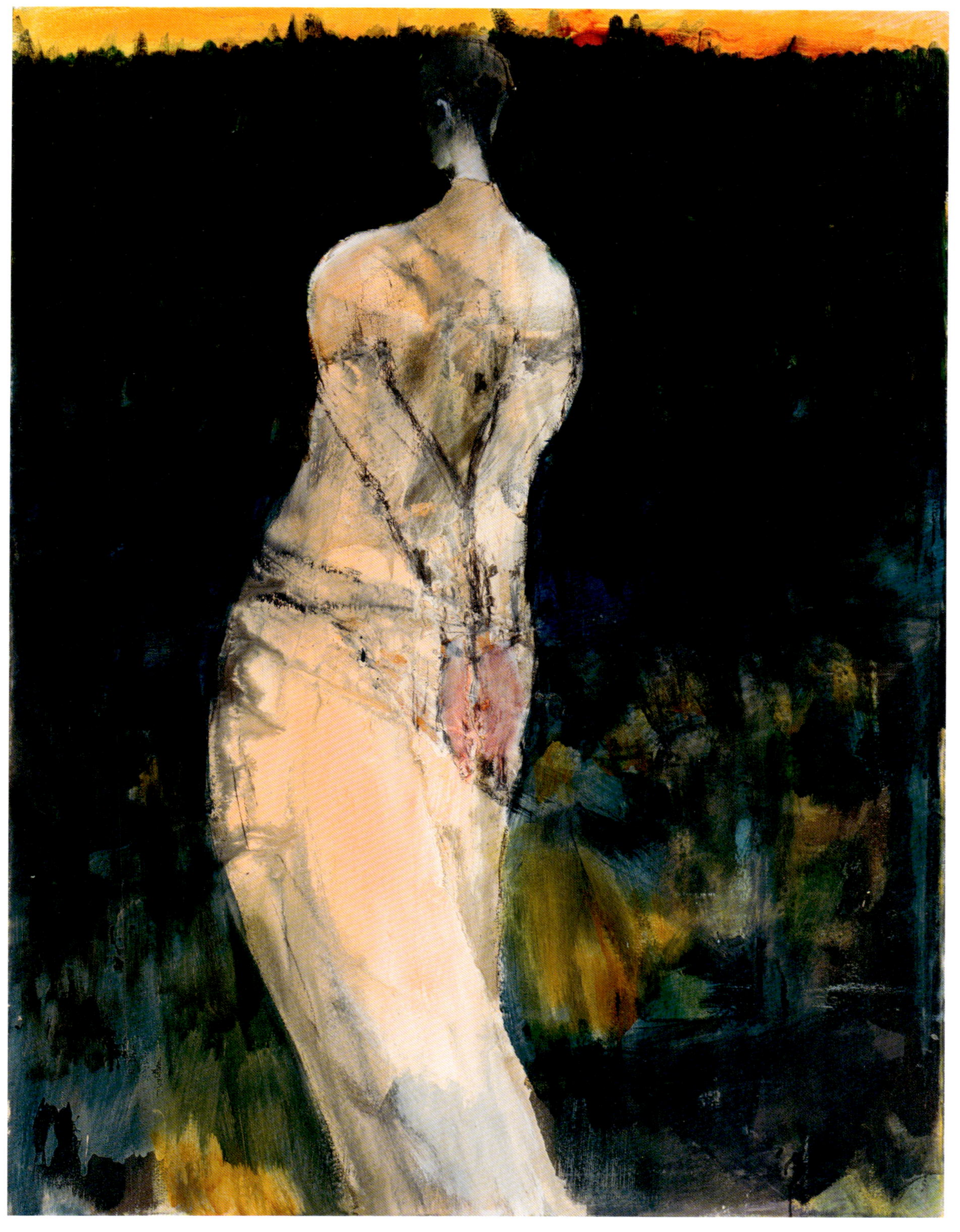

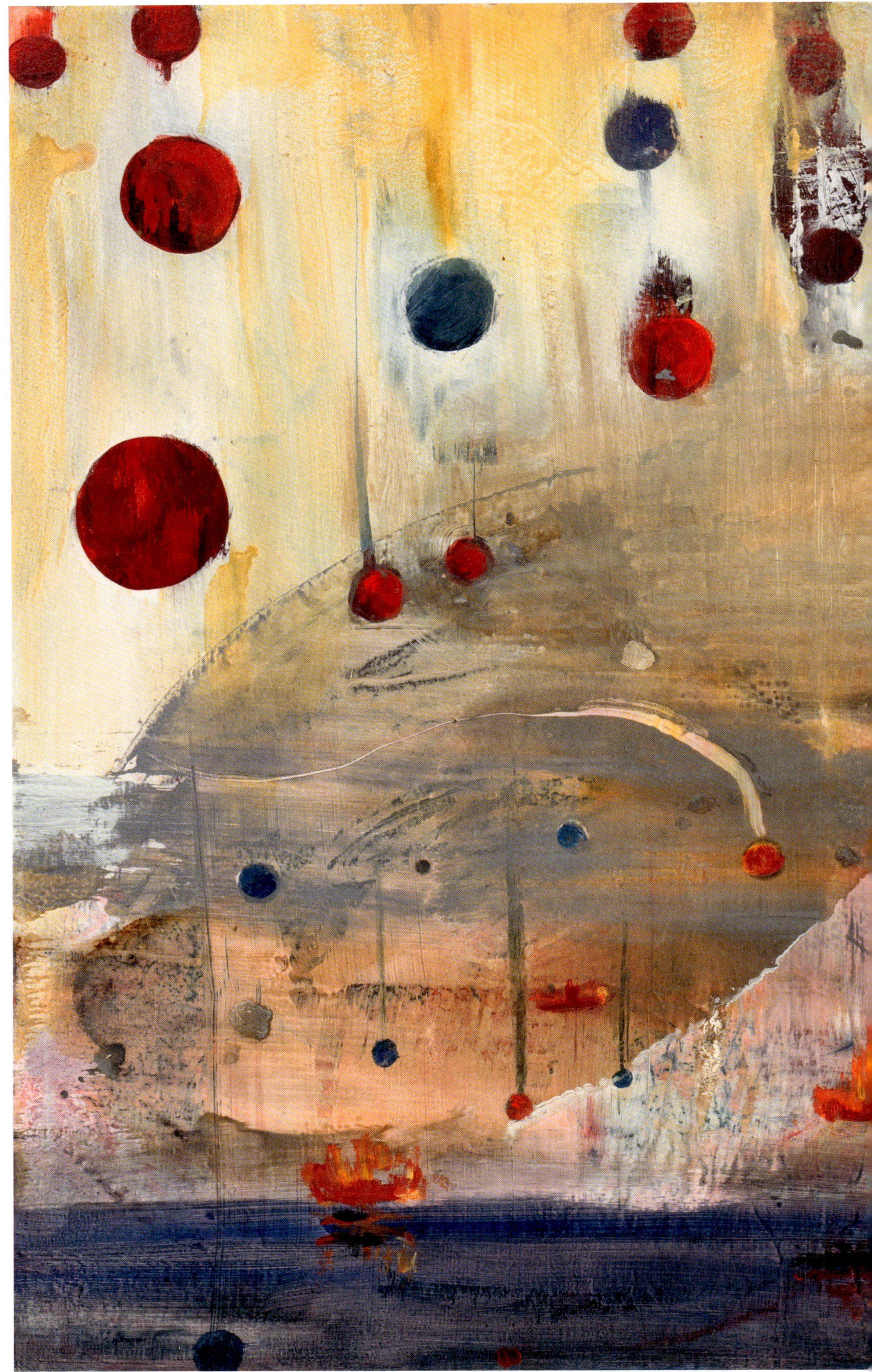

ASTRAL BLANKET 2017 Oil on canvas 90 × 150cm

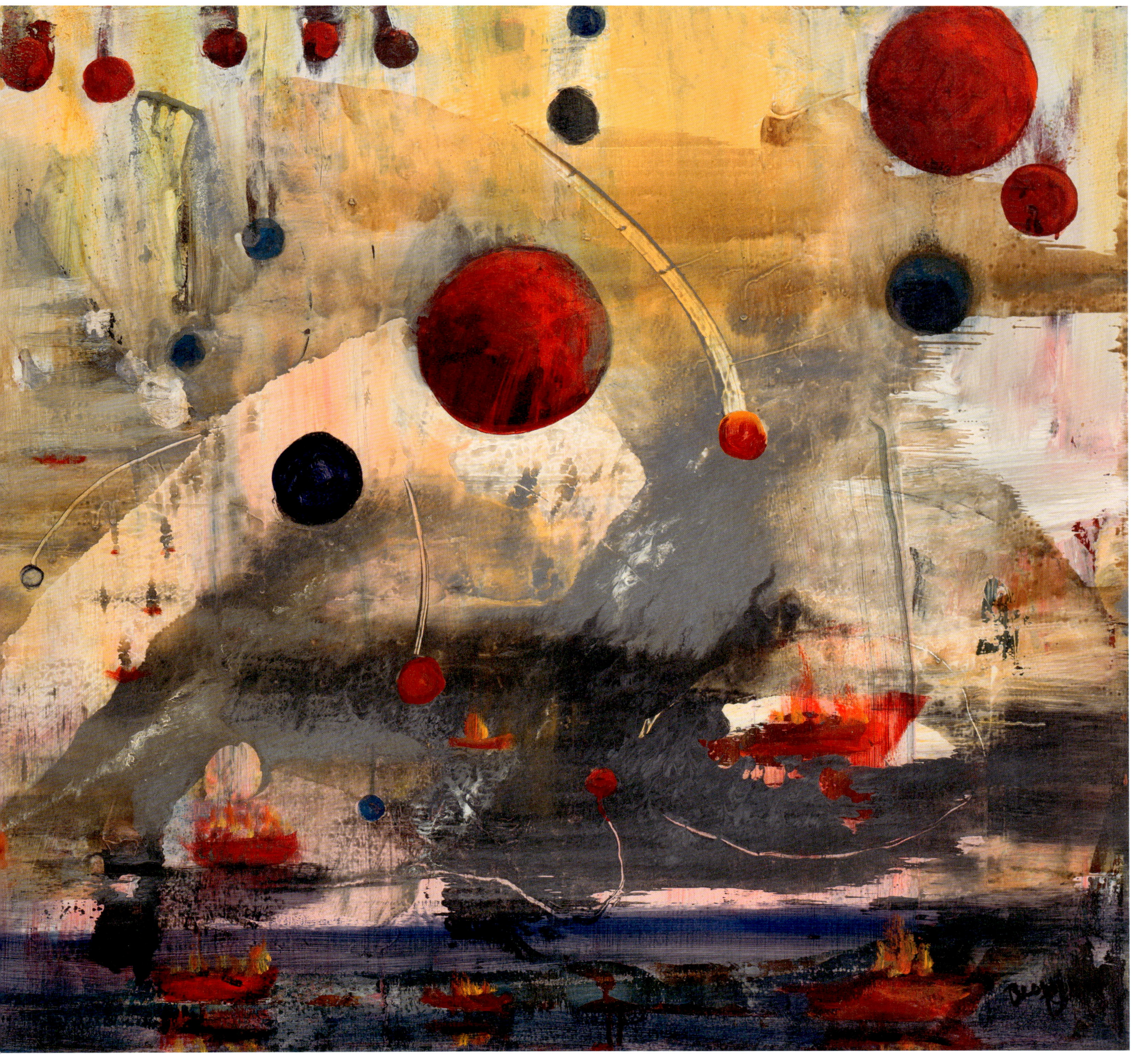

AS IT IS IN HEAVEN 2018 Oil on canvas 170 × 250cm

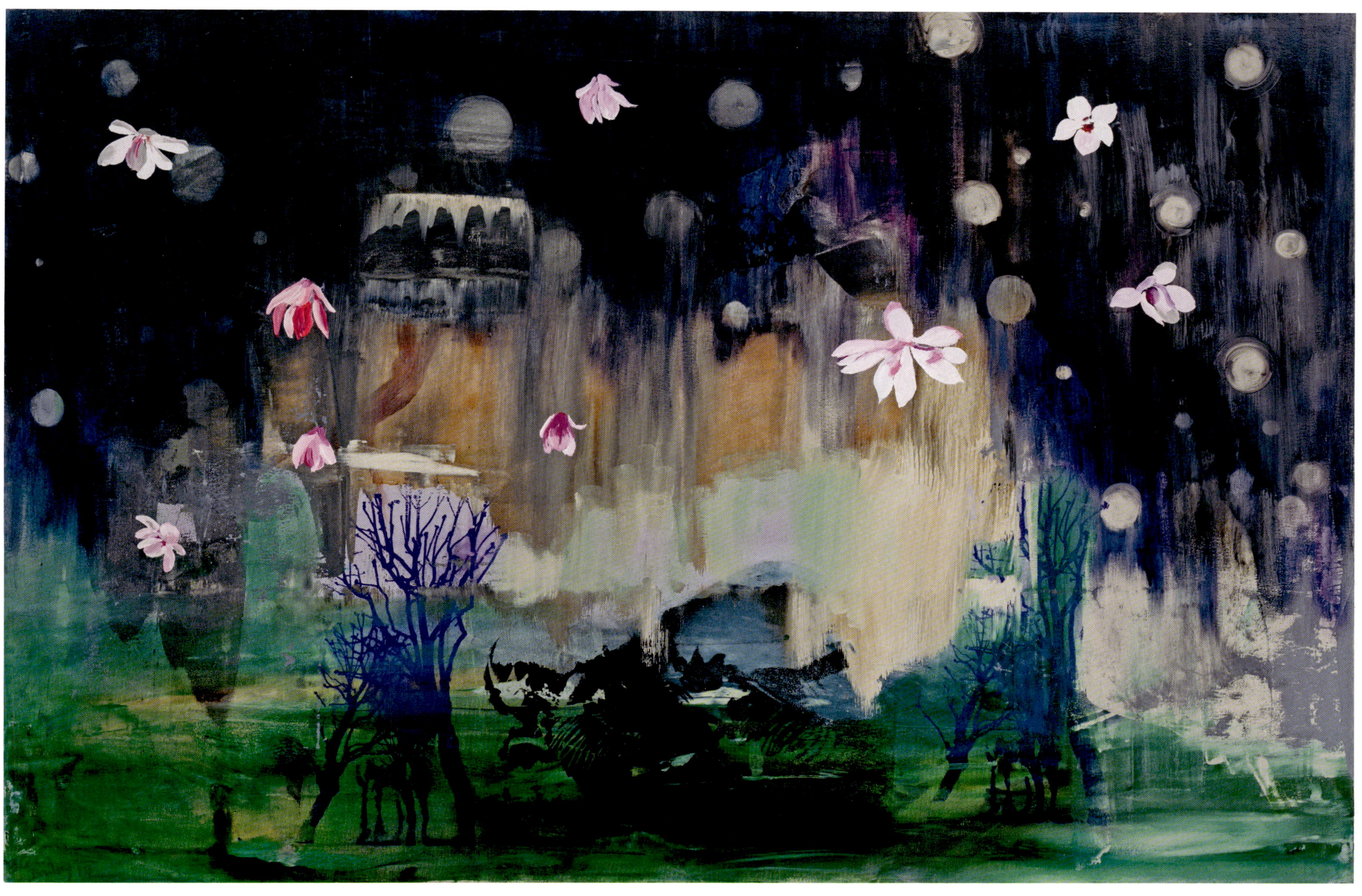

PAKENHAM'S PRESENT 2018 Oil on canvas 61 × 80cm

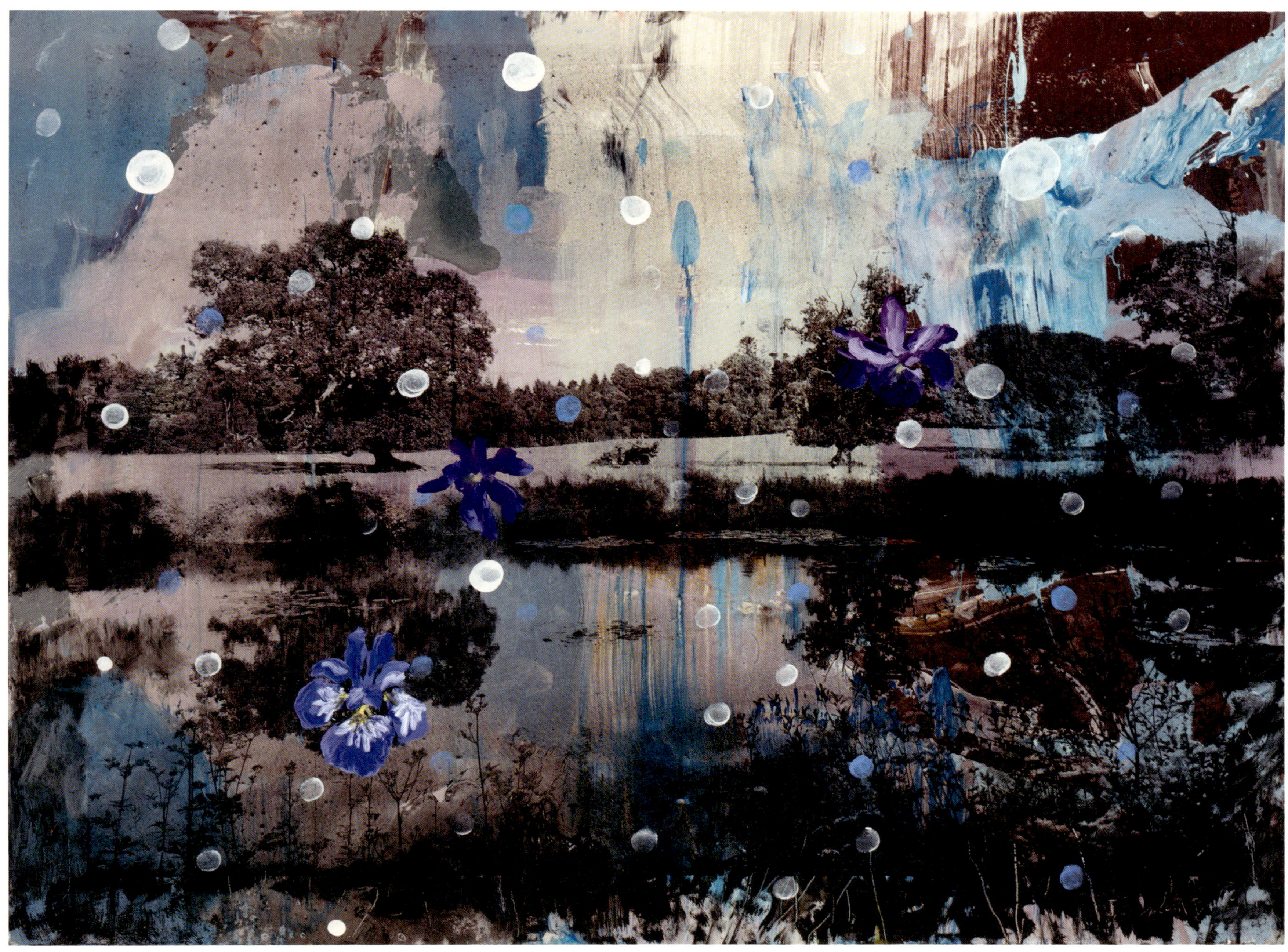

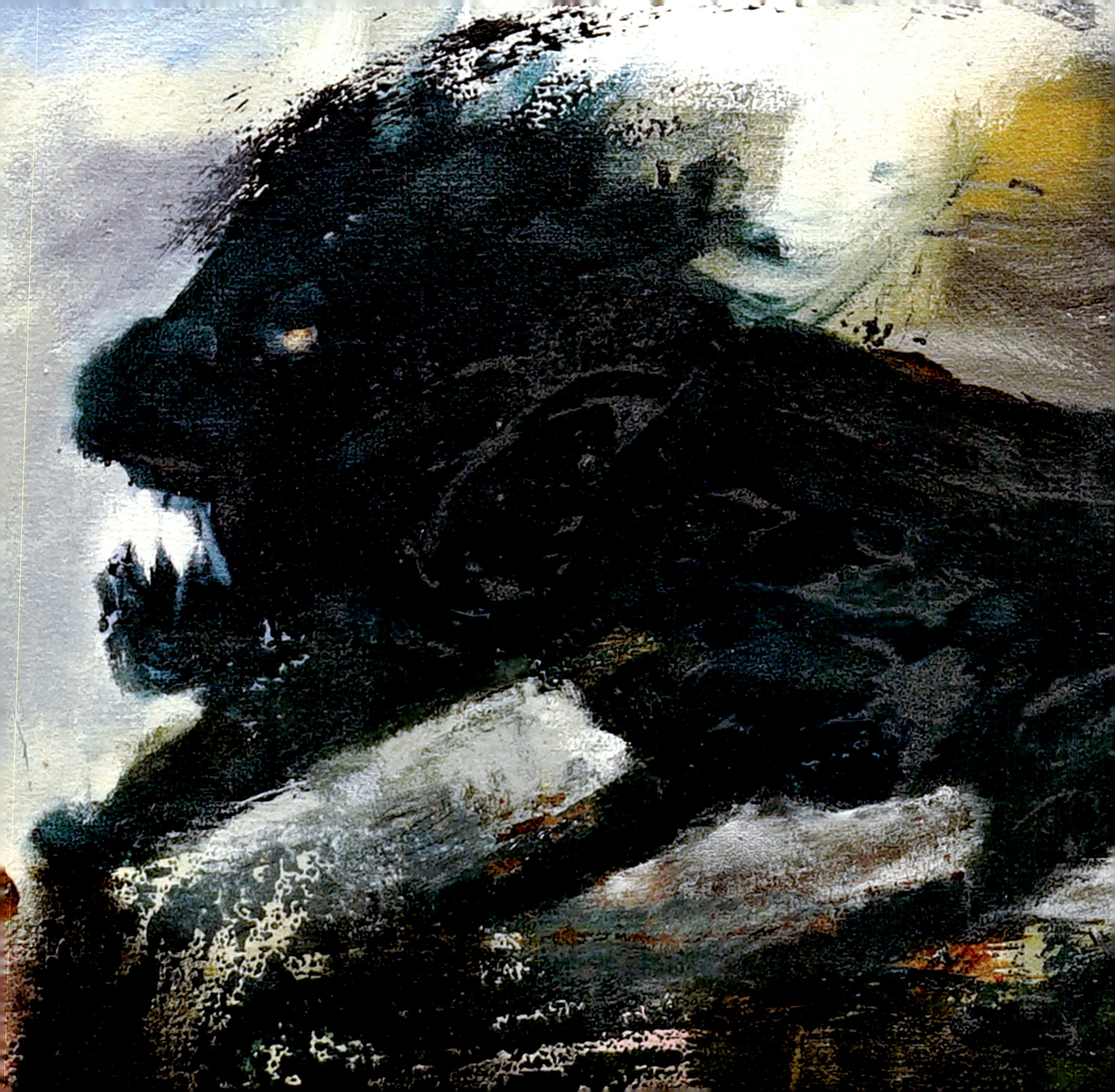

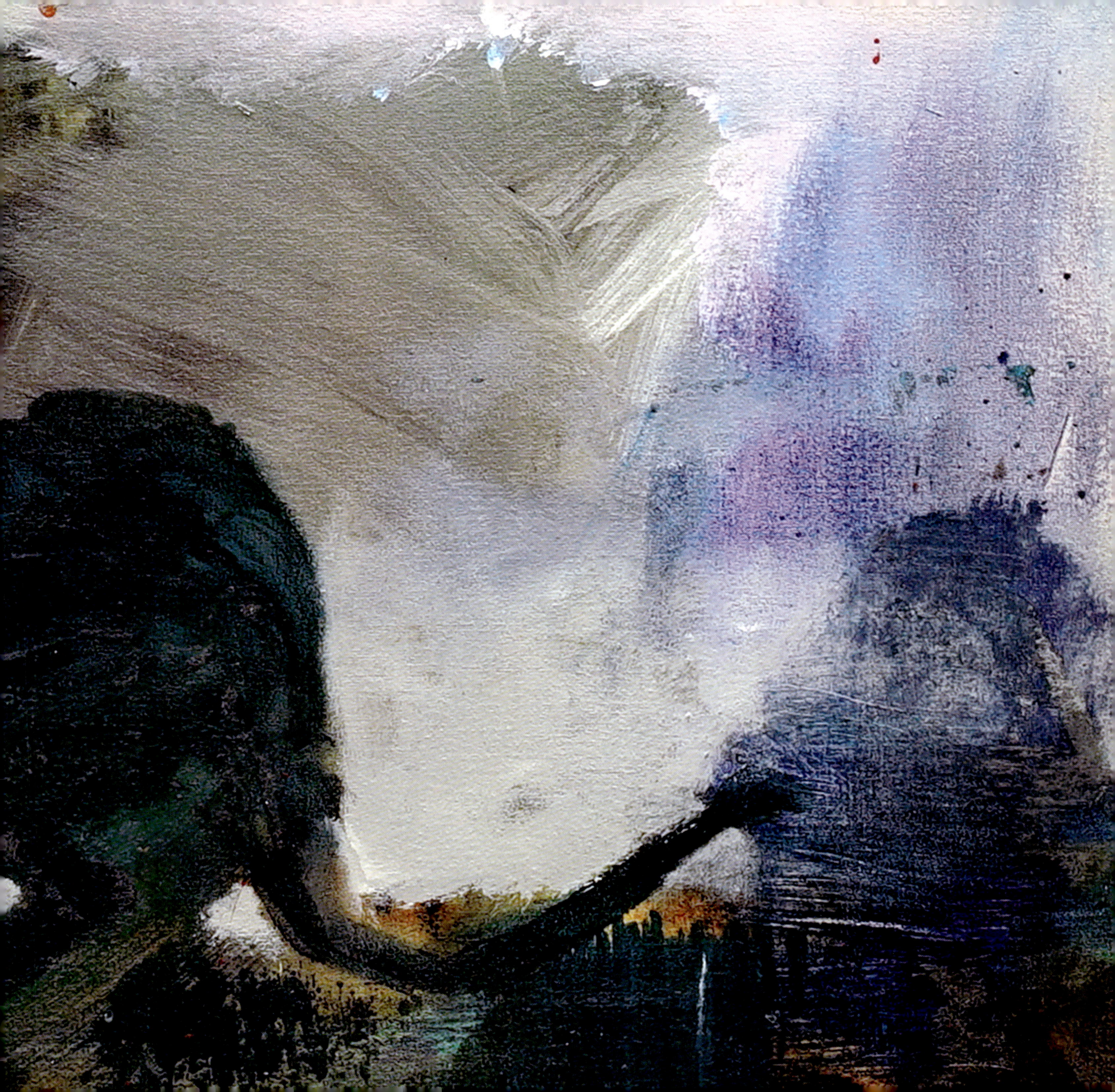

PURPLE CATS 2018 Oil and enamel on canvas 13 × 18cm

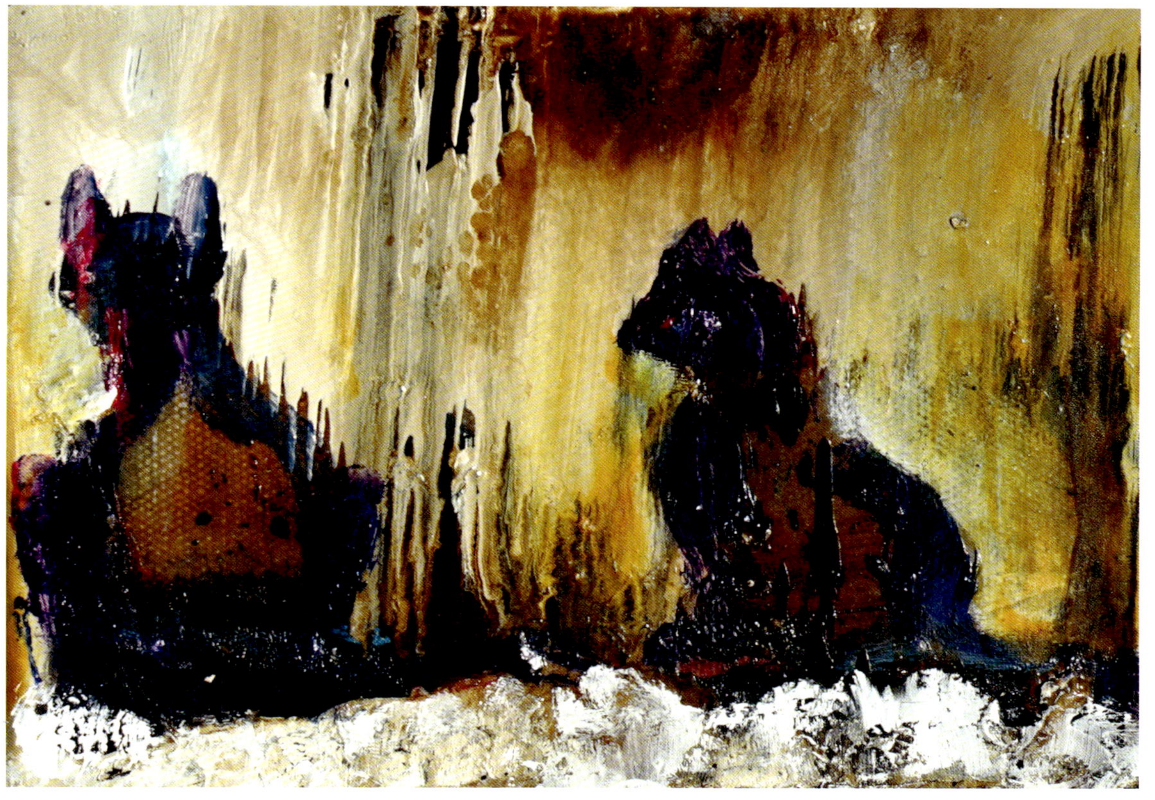

LITTLE BRITAIN 2018 Oil and enamel on canvas 60 × 75cm

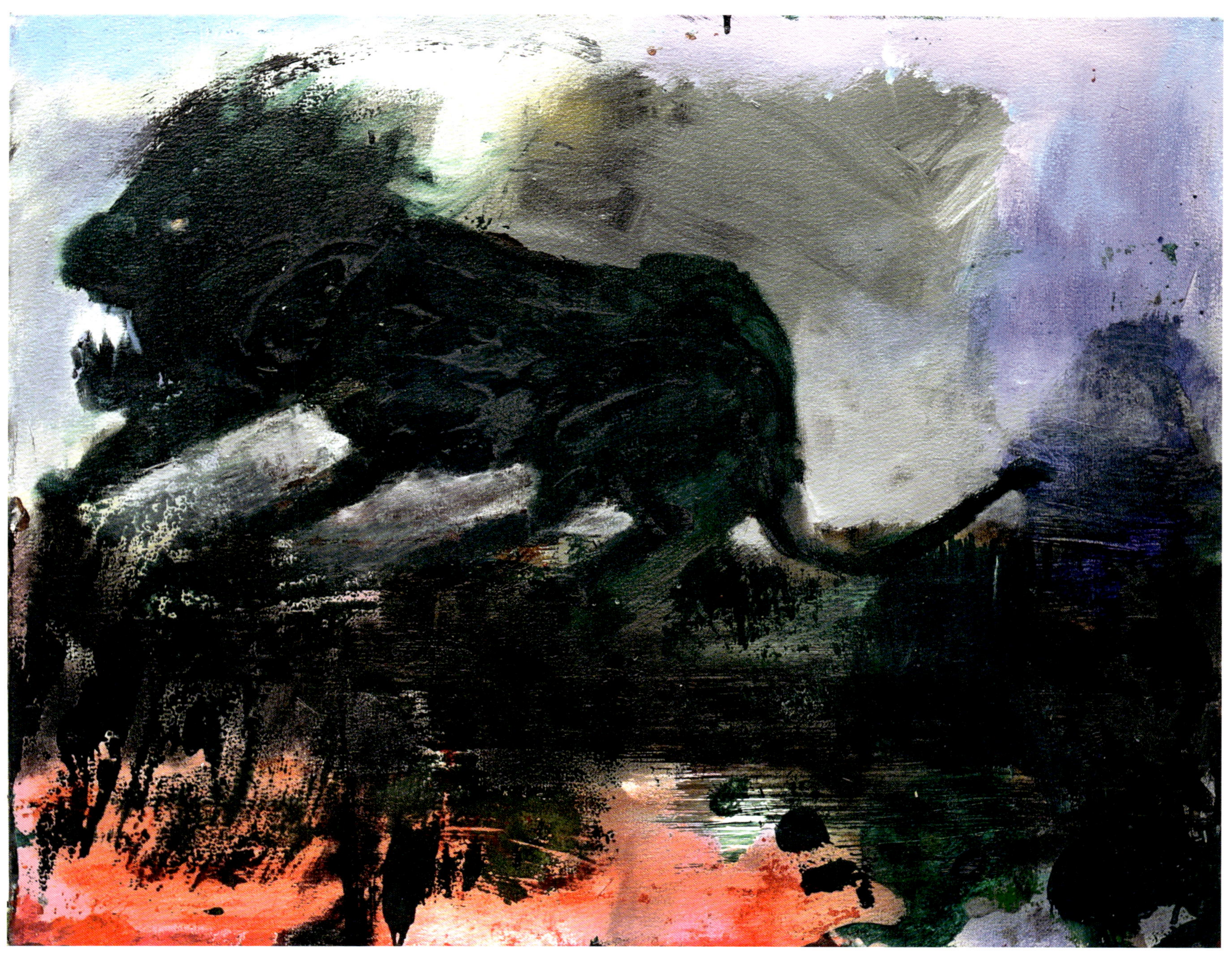

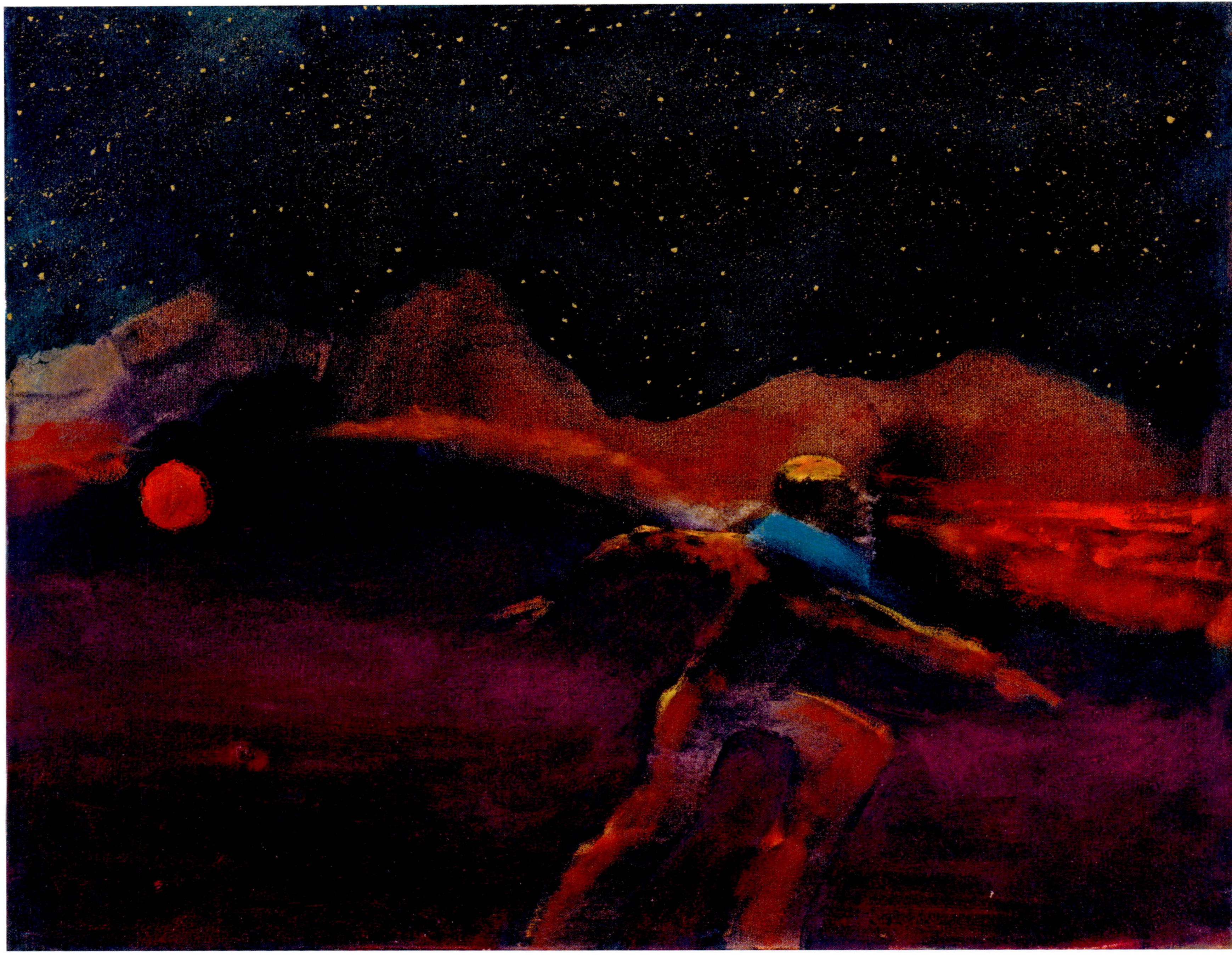

MIDNIGHT WALKER 2018 Oil on canvas 60 × 75cm

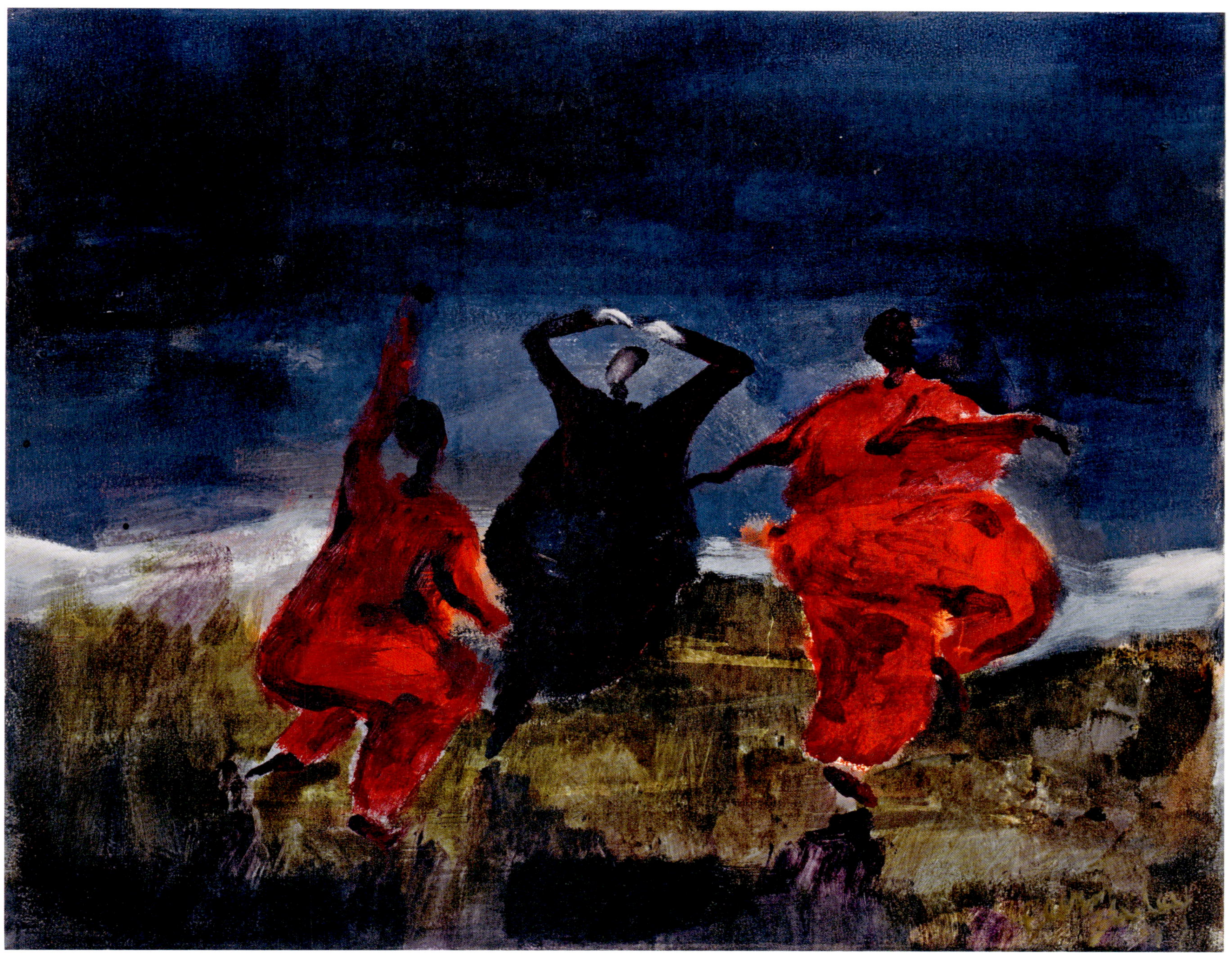

THE WEIRD SISTERS 2018 Oil on canvas 60 × 75cm

BURNING LOVE 2018 Oil on canvas 60 × 75cm

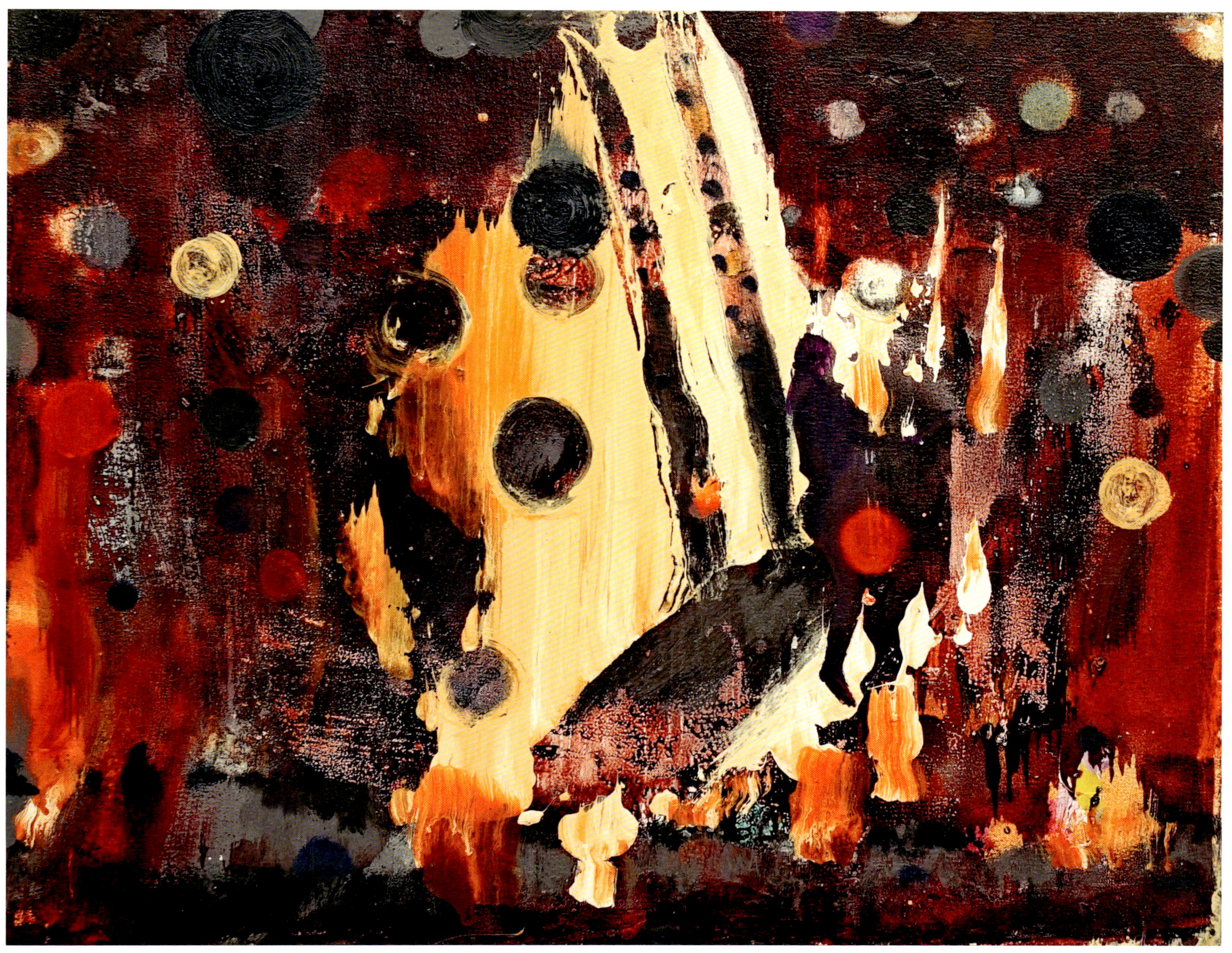

JEWEL REVOLUTION 2018 Oil on canvas 90 × 120cm

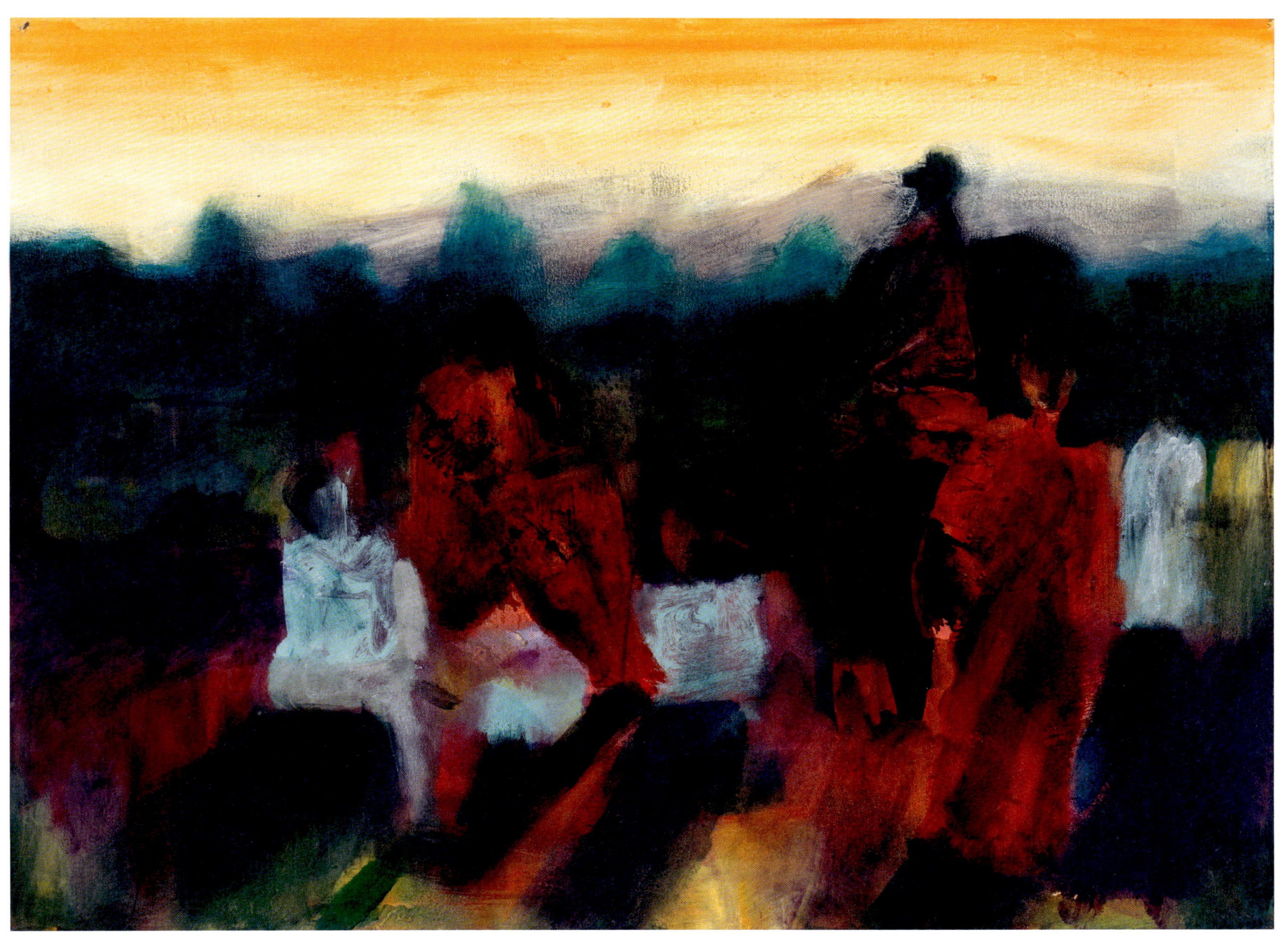

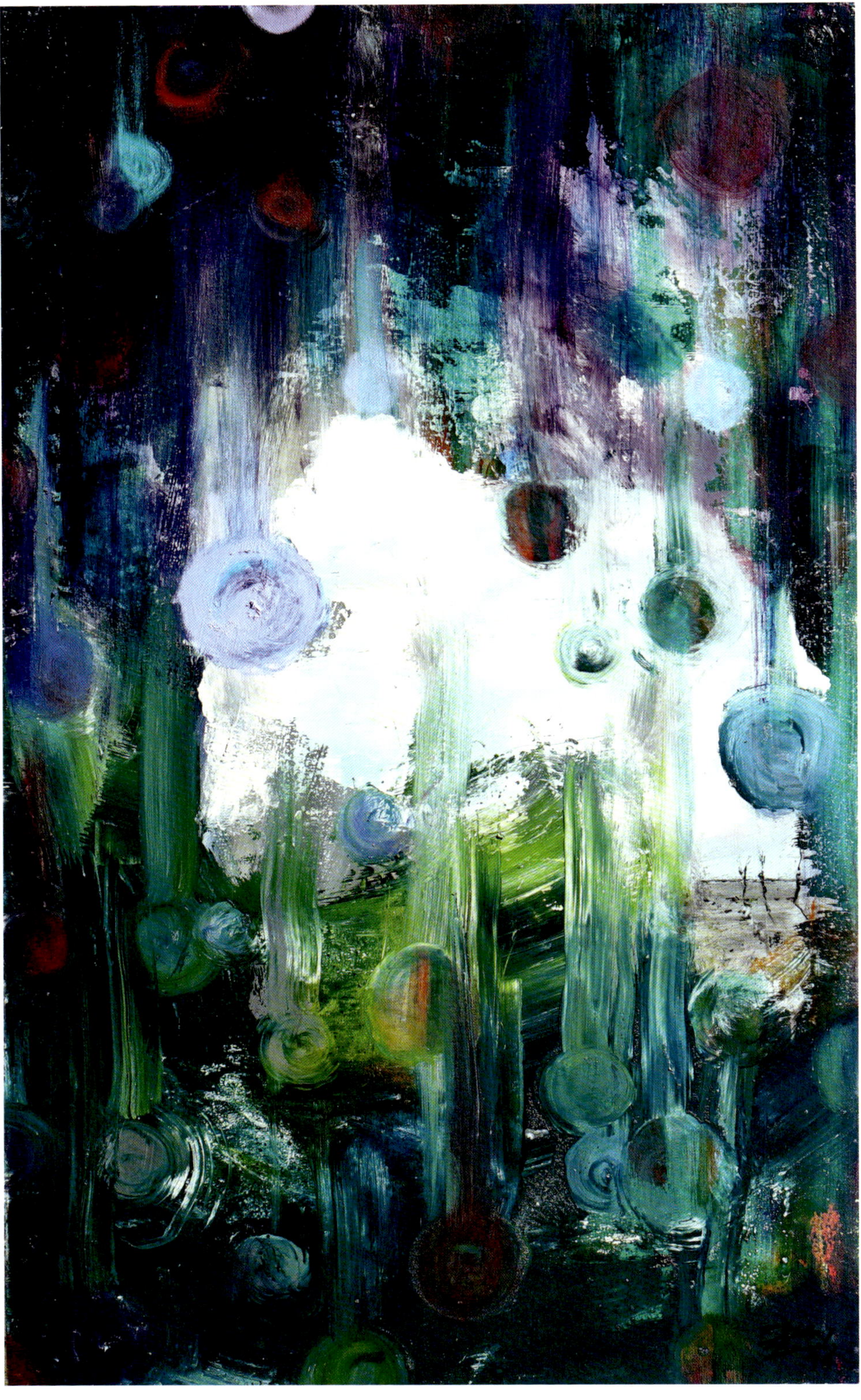

VIEW FROM THE CAVE OF THE EARTH THAT WAS 2018 Oil on canvas 150 × 90cm

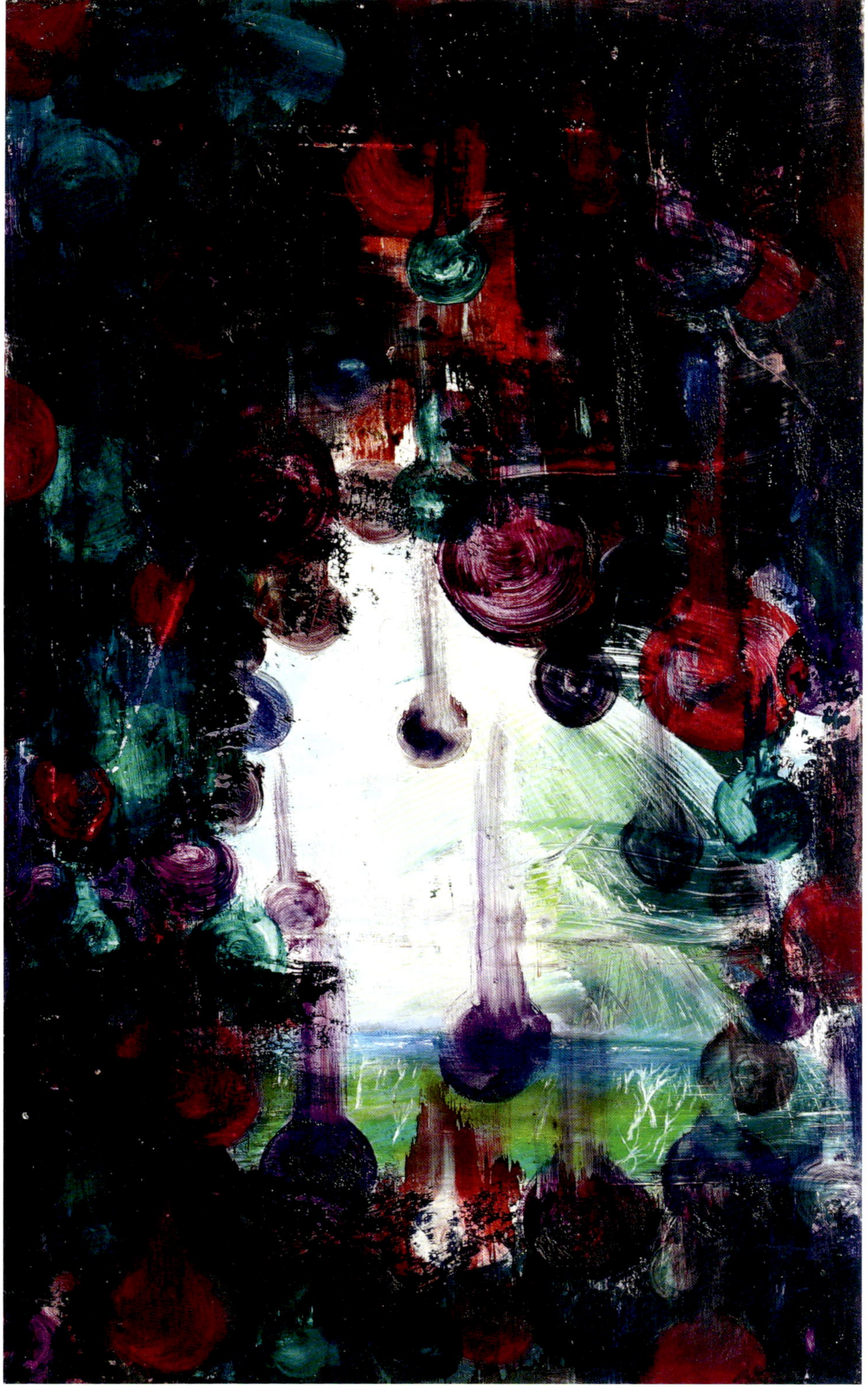

ANGELS FALLING INSIDE THE CAVE 2018 Oil on canvas 150 × 90cm

SUMMER SNOW ON PLUTO 2018 Oil on canvas 170 × 250cm

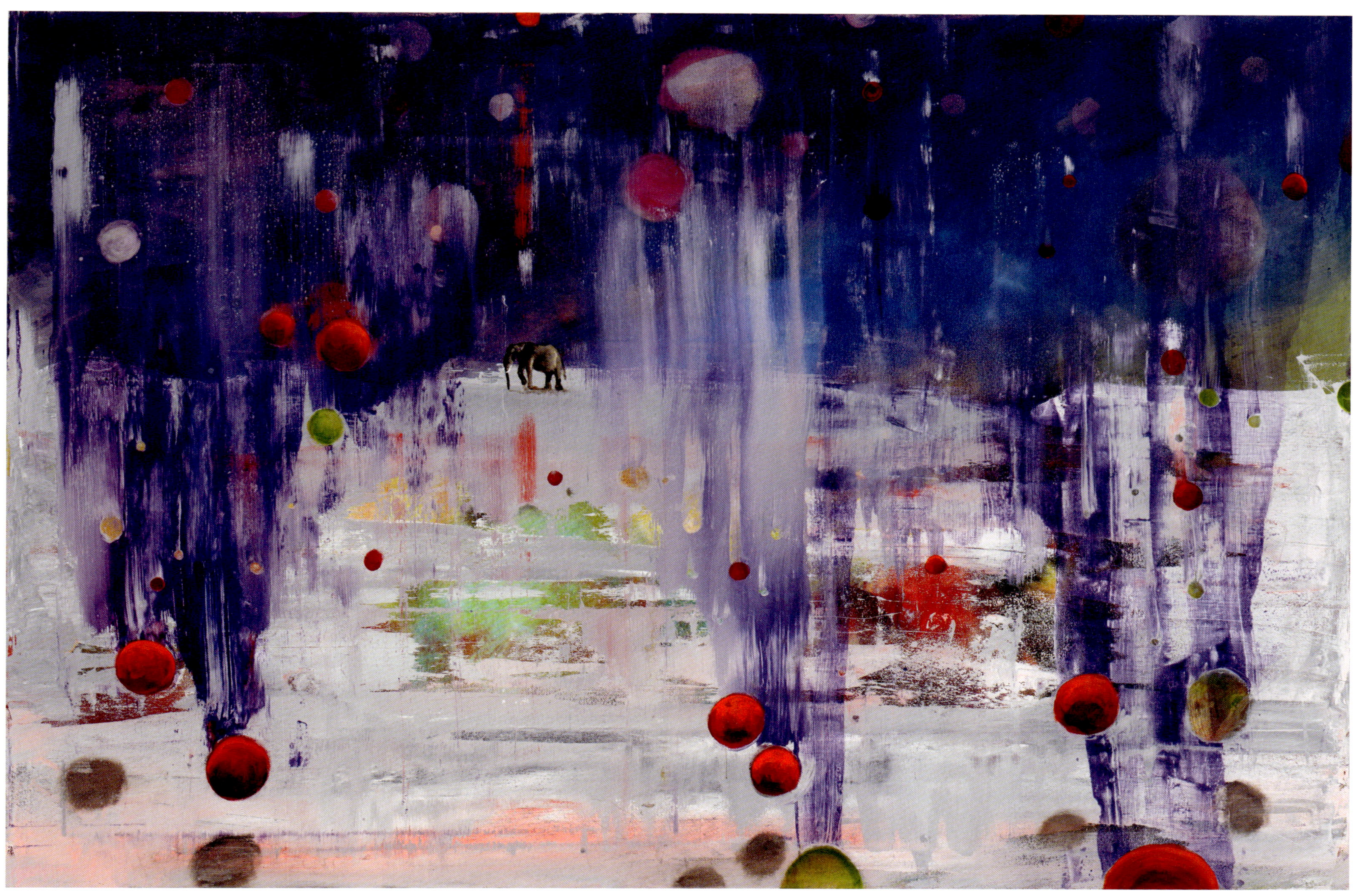

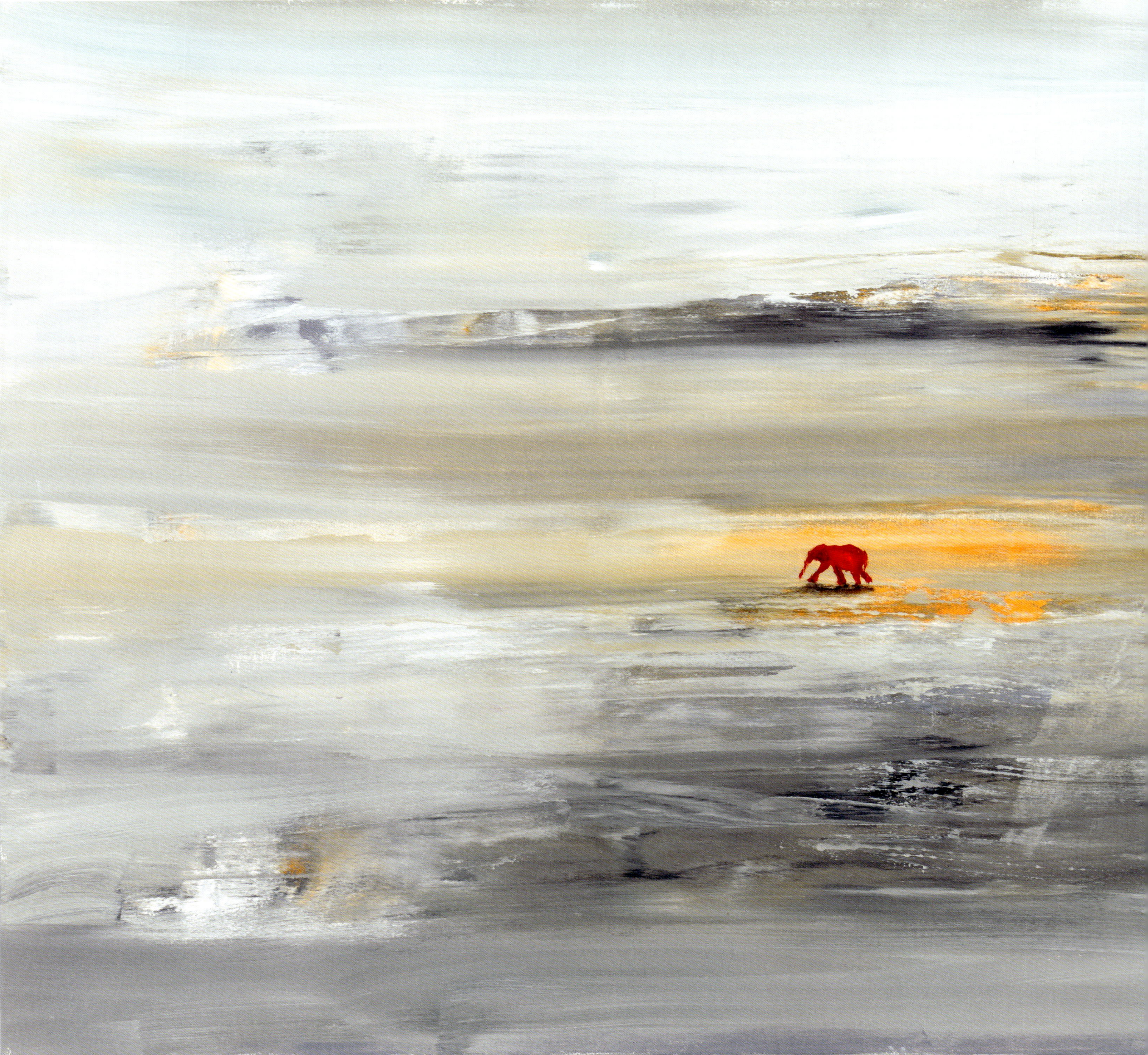

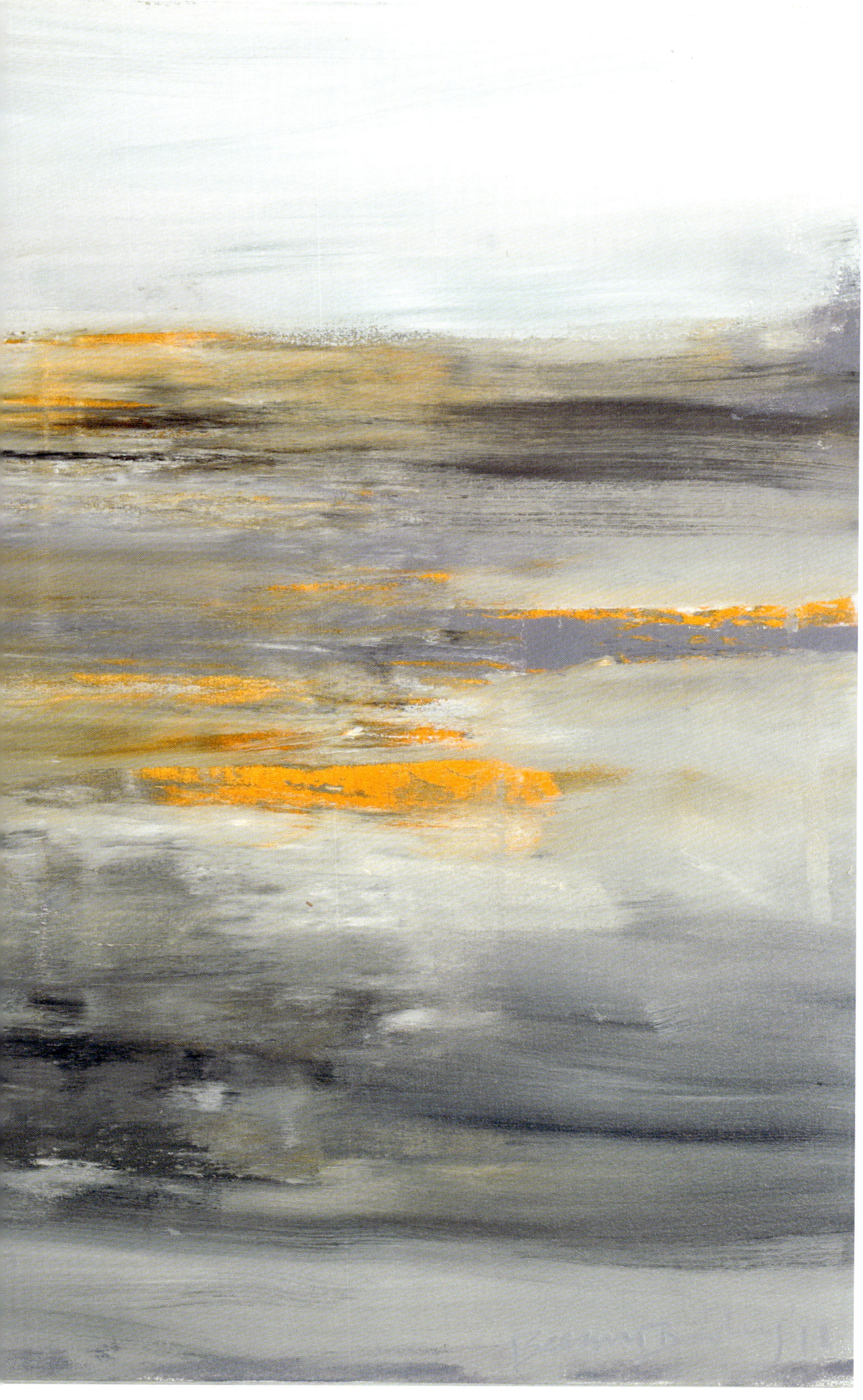

LONELY WALK 2018 Oil on canvas 90 × 150cm

DON'T GO GENTLY INTO THAT GOOD NIGHT 2018 Oil on canvas 90 × 120cm

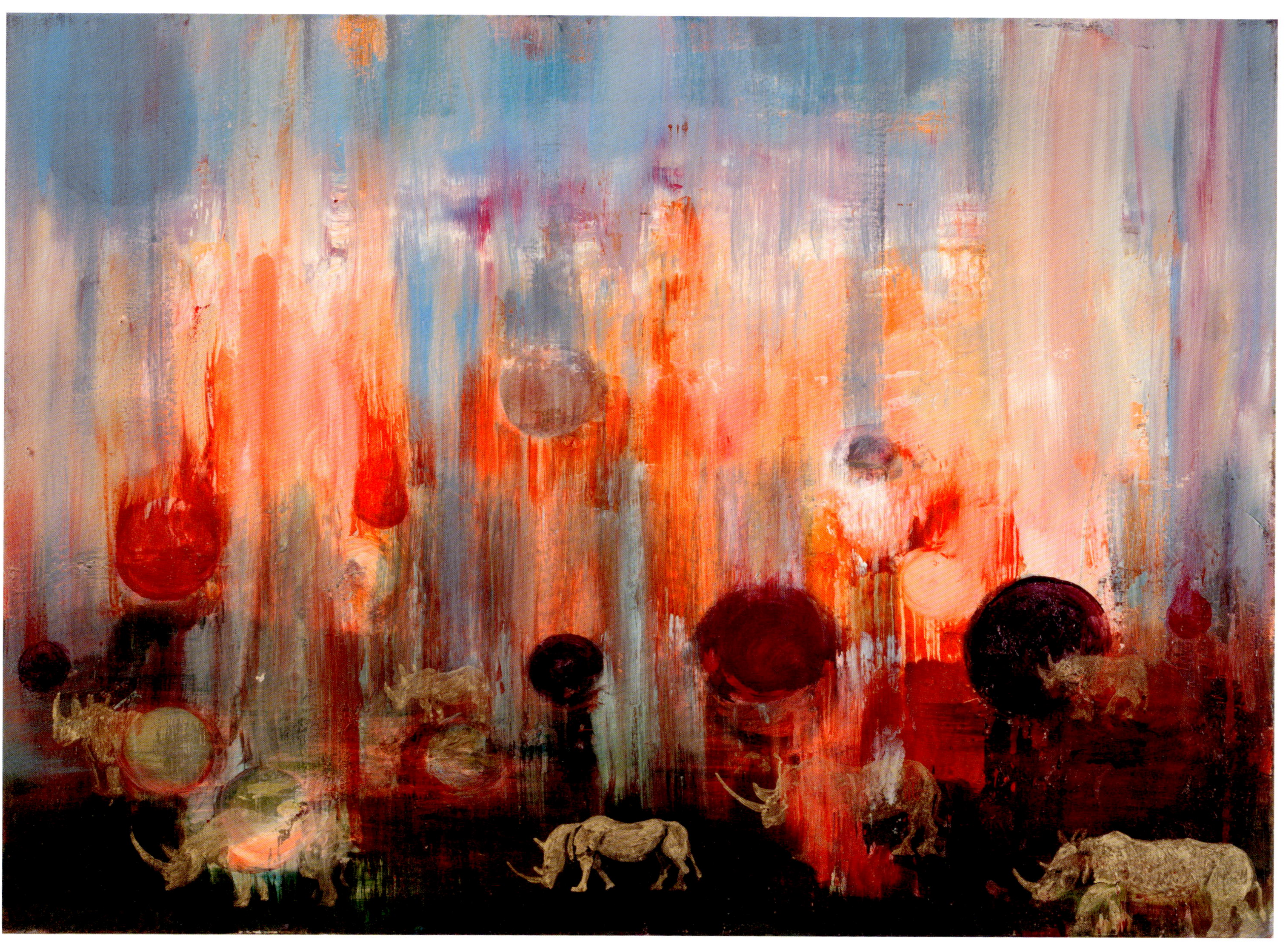

21ST BIRTHDAY PARTY 2018 Oil on canvas 92 × 122cm

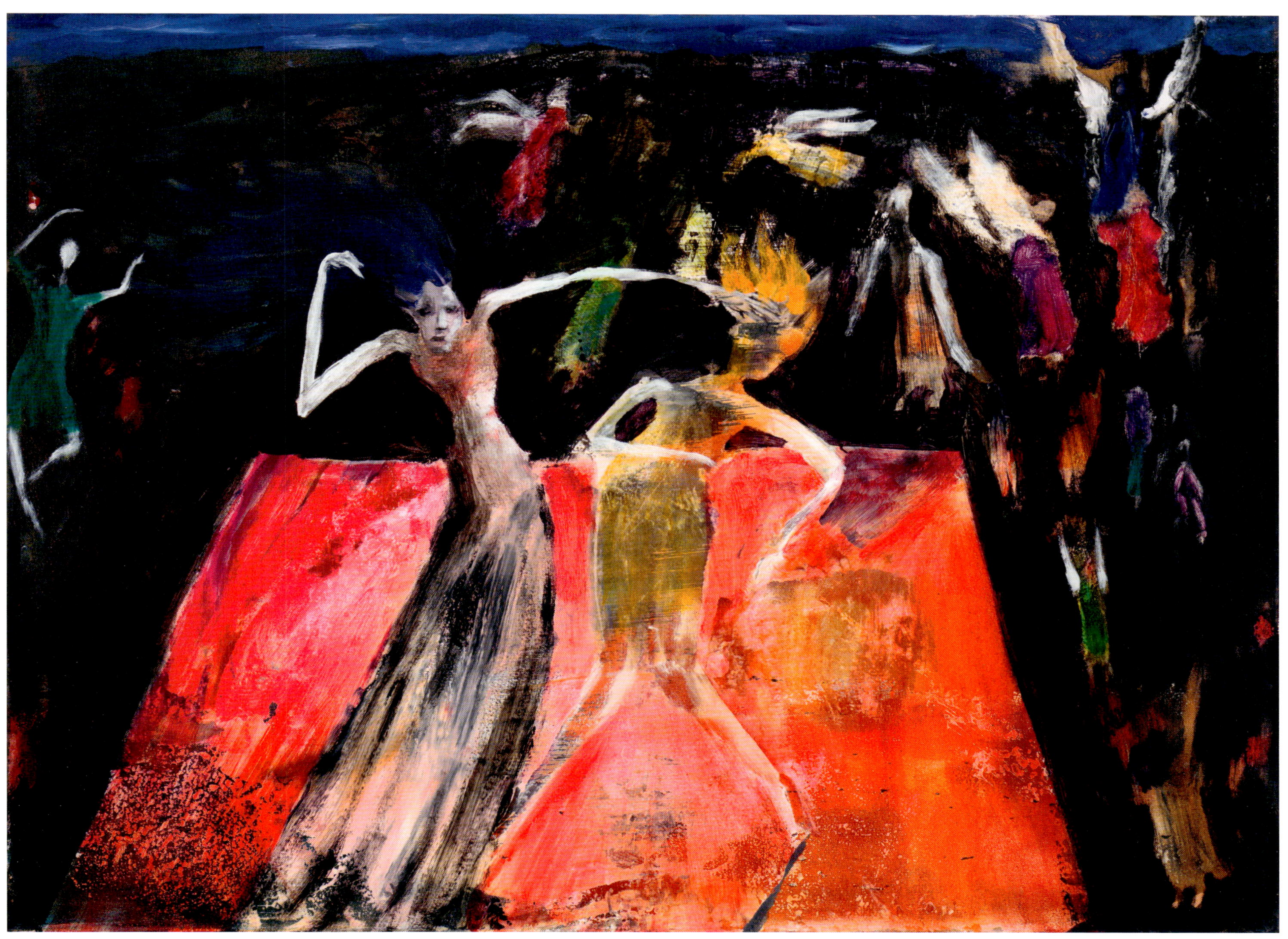

THE RESURRECTION OF MAMMIWATTI 2018 Oil on canvas 250 × 170cm

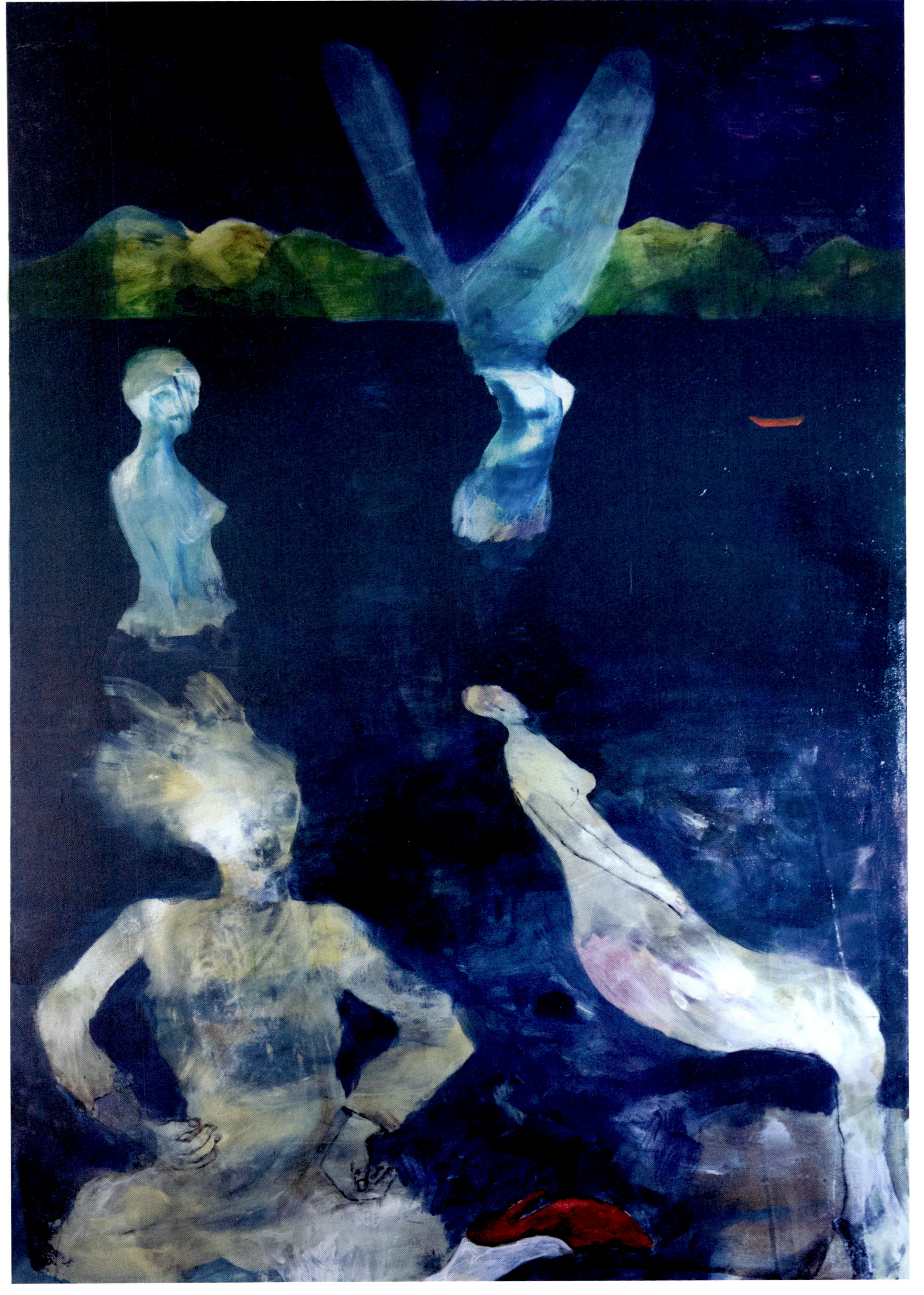

RAINBOW RACE 2018 Oil on canvas 92 × 122cm

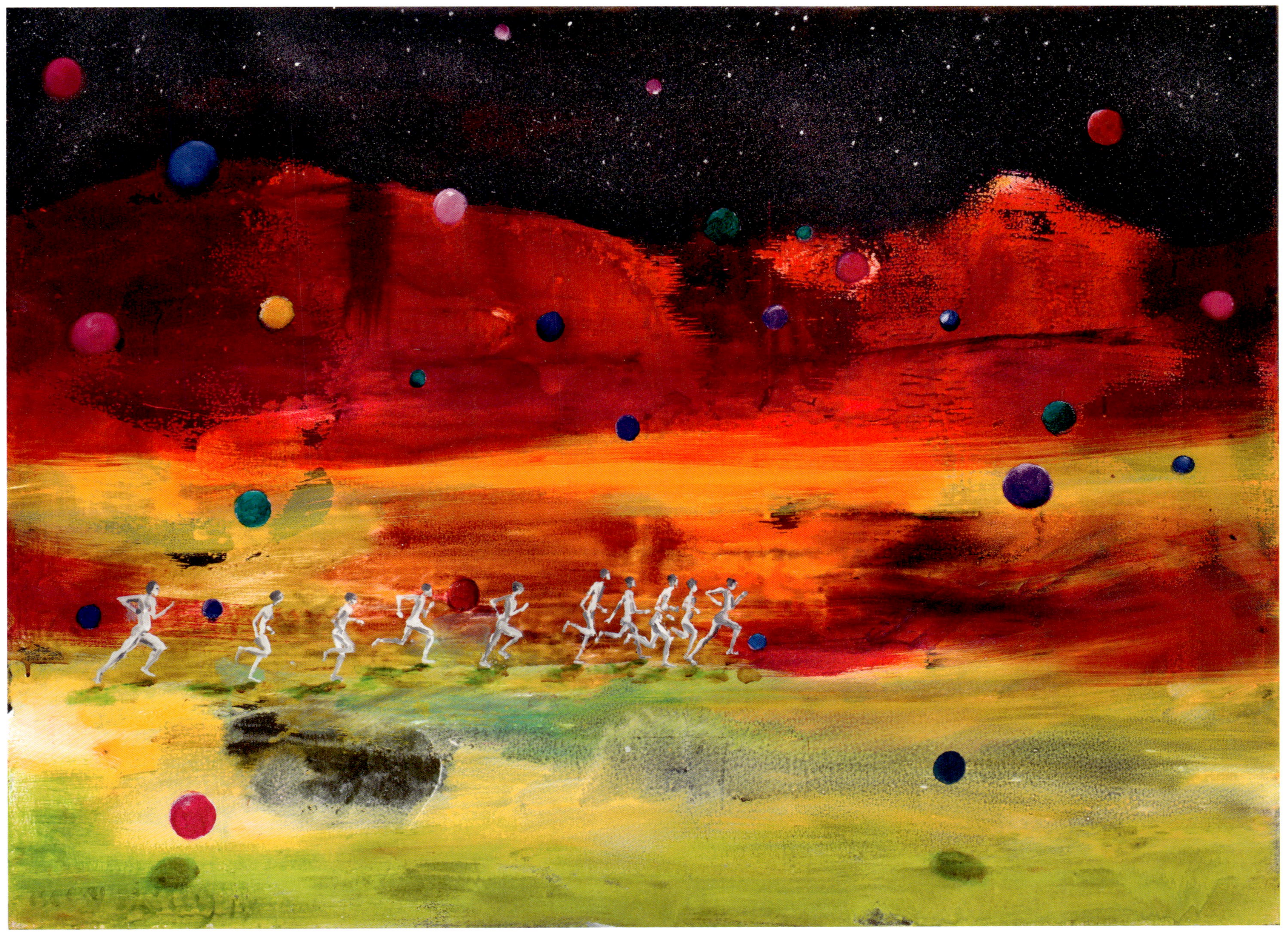

GLASS PURPLE PLANETS 2018 Oil on canvas 250 × 170cm

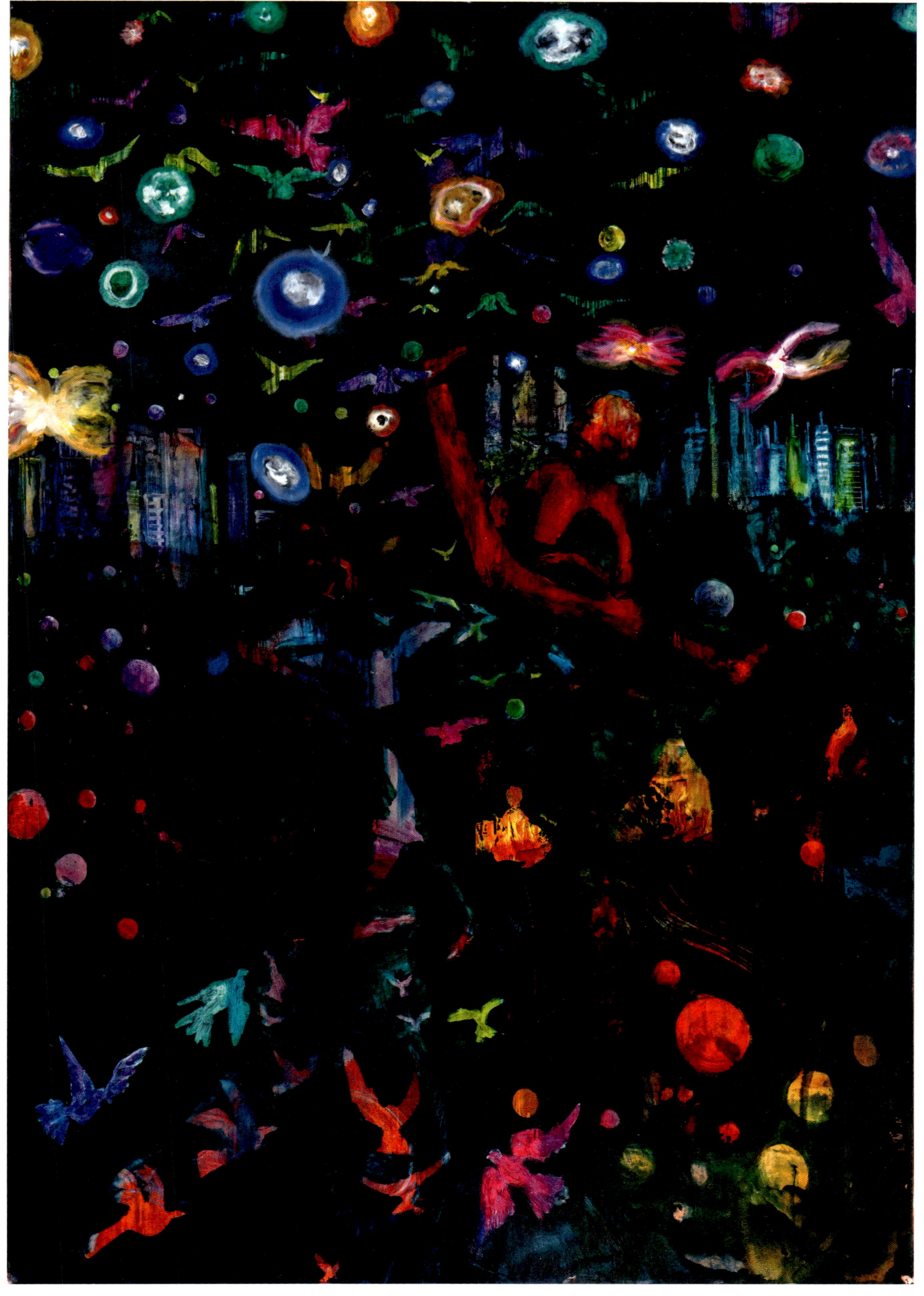

THE SKY FELL DOWN AS THE FAT MAN DANCED 2018 Oil on canvas 170 × 250cm

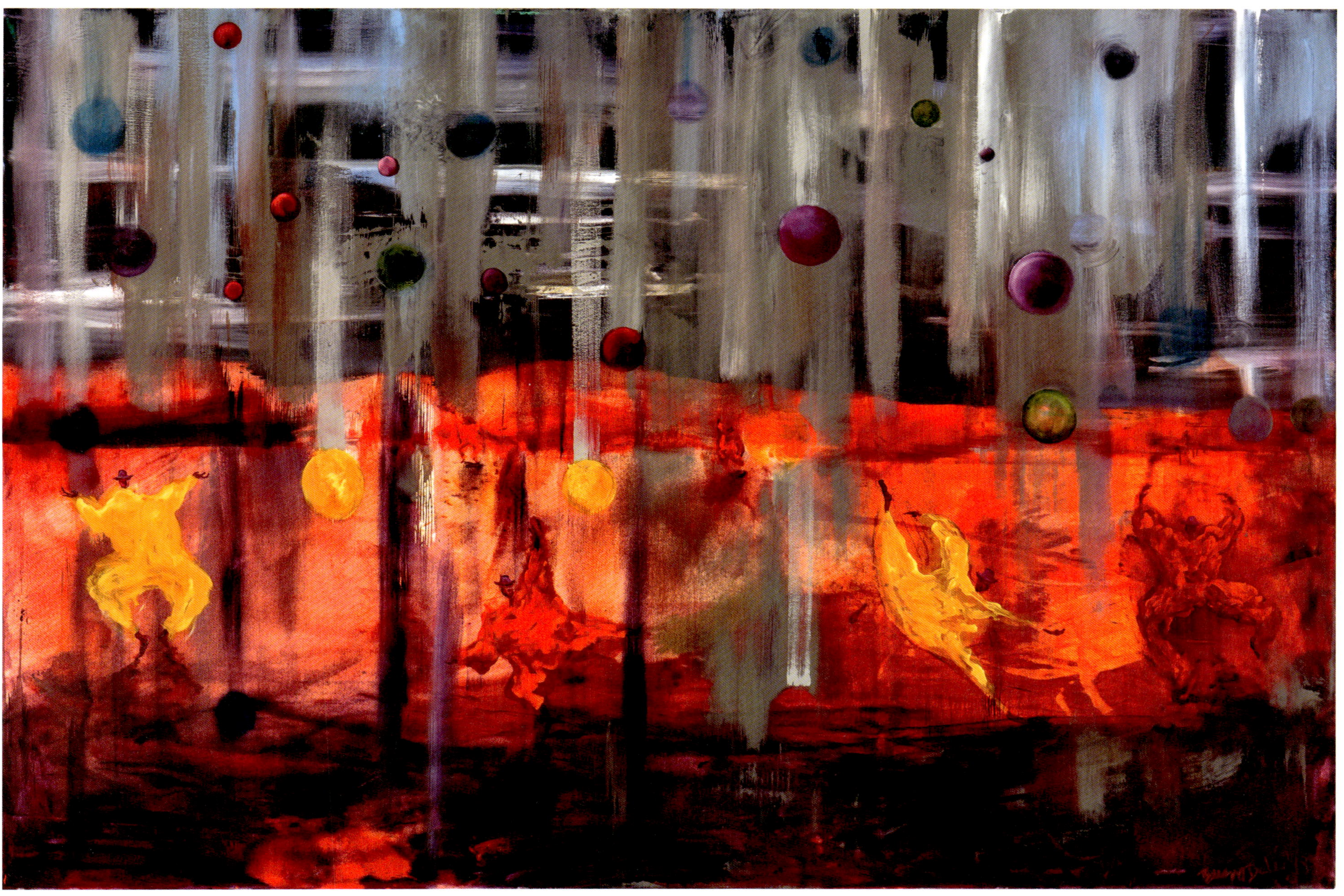

THE MOON CRIED WHEN THE ELEPHANT DIED AND THE POACHER RAN TO HIDE 2018 Oil on canvas 90 × 120cm

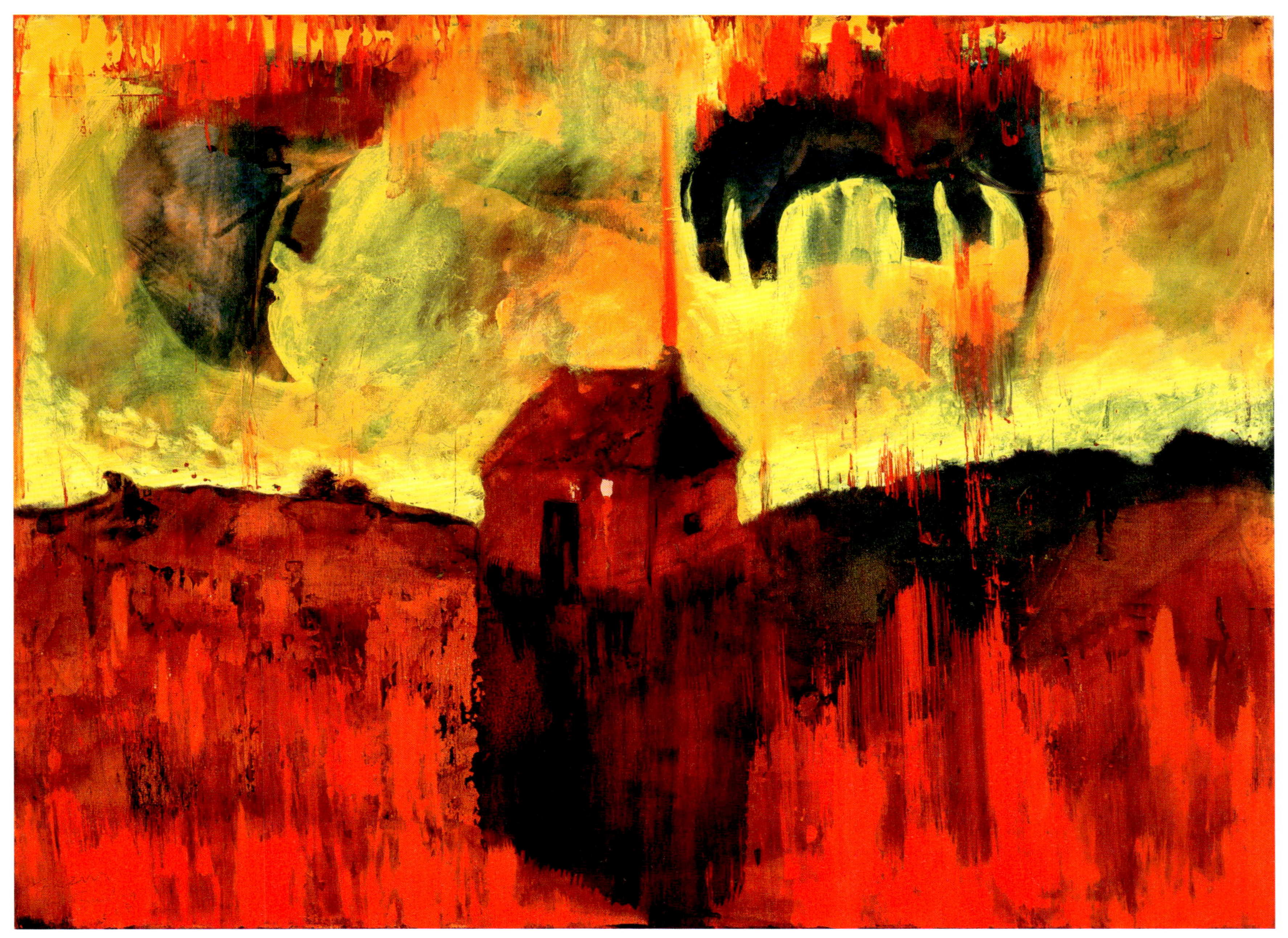

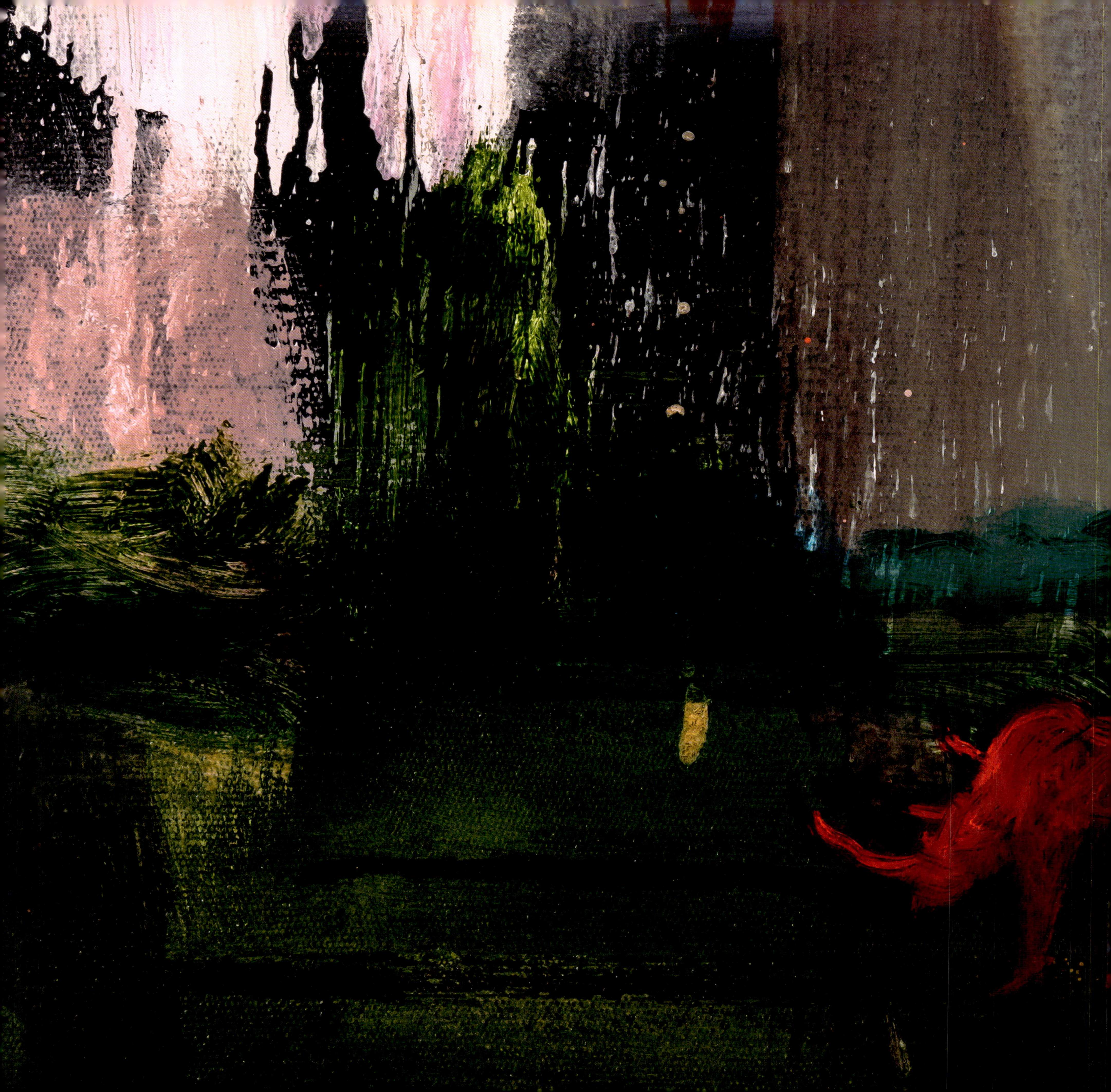

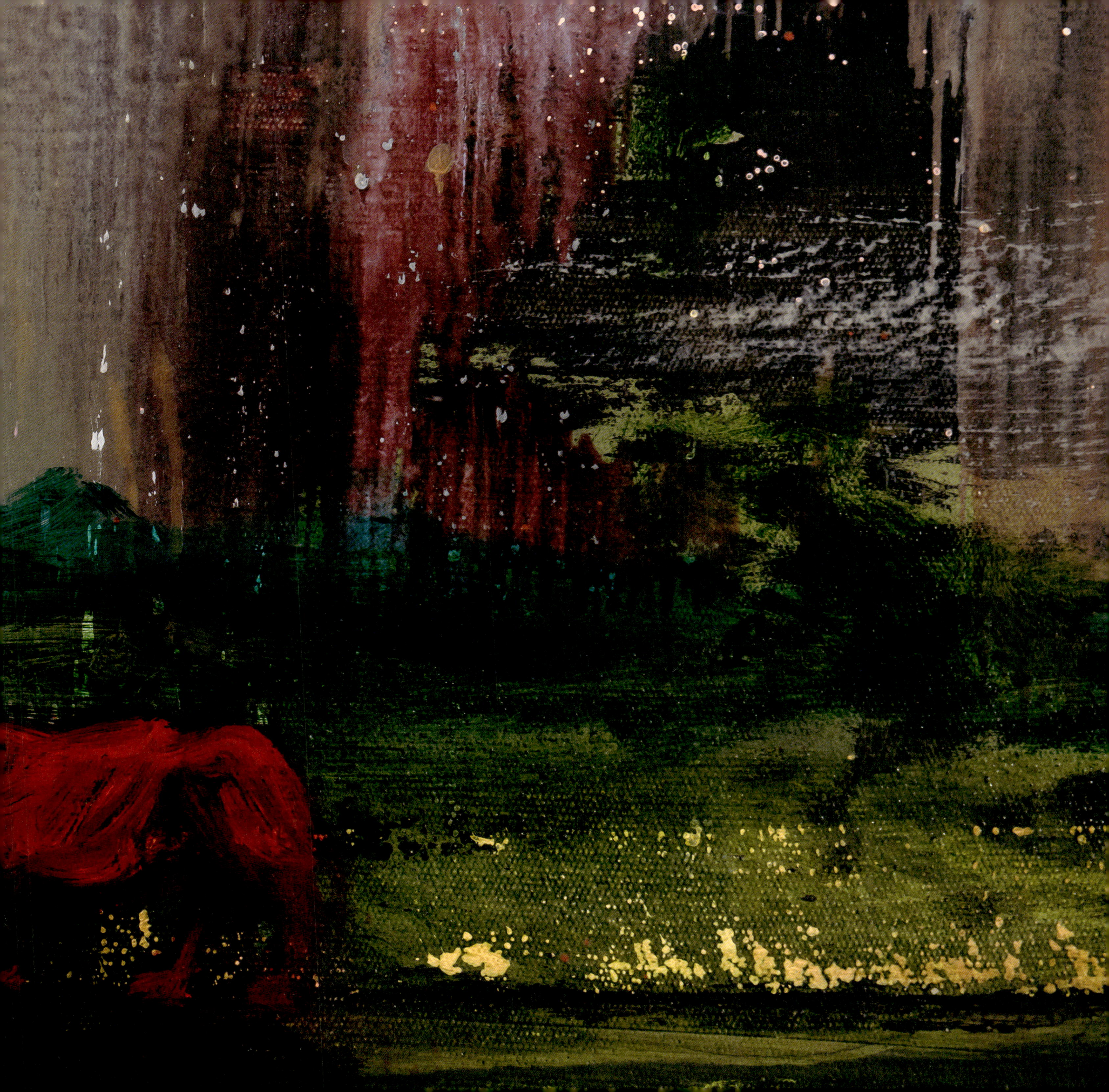

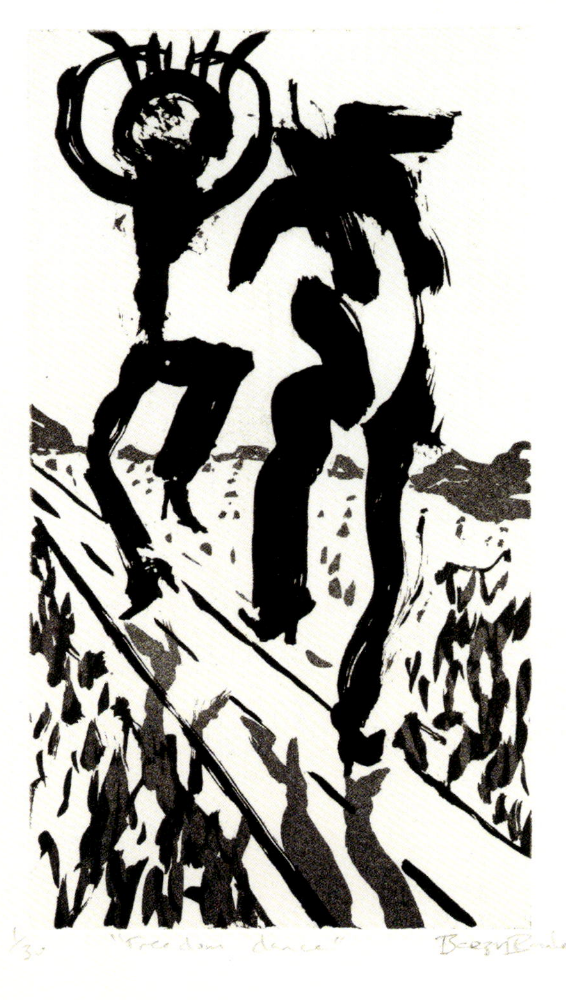

FREEDOM DANCE 2018 Copperplate etching 50 × 33cm

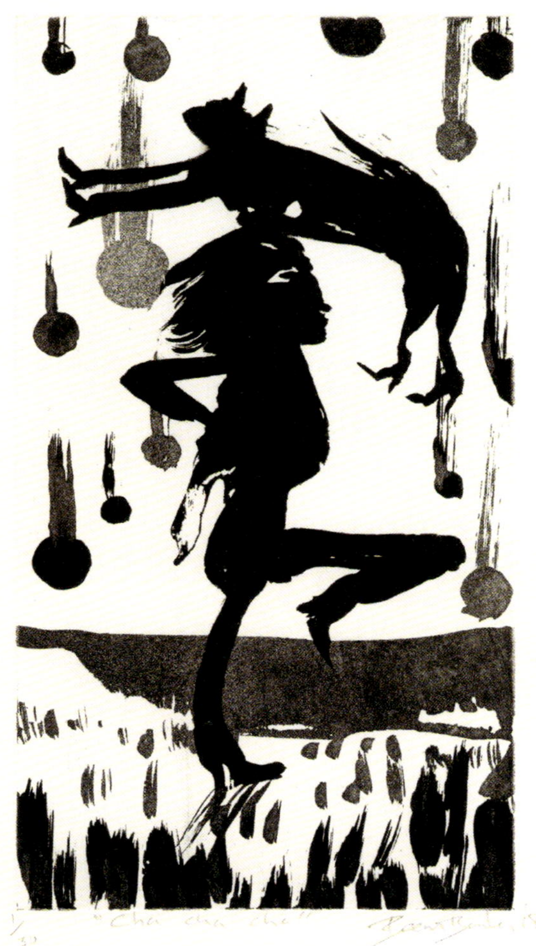

CHA CHA CHA 2018 Copperplate etching 50 × 33cm

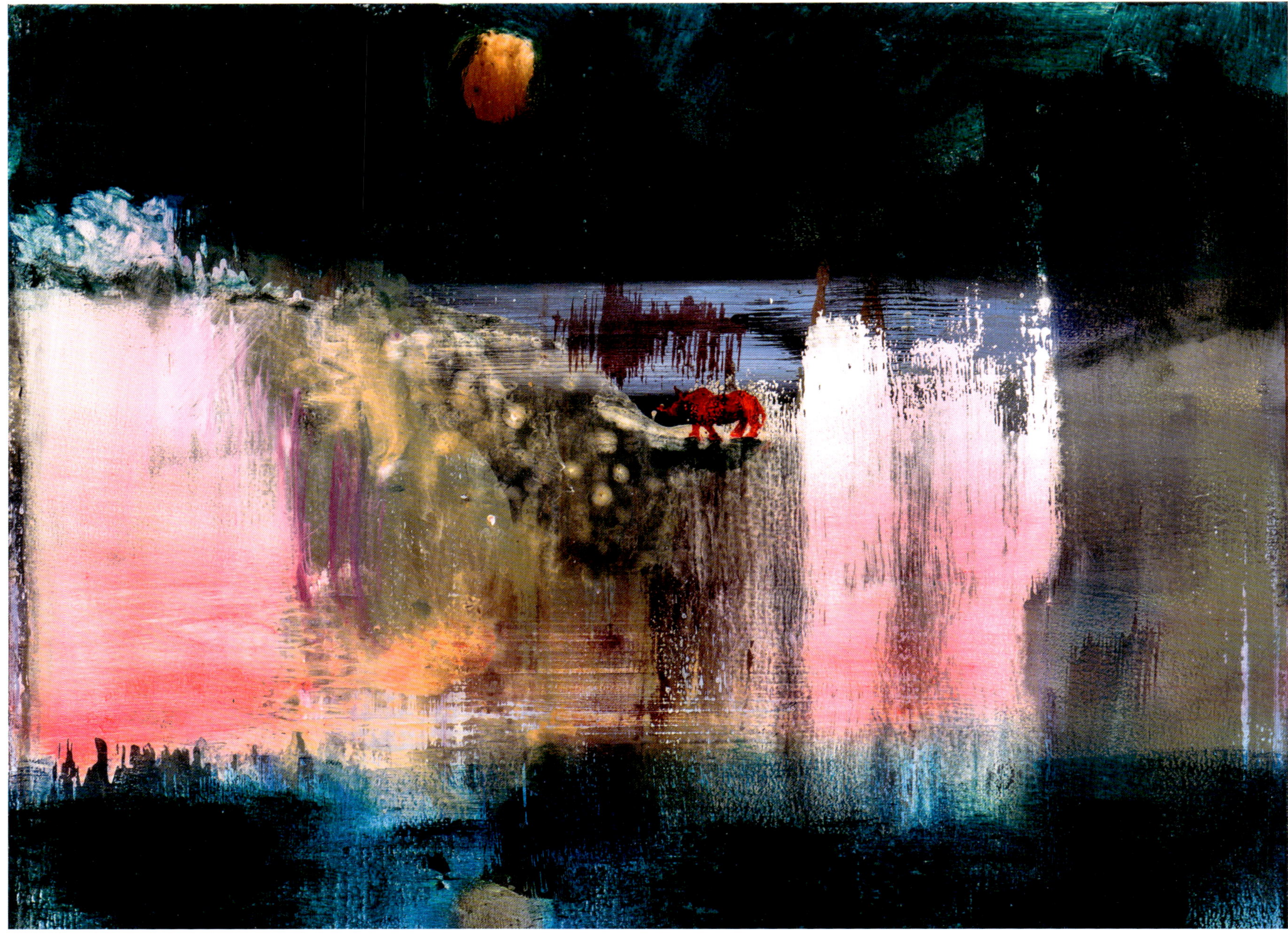

LONELY PLANET 2018 Oil on canvas 60 × 75cm

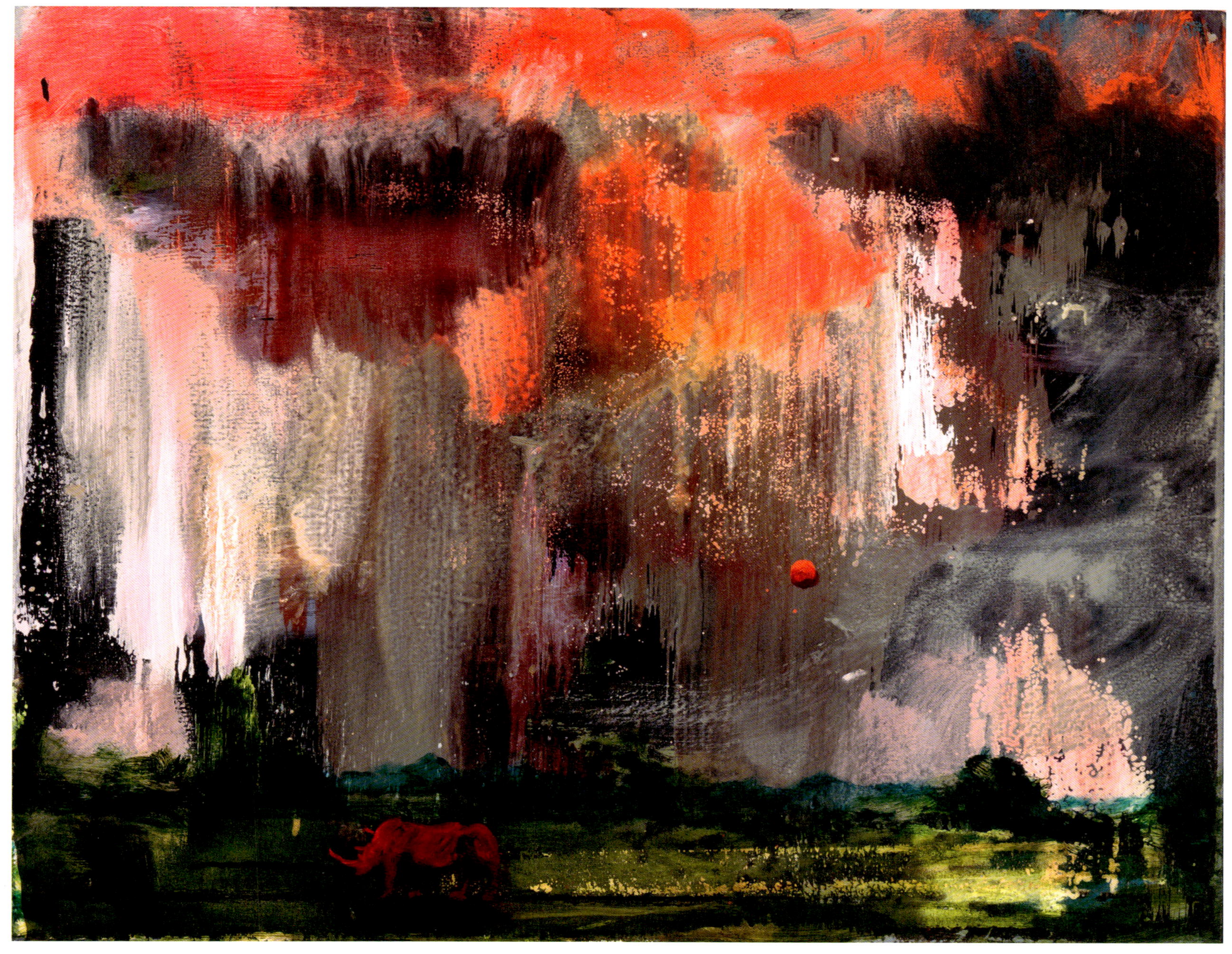

THE NIGHT OF THE RED MOON 2018 Oil on canvas 60 × 75cm

THE GRASS IS REDDER ON THE OTHER SIDE 2018 Oil and silkscreen on canvas 170 × 250cm

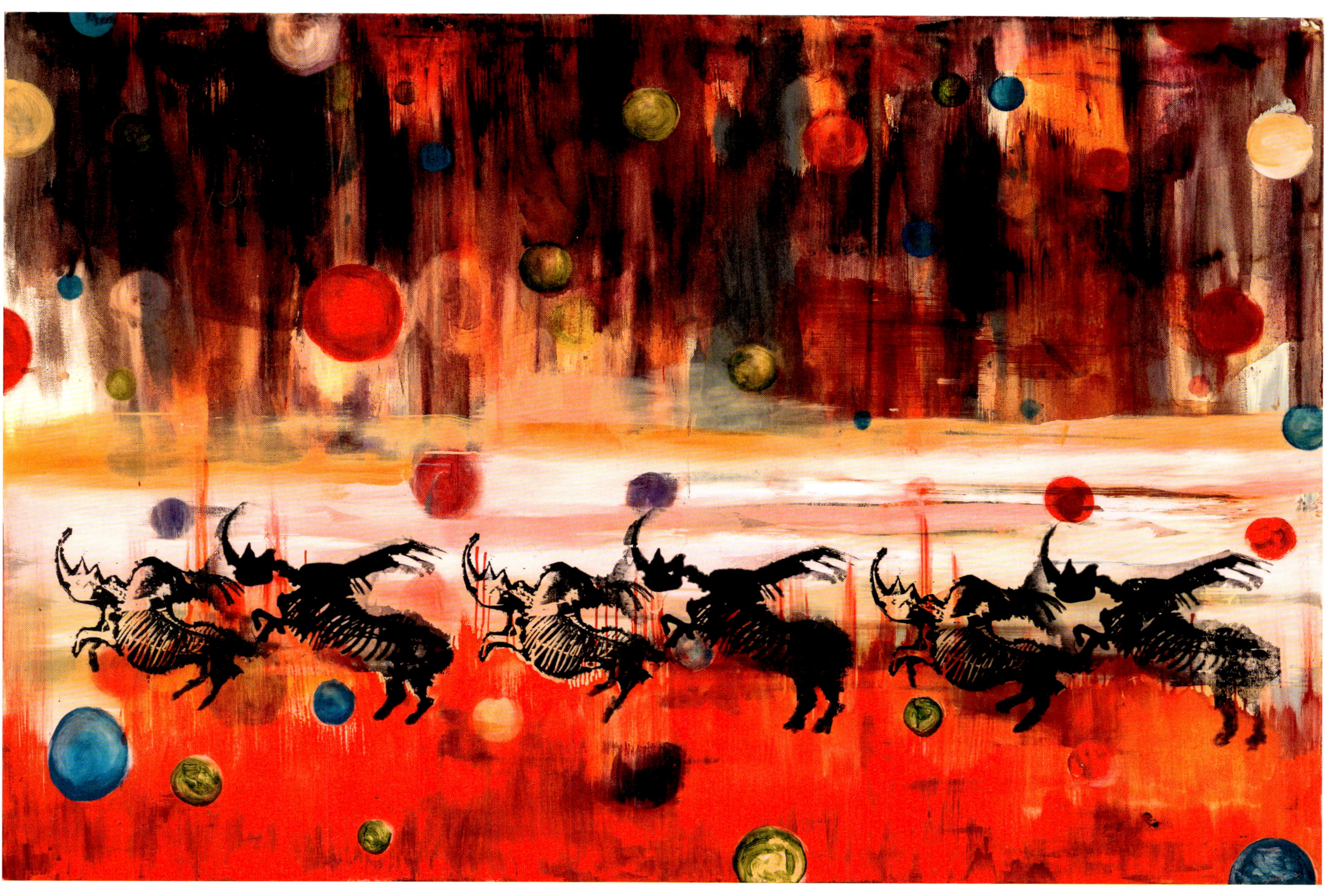

YOU CAN RUN BUT YOU CAN'T HIDE 2018 Oil on canvas 70 × 90cm

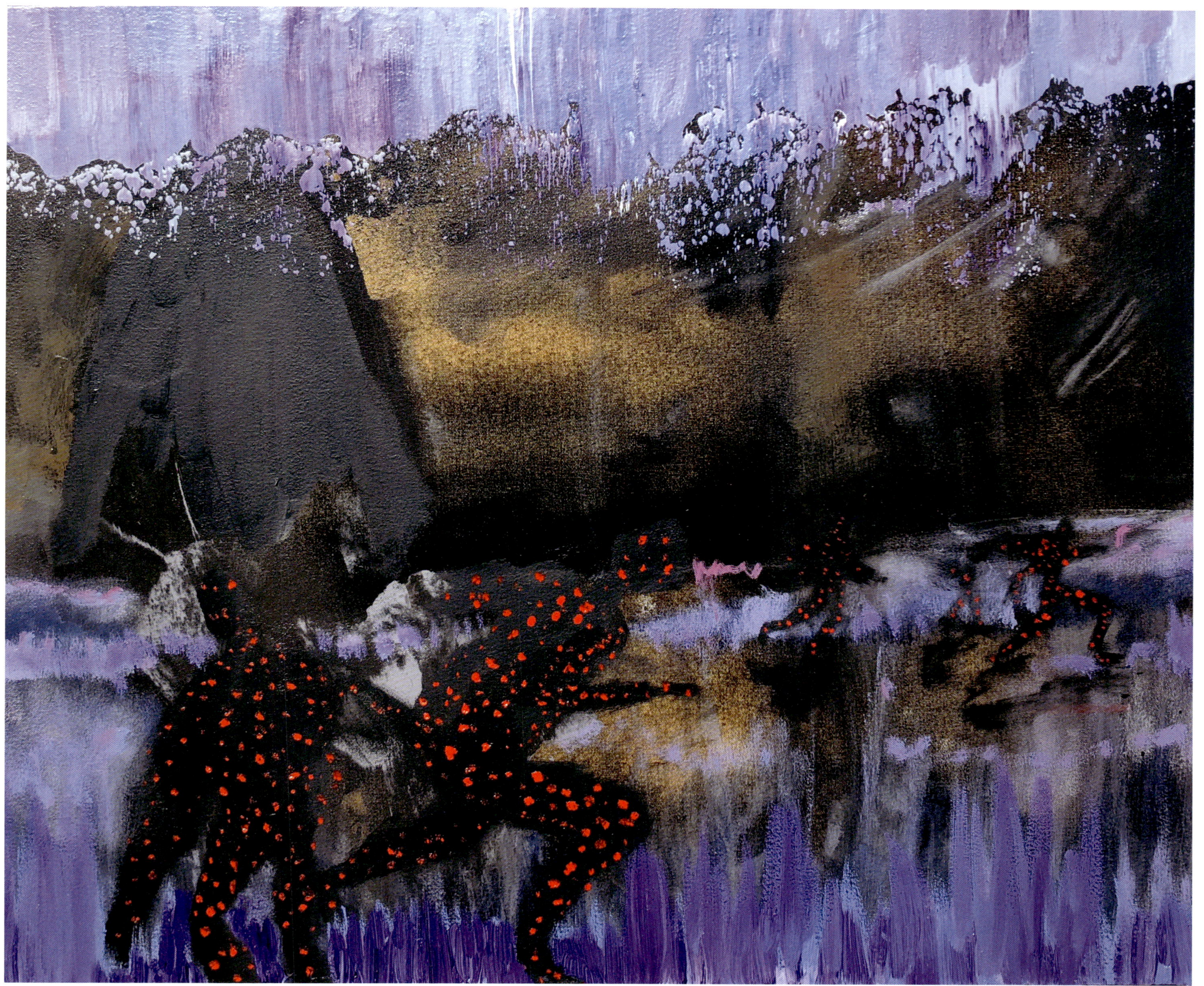

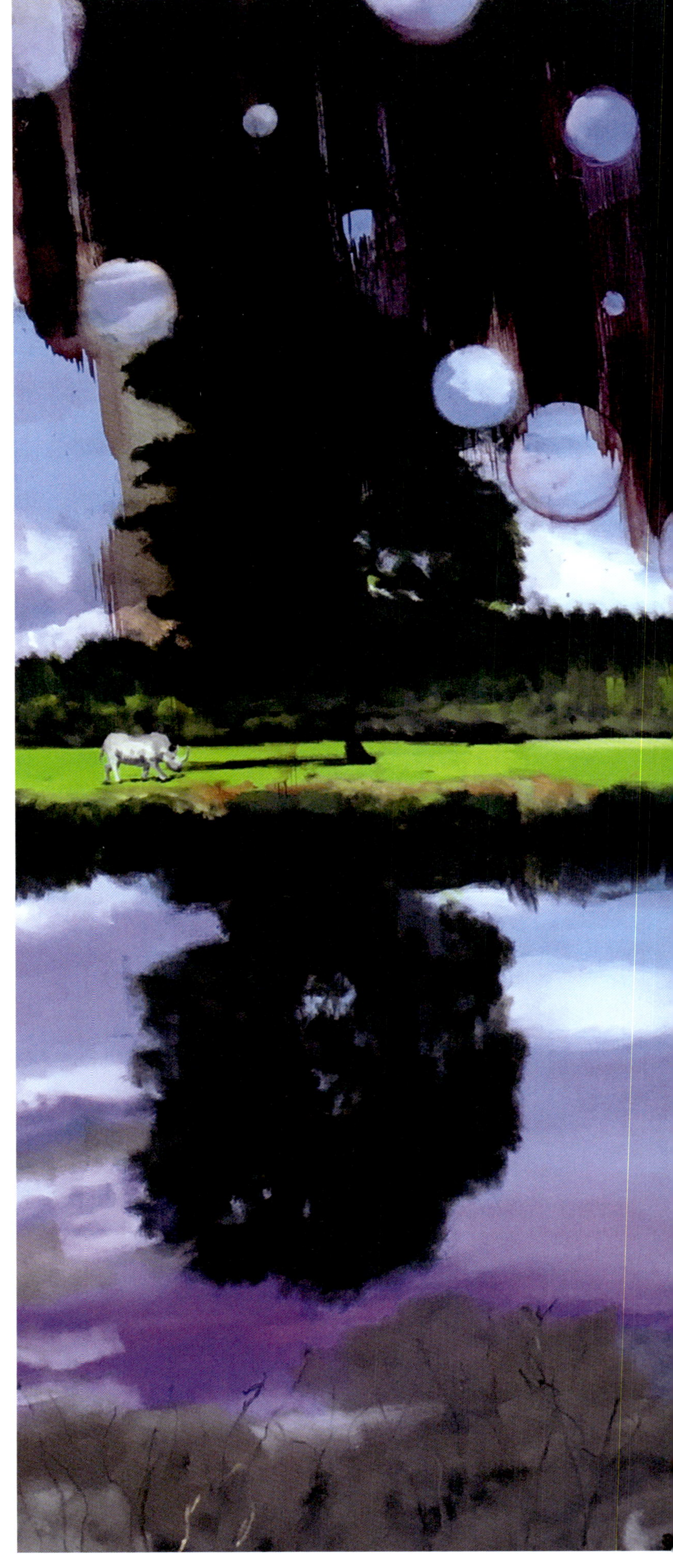

THE GRASS IS ALWAYS GREENER ON THE OTHER SIDE 2018
Oil on canvas 170 × 250cm

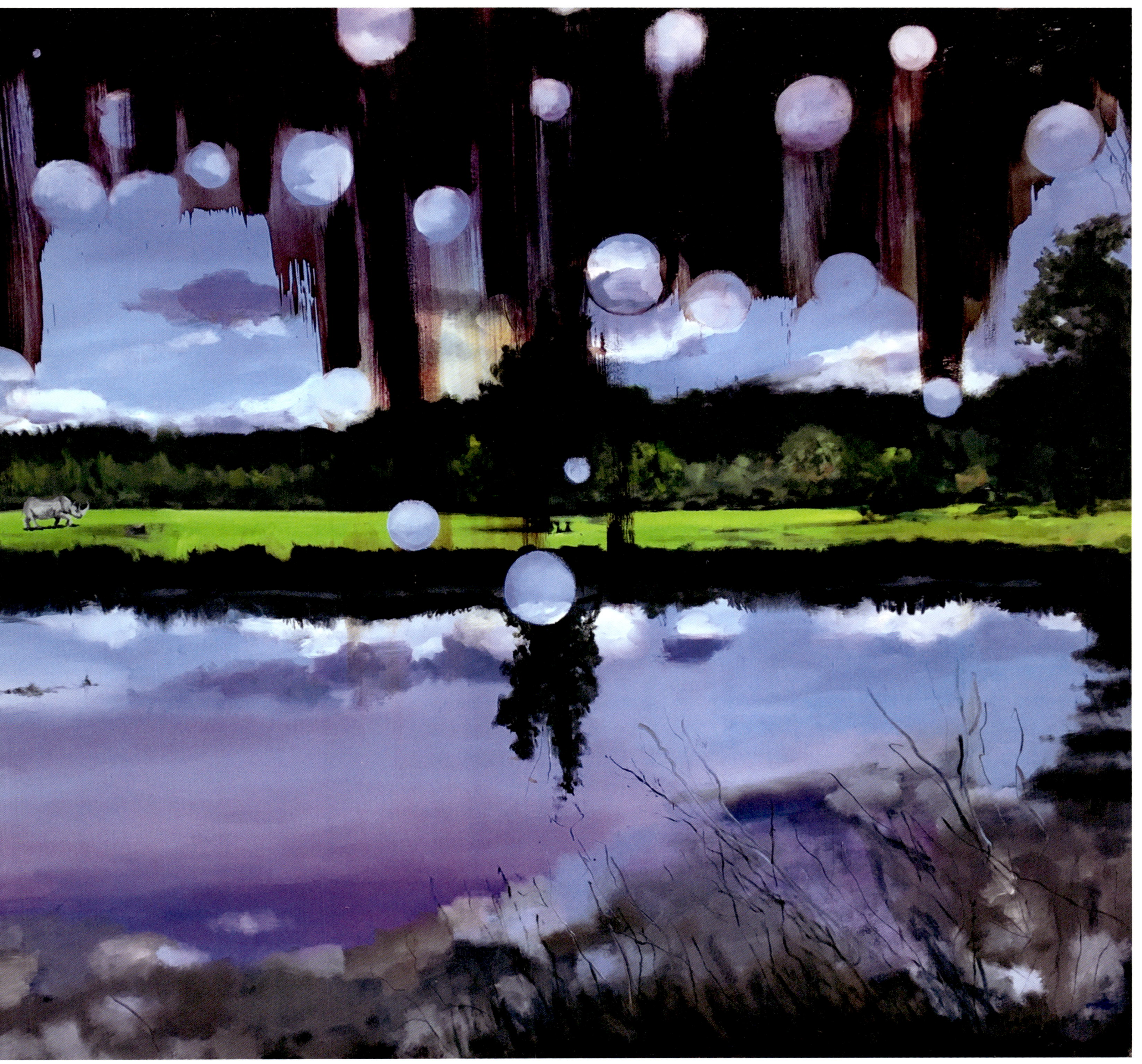

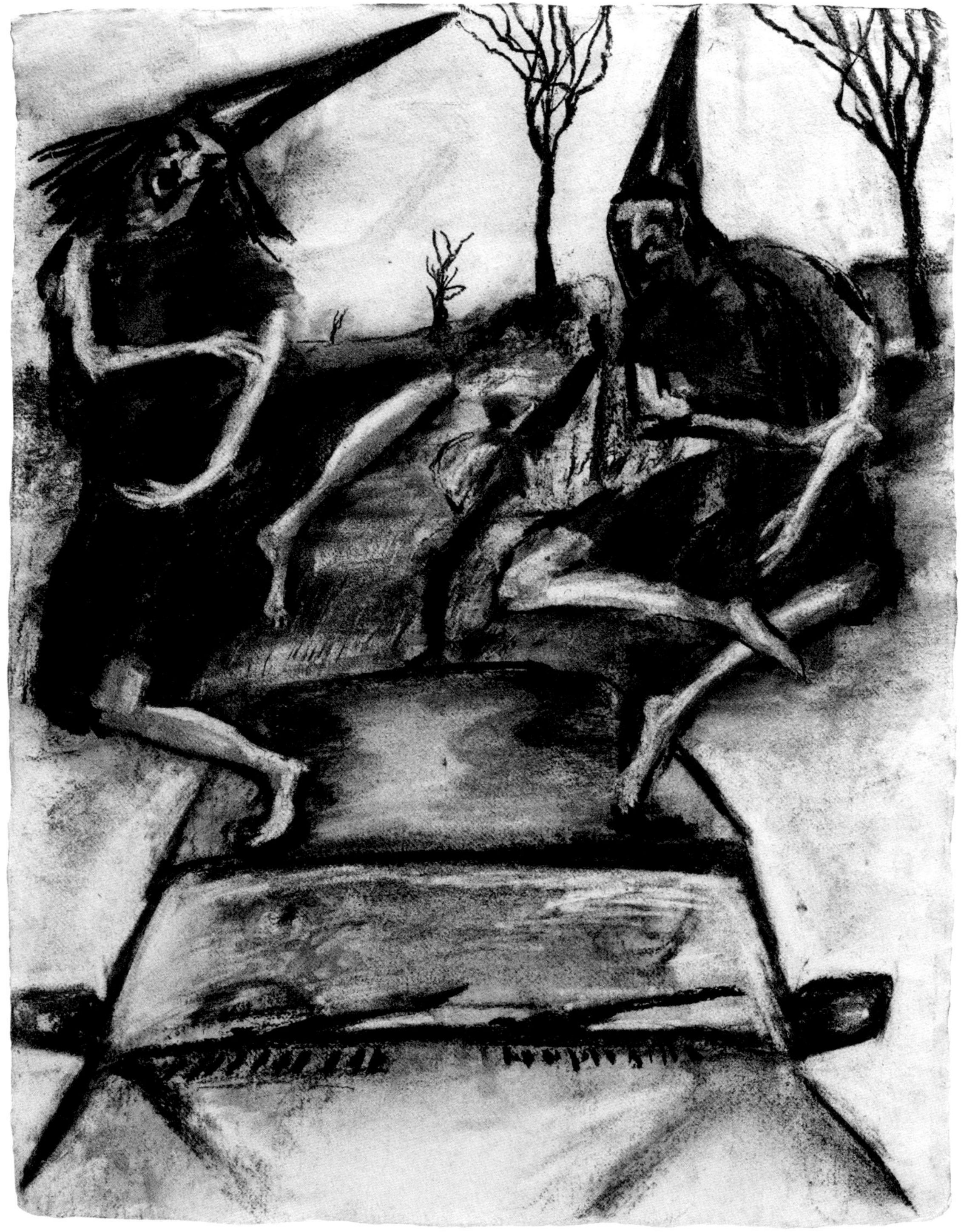

CLICKITY CLACK ON THE ROOF OF THE ROLLS 2018 Charcoal on handmade paper 75 × 57cm

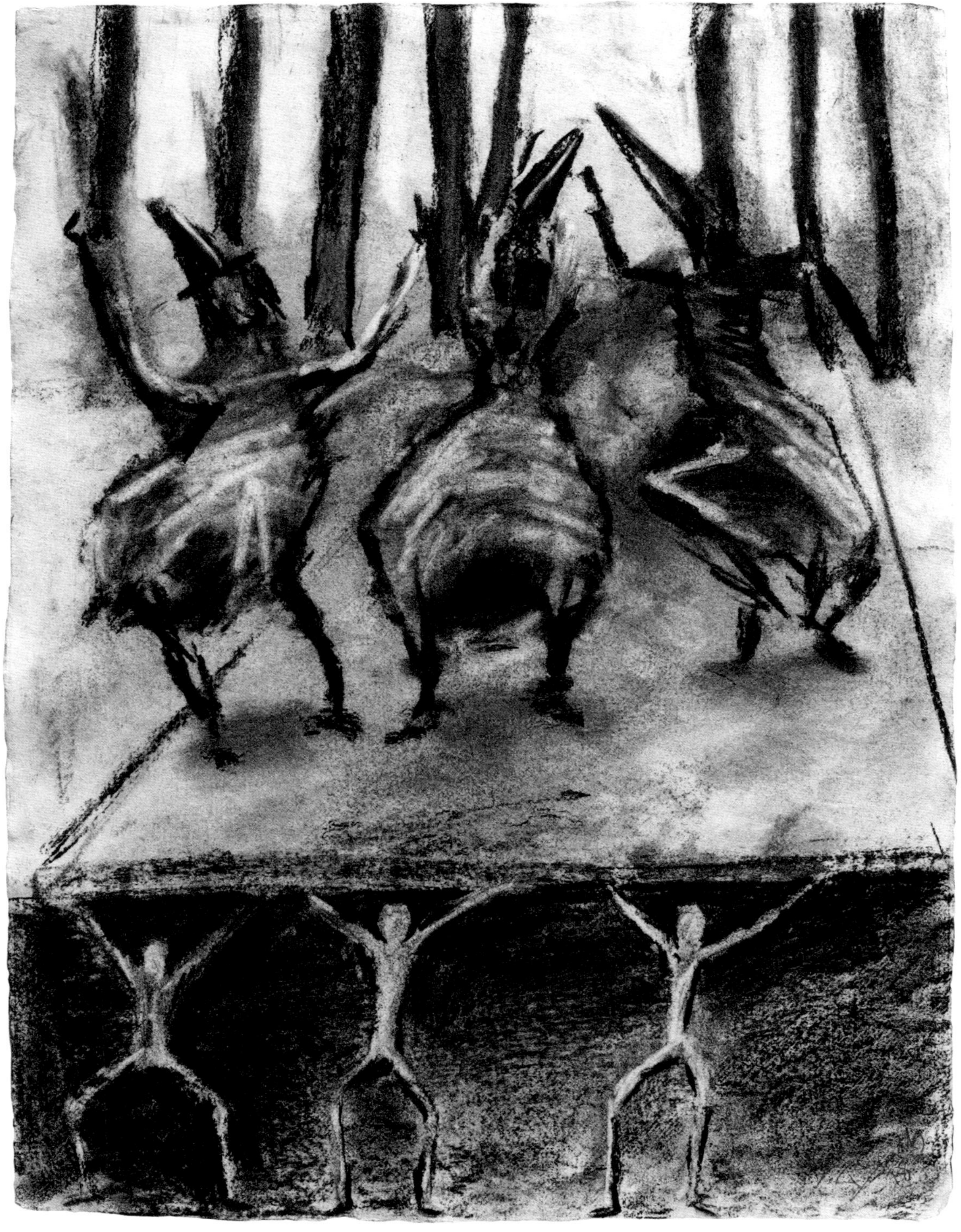

UPON THE STAGE OF LIFE THE WITCHES DANCED 2018 Charcoal on handmade paper 75 × 57cm

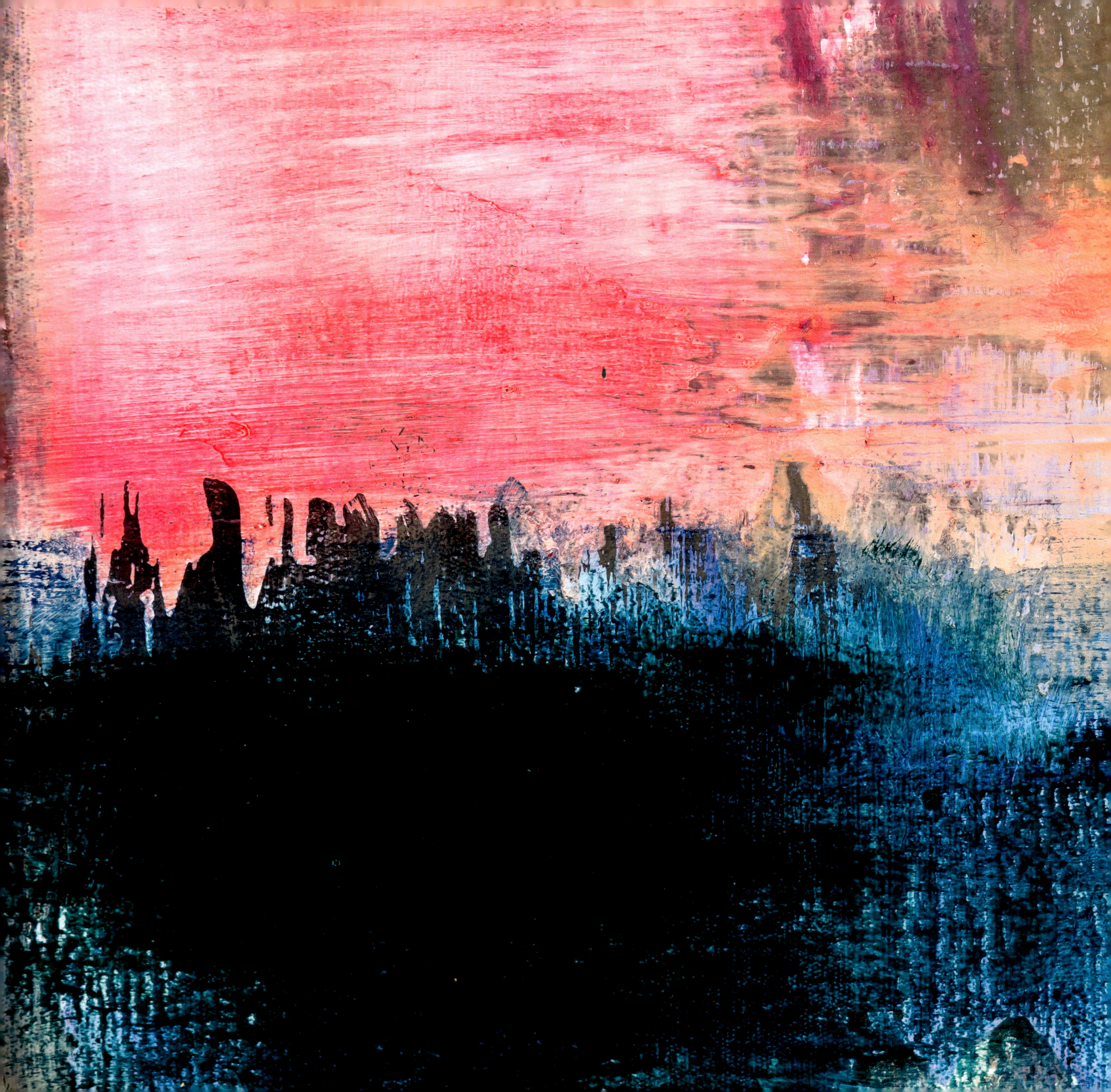

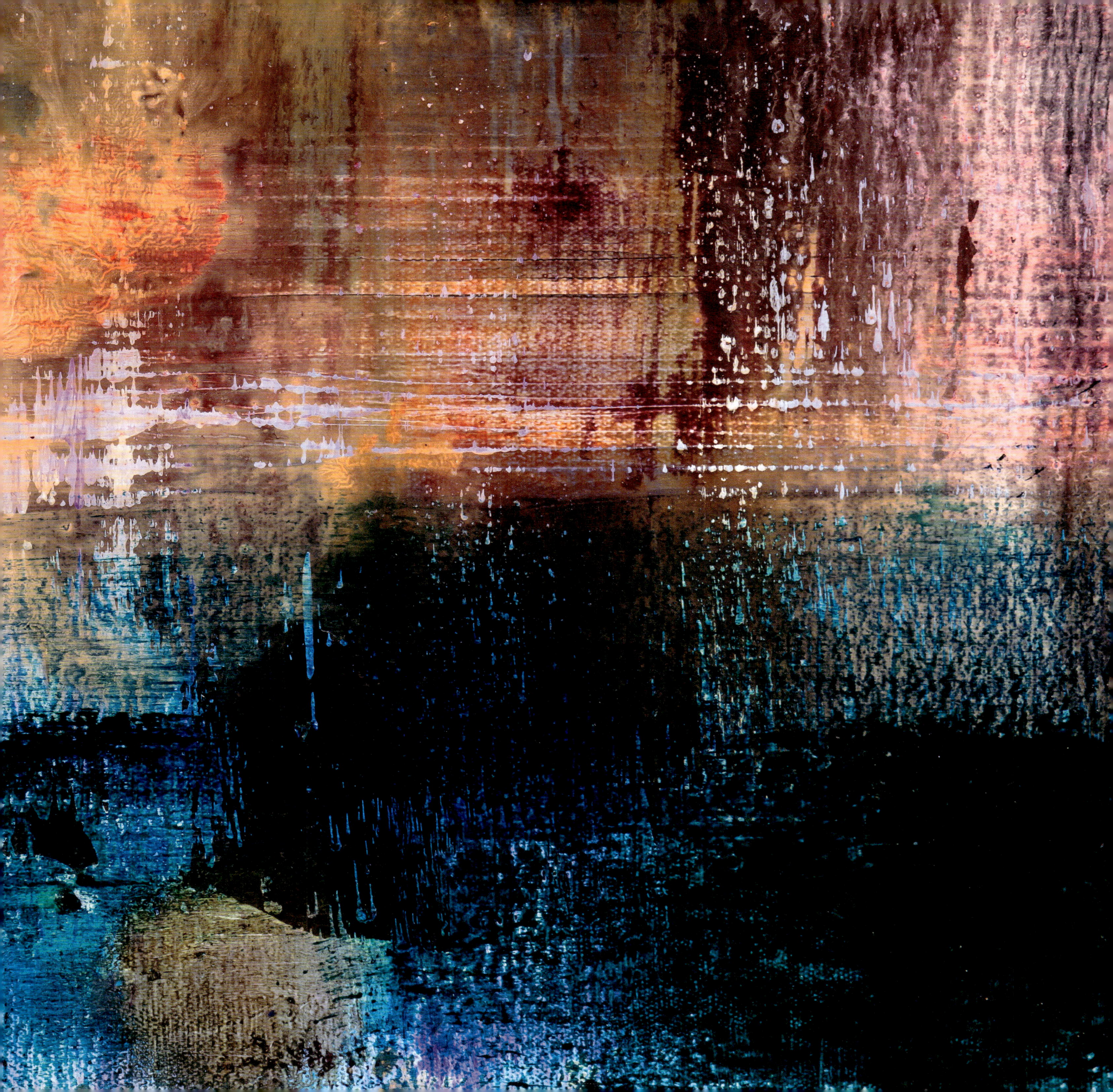

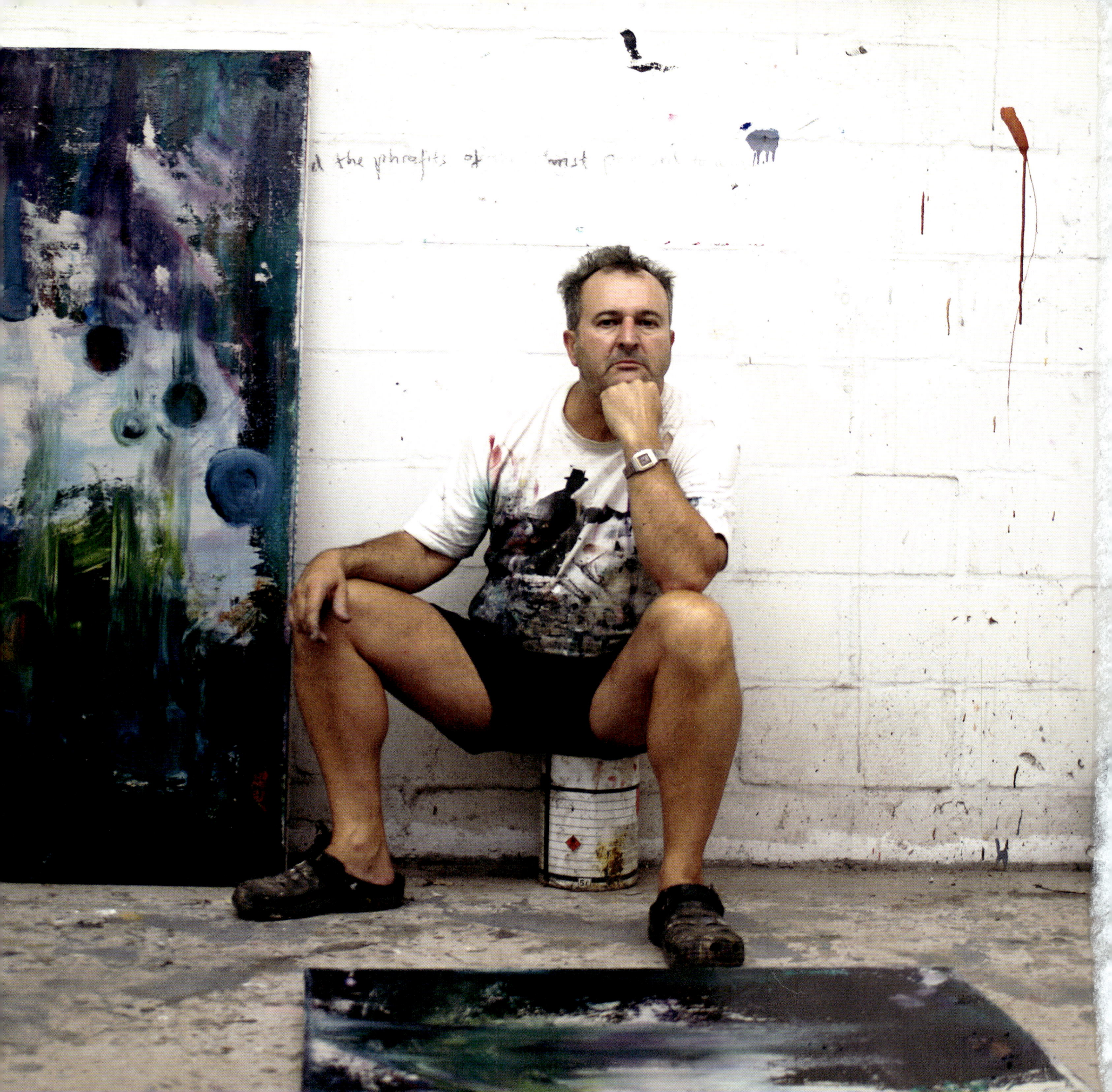

Biography

Beezy Bailey (b. 1962, Johannesburg, South Africa) is a multi-disciplinary artist whose practice includes painting, sculpture, drawing, printmaking and ceramics.

He studied Fine Art at the Byam Shaw School of Art, in London (1983–6). Over a thirty-five-year career, he has exhibited in South Africa and internationally. In 2011 he had a solo exhibition at the Chenshia Museum in Wuhan, China; and in 2015 he was part of the official programme at the Venice Biennale. He has a history of close collaboration with other artists, most notably David Bowie, Brian Eno and Dave Matthews.

Bailey's work is represented in important art collections around the world, including the David Bowie Collection, the Getty Family Collection and the Oppenheimer Collection. His work is also in the permanent collections of Sasol, Standard Bank, Investec Bank, the Kunsthaus Zurich, and the South African National Gallery.

Selected Exhibitions

2018
Light Beyond the Dark, solo exhibition, Everard Read Gallery, London

2017
Summer Exhibition, Everard Read Gallery, London
People and Portraiture, CIRCA Gallery, Cape Town

2016
Inaugural Exhibition, Everard Read Gallery, London
1000 Year Dance Cure, inaugural exhibition, CIRCA Gallery, Cape Town
Winter Collection, group exhibition, Everard Read Gallery, Cape Town

2015
The Sound of Creation, Sound Paintings by Beezy Bailey and Brian Eno, 56th International Art Exhibition, La Biennale di Venezia, Venice

2014
Landscapes with a Twist, solo exhibition, Everard Read Gallery, Johannesburg
Itica Pritica, two-man exhibition with Dave Mathews, Everard Read Gallery, Cape Town

2013
As it is in Heaven, solo exhibition, Everard Read Gallery, Cape Town
Itica Pritica, two-man exhibition with Dave Matthews, Robert Miller Gallery, New York

2012
As it is in Heaven, solo exhibition, CIRCA Gallery, Johannesburg
Winter Exhibition, group exhibition, Everard Read Gallery, Cape Town
10,000 Trees Landscape, greening project for the Cape Flats, Cape Town

2011
Icon-Iconoclast, solo exhibition, Everard Read Gallery, Johannesburg
Fifteenth Anniversary, group exhibition, Everard Read Gallery, Cape Town

2009
Dancing Christ, solo exhibition, Spring Art Tour, Everard Read Gallery, Cape Town
Sex Power Money, group exhibition, Everard Read Gallery, Cape Town

2008
Being Blown Backwards into the Future, solo exhibition, Everard Read Gallery, Johannesburg

2007
Fallen Angels & Other Dreams, solo exhibition, Everard Read Gallery, Cape Town

2006
Collaborative work produced with Zwelethu Mthethwa was acquired by the Kunsthalle Wien, Vienna
A collection of forty-five paintings was acquired by the Ojai Valley Museum in California

2005
Solo exhibition, Everard Read Gallery, Johannesburg

2004/5
Collaboration with Zwelethu Mthethwa, Prague Biennale

2004
Solo exhibition, Everard Read Gallery, Johannesburg
Solo exhibition, Knysna Fine Art, Knysna

2002
Brian Eno and Joyce Ntobe project (collaboration with Zwelethu Mthethwa)
Curated the Art for Aids Orphans auction, November 2002

2001
Photographic collaboration with Zwelethu Mthethwa
Vanessa Branson commission: statues and a mural in the UK
Ongoing exhibition of graphic works and watercolours at the Art Factory, Cape Town

2000
Back to the Drawing Board, Pa Kua Gallery, Cape Town. Solo exhibition of ink-on-paper life drawings with live drawing performance on the opening night.

1999
Abakwetha – Farmer, Warrior, Statesman. Intervention, Parliament, Cape Town. Part of a public sculpture festival to commemorate Heritage Day. The bronze statue of Boer War General Louis Botha, outside Parliament, was transformed into a Xhosa initiate wearing a traditional blanket and hat, with his face painted with white clay. The statue's transformation received extensive international press and TV coverage.
Ju-ju and the Blue Zulu, performance at Red Eye, Durban Art Gallery. Bailey appeared at the pop-culture event Red Eye as Flying Man San and – naked but for a coat of blue paint, wings, goggles and a propeller hat – painted a self-portrait using an ultra-long brush.
Learning to Fly Again, Art Factory, Cape Town, solo exhibition of prints and paintings on the theme of a fantastical flying contraption, depicting Flying Man San's attempts to touch the sky.
Lee Ping Zing, performance at Womad Music Festival, Benoni

1998
Solo exhibition, Art Factory, Cape Town, an exhibition of ceramics and hand-coloured prints produced at the Art Factory.
Fabric of the People, Art Factory, Cape Town. Choreographed by South African director Brett Bailey, this open-air theatre event showcased fabric, clothing and homeware designed by Bailey for the Art Factory, using untrained models and actors, including street people.

Beezy Bailey Art Factory opening, Cape Town. The Art Factory was a project aimed at closing the gap between fine art and popular culture. Bailey collaborated with Koos Malgas of the Owl House on the design of the building's facade. The Factory included ceramics and printmaking studios, an art gallery, and a shop that sold printed fabrics and homeware.
Group exhibition, Augsburg: exhibition by five South African artists – Beezy Bailey, Gail Catlin, Paul du Toit, Xolile Mtakatya and Robert Slingsby.
Driftscapes, Hänel Gallery, Cape Town, solo exhibition of mixed media works incorporating found objects, driftwood and plywood constructions, and coastal landscape paintings.

1997
District Six Sculpture Festival, District Six, Cape Town. An outdoor group exhibition in commemoration of communities forcibly removed from their homes in District Six during apartheid. Bailey's contribution was to paint the trunk of a dead tree a blazing, fluorescent red.
'A highly effective and affecting symbol for the day' – Sue Williamson, *ArtThrob*, October 1997.

1996
Through the Looking Glass, Jibby Beane Gallery, London. Lee Ping Zing paintings were included in a group exhibition of works projected onto the exterior of the gallery, alongside contributions from David Bowie, Brian Eno and Langlands & Bell.

1995
Beezy Bailey/Joyce Ntobe, Goodman Gallery, Johannesburg. An exhibition of paintings and chainsaw-carved wooden heads, alongside conceptual works by Bailey's alter ego, the black domestic worker Joyce Ntobe.
Collaboration with David Bowie, London and New York. Paintings and drawings created with David Bowie were exhibited in joint exhibitions in London and New York; collaborative works were also included in David Bowie's solo exhibitions at The Gallery in Cork Street, London, in April 1995 and at the Daniel Blaise Thorens Gallery, Basel, in May 1996.

1994
Exquisite Corpses, Chelsea Gallery, Cape Town, a solo exhibition of etchings produced in collaboration with various South African artists, including Norman Catherine, Barend de Wet and Billy Mandindi.
Vote for South Africa, South African Association of Arts Performance work to mark the first democratic elections in South Africa.
Touring print exhibition, Florida State University: prints by Bailey and his alter ego, the black domestic worker Joyce Ntobe, were included in a group exhibition of prints that toured three American states.

1993
Two Collaborations, South African Association of Arts, Cape Town. Bailey exhibited concrete sculptures made in collaboration with Koos Malgas (assistant to Helen Martins at the Owl House sculpture garden in the Karoo) and painted photographs in collaboration with Adam Letch.
The Incisive Eye, group exhibition, Arts Association of Bellville, Cape Town
The Cape of Great Hope, group exhibition, Visual Arts Foundation, Johannesburg
Made in Wood, group exhibition, South African National Gallery, Cape Town

1992
Landscapes, exhibition with two artists at The Art Scene, Cape Town
Joyce Ntobe/Beezy Bailey, Market Galleries, Johannesburg. 'Group exhibition' in which Bailey exhibited linocuts and sculptures by Joyce Ntobe, and works based on material from the Drum/Bailey African Photo Archives.
Joyce Ntobe/Beezy Bailey: South African Association of Arts, Cape Town

1991
New Directions, group exhibition of sculpture, Centre for African Studies and Michaelis School of Fine Art, University of Cape Town
Solo exhibition, Gallery on the Market, Johannesburg
Solo exhibition, Desré Resnick Art Gallery, Cape Town

1990
Solo exhibition, South African Association of Arts, Cape Town

1989
Artist in residence, South African National Gallery, Cape Town
Solo exhibition, Karen McKerron Gallery, Johannesburg
Solo exhibition, Cadres d'Ésprit, Cape Town

1988
Harbour Paintings, solo exhibition, The Art Scene, Cape Town
Dove of Peace, solo exhibition, The Art Scene, Cape Town
Cape Town Triennial, national touring group exhibition and competition, South African National Gallery, Cape Town, and Johannesburg Art Gallery
Introducing Beezy Bailey, solo exhibition, Vanessa Devereux Gallery, London
Live Painting Performance, 5 Roodehek Street, Cape Town

1987
Landscapes from France and Namibia, exhibition with two other artists, Karen McKerron Gallery, Johannesburg
Standard Bank Drawing Exhibition, group exhibition, South Africa
Solo exhibition, Gallery 47, London
Solo exhibition, Gallery International, Cape Town
First South African exhibition, Karen McKerron Gallery, Johannesburg

1986
First solo exhibition, Art Show Gallery, London
International Contemporary Art Fair, Olympia, London

Details

6–7
THE GRASS IS REDDER ON THE OTHER SIDE 2018

10–11
THE MOON CRIED WHEN THE ELEPHANT DIED
AND THE POACHER RAN TO HIDE 2018

12
GLASS PURPLE PLANETS 2018

25
AS IT IS IN HEAVEN 2018

26–7
THE DEATH OF NELSON MAKUBA 1987

52–3
DANCING SOLDIERS 2015

70–1
BLUE GUMS ON MONAGHAN FARM 1991

86–7
MENTAL PRINCESS 2000

104–5
HOMECOMING 2010

120–1
PLAY US A SONG, YOU'RE THE PIANO MAN 2009

134–5
JASPER IN NEW YORK 2011

162
MY HANDS ARE TIED 2017

175
THE NIGHT OF THE RED MOON 2018

176–7
ASTRAL BLANKET 2018

188–9
LITTLE BRITAIN 2018

220–1
THE NIGHT OF THE RED MOON 2018

234–5
LONELY PLANET 2018

Front cover
WILD HORSES ON MARS 2017

Frontispiece and back cover
Beezy Bailey at home in Cape Town, photographed by Bruce Weber, 1995

236
Beezy Bailey in his Cape Town studio, photographed by Jasper Bailey, 2018

Acknowledgements

I would like to thank all those people who have helped to make this book a reality, particularly: Herman Lelie and Stefania Bonelli for their elegant design, and for their patience and belief in my work; Brian Eno for his inspiration in all things, and for his Foreword; the late great David Bowie for the ride in the spaceship of his creative universe, and for his generous remarks; Bruce Weber for the use of his photographs of me at home in Cape Town; Richard Cork and Roslyn Sulcas for their understanding of my work and for their writing; Georgie Shields, Mark Read, Charles Shields and the Everard Read Gallery for their support at all levels; Frank Kilbourn for his vision and generous support; Jasper Bailey for his photographs and scans; Tacita Rumble for her tireless scanning; and finally David Jenkins at Circa for taking this project on, and for his consistent direction.

Beezy Bailey, Cape Town, November 2018